THE
KNIGHT
IN MEDIEVAL
ENGLAND
1000–1400

This engaging double brass is of Sir John de Wauton and his wife, of Wimbish, Essex

THE

KNIGHT

IN MEDIEVAL
ENGLAND
1000–1400

PETER COSS

ALAN SUTTON

First published in the United Kingdom in 1993 by
Alan Sutton Publishing Ltd · Phoenix Mill · Far Thrupp
Stroud · Gloucestershire

First published in the United States of America in 1993 by
Alan Sutton Publishing Inc. · 83 Washington Street · Dover · NH 03820

British Library Cataloguing in Publication Data

Coss, Peter R.
  Knight in Medieval England 1000–1400
  I. Title
  305.520942

  ISBN 0–7509–0059–8

Library of Congress Cataloging in Publication Data applied for

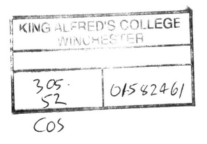
Typeset in 11/12pt Erhardt.
Typesetting and origination by
Alan Sutton Publishing Limited.
Printed in Great Britain by
The Bath Press Ltd, Avon.

Contents

For Angela

List of Illustrations

COLOUR PLATES

between pp. 74 and 75

BLACK AND WHITE PHOTOGRAPHS

Acknowledgements

I would like to thank all those who have helped in the preparation of this book, including the staff of libraries and record offices who have given freely and courteously of their time. Particular thanks are due to Mr Russell Baston, Dr Paul Brand, Dr Caroline Barron, Dr Philip Dixon, Mr Thomas Faulkner, Dr Simon Lloyd and Mr Andrew McGuiness for allowing me to draw upon their specific expertise. I am most grateful to Dr Barron and to Dr Anne Polden for allowing me to use their unpublished work, and to Dr Grenville Astill and Dr William M. Delehanty for permission to draw upon their doctoral theses. I would also like to thank Mr Alan Sutton who greatly encouraged this project from the beginning, and Rosemary Aspinwall and Jaqueline Mitchell of Alan Sutton Publishing for their good-humoured help at various stages of this work and for seeing it through to publication.

I owe very special thanks to Mr David Hill of Stourbridge for putting aside an extremely heavy workload to lavish care and attention upon the heraldic illustrations, to Dr Lindy Grant of the Courtauld Institute for giving generously of her time and knowledge to ensure that my visit to the Conway Library was an extremely profitable one, and to Dr Malcolm Norris, president of the Monumental Brass Society, for his great generosity not only in providing photographs from his own extensive collection but also for bringing a range of items to my attention. And, finally, the debt to my wife, Angela Coss, is once again immeasurable and is present throughout the work.

Photographs were supplied by or reproduced by the kind permission of the following: The British Library (Plates 1, 2, 3, 5, 7, and Figs.10, 15, 18, 19, 20, 23, 27, 28, 29, 37, 52, 55, 56, 62, 66, 69, 70, 71, 72); Mr David Hill of Stourbridge (Plates 10, 11, 12, 13, and Fig. 14); Mr Paul Felix (Plate 6); The University of Birmingham Library (Plate 9); Mr Thomas Faulkner (Plate 4); The Conway Library, Courtauld Institute of Art, University of London (Figs. 2, 4, 12, 25, 30, 32, 33, 34, 42, 43, 53, 58, 59, 60); The Public Record Office, Chancery Lane [Crown Copyright] (Figs. 5, 9, 13, 24, and 26 [Photograph by A.C. Cooper Ltd, London]); The Museum of Antiquities of the University of Newcastle upon Tyne and the Society of Antiquaries of Newcastle upon Tyne (Fig. 11); Mr James Austin, Cambridge (Fig. 16); The Bodleian Library, University of Oxford (Figs. 17, 63, 64); The Master and Fellows of Corpus Christi College, Cambridge (Figs. 21, 35); The Department of Medieval and Later Antiquities, The British

Museum (Fig. 22); F.H. Crossley and Maurice H. Ridgway (Fig. 33); The Pierpont Morgan Library, New York (Fig. 36); Society of the Antiquaries of London (Figs. 38, 39, 40); Mr Malcolm Norris (Figs. 1, 45–51); The Honourable Michael Willoughby (Fig. 54); Dr Philip Dixon (Fig. 61); The Huntington Library, San Marino, California (Figs. 65, 67, 68). While every effort has been made to acknowledge all copyright holders I would like to apologize should any omissions have been made.

ONE

Introduction

In July 1466 King Edward IV commanded that the manor of Caister should be restored to Sir John Paston. In doing so he declared himself satisfied that Paston and his uncles were 'Gentlemen discended lineally of worshipfull blood sithen the Conquest hither', that is since 1066. The king had very probably been presented with a proclamation of the Pastons' ancestry, an account of which still survives.[1] Its essence is as follows:

They showed divers great evidences and court rolls, how that they and their ancestors had been possessed of a court and seignory in the town of Paston, and of many and sundry bondmen, since the time that no mind is to the contrary; and how that Agnes Paston, wife to the said William Paston, father to the said John, William, and Clement, in title of her dower, is in possession of bondholders and also of bondmen, whose ancestors have been bondmen to the ancestors of the said John Paston since the time that no mind is to the contrary. And they showed divers fines, some levied in the time of the beginning of the reign of our noble progenitor Edward the First, son of King Henry, son of King John, of livelihood whereof they and their ancestors have been possessed ever since to this day.

Also they showed divers inquests which is a matter of record. Also they showed divers deeds and grants before time of mind, how that their ancestors had licence to have a chaplain . . . and that divers of their ancestors had given livelihood to houses of religion to be prayed for, and confirmations under the great seal of our noble ancestor King Henry the Third, son of King John, confirming the same grants.

Also they showed divers old deeds, some without date, sealed under authentic seals, of divers particular purchases in the town of Paston, reciting in the said deeds that the land was held of the ancestors of the said [John] Paston as of the chief lord of the fee, and by homage, and had ward, marriage, and relief. . . . Also they showed a great multitude of old deeds, without date and with date, wherein their ancestors were always set first in witness and before all other gentlemen. Also they showed how that their ancestors had in old time and of late time married with worshipful gentlemen, and proved by deeds of marriage and by other deeds how their ancestors had endowed their wives, and by descents of livelihood and by testaments and wills of their ancestors under seal; and made open by evident proof how they and their ancestors came lineally descended of right noble and worshipful blood and of great lords sometime living in this our realm of England. And also they made open proof how they were near of kin and blood to many of the most worshipful of the country, and also near to many and sundry great estates and lords of this realm, and was openly proved and affirmed without contradiction or proof to the contrary. . . .

They showed a lineal descent how their first ancestor Wulstan came out of France, and Sir William Glanville together, his kinsman, that after founded the priory of Bromholm by the town of Paston and the town of Bentley, and how Wulstan had issue Wulstan, who bore arms gold floret azure, and how he had issue Ralf and Robert, which Ralf senior bore arms as his father and Robert the younger bore silver floret azure. And Robert had issue Edmund and Walter, which Edmund the elder bore as his father, and his brother, because he married Glanville's daughter, a chief indented gold, the field silver floret azure . . . and how Sir John Paston was heir to all these, for they died without issue. And this was shown by writing of old hand and by old testaments and evidences.

The Pastons' account of themselves was a tissue of lies. They were, in fact, the family of the late judge, William Paston (d. 1444), who was himself the son of a thrifty yeoman, or of 'a good pleyn husbond' as a hostile contemporary put it. But the Paston lies were absolutely the correct ones to tell, for they encapsulated the central claims of the English nobility and gentry. The Paston proclamation is nothing less than a roll call of the attributes of gentility, as they were seen in the fifteenth century. It was deemed necessary to be a lord of the manor with a hall and a court, and to have unfree (or customary) tenants attending that court. It was advisable to have a clearly recognized central residence, preferably located in a settlement from which was derived one's name. One should also have one's own chapel in the manor-house for private worship under ecclesiastical licence, and to be a proven benefactor to monastic houses. It was also essential to hold by military tenure, which was held to have originated with the Conquest when all England was forfeit to the Conqueror and when land needed to be parcelled out to provide knights for the royal army, and to have free tenants who held their lands on the same terms. This meant that they should perform the act of homage, and that they were subject to the same feudal incidents of wardship and marriage (the right to the custody of the lands and person of an heir who succeeded under age and to determine his or her marriage if they were still single) and of relief (a sum of money paid upon succeeding to an inheritance). Furthermore, one needed to be connected by blood and by marriage to many another gentle family, and all of this needed to be authenticated by the correct documentation, going back to at least the thirteenth century.

The very heart of their élitist ideology, however, was expressed by the Pastons in their final paragraph. They were descended from the knights who came over with the Conqueror in 1066. Their status was expressed in their heraldic devices. These proclaimed not only their proud ancestry and their noble connections, but also their antiquity, as the chivalry that separated them from the rest of the populace was held to have 'come out of France'. These were the elements, then, that the king was concentrating upon when he accepted that the Pastons were gentlemen descended of worshipful blood in unbroken line since the Norman Conquest.

The emphasis placed upon the attributes of chivalric knighthood is not without its irony, for by the mid-fifteenth century it had long since ceased to be essential to actually be a knight in order to claim gentility. Knights by now were comparatively few in number, while both esquire and simple gentlemen existed as levels within gentle society inferior to that of the knight. Nevertheless, not only was knighthood itself incremental in terms of status – with Sir John Paston's knighthood the family can be said to have fully arrived – but there remained added cachet in being able to exhibit knights among one's ancestry. Moreover, whether knight or not, true social status was expressed heraldically, that is to say in a manner once appropriate only to knights.

• In the minds of contemporaries lordship or seignory and knighthood were intimately connected. If lordship was not, or at least no longer, synonymous with knighthood, knighthood was certainly felt to be dependent upon lordship, as Caxton's translation of Ramon Lull's *Order of Chivalry* makes clear:

> So high and noble is the order of chivalry that it sufficeth not that there be made knights of the most noble persons or that there should be given them the most noble beasts and the best, the most noble arms and the best; but it behoveth that he be made lord of many men, for in seignory is much nobleness . . . and it behoveth also that the common people labour the lands to bring forth fruits and goods whereof the knight and his beasts have their living.[2]

The Pastons, then, knew the right lies to tell, just as they knew the right things to do. It is hardly surprising, for example, that William Paston had recently laboured to turn Paston itself into precisely the seignory that Sir John said it was, and to have provided it with manor-house and chapel.[3] The question that needs to be asked, however, is not whether the Pastons were telling the truth; patently they were not. It is whether the central myths of the English gentry were themselves historically accurate, most especially with regard to the central phenomenon of knighthood. The question is made more difficult, and indeed more fascinating, by the very fact that these people projected their own values onto the past; and knighthood was in many respects a backward-looking institution. What they envisaged was an essentially unchanging world, at least since the Norman Conquest, in which chivalric knighthood played a vital role.

Until recently, historical scholarship in this country would have agreed, in broad terms at least, with the Pastons' sense of knighthood's historical role. An invasion army in 1066 and the subsequent need for the tenants of the Crown to supply cavalry for the feudal host brought noble knighthood and hence chivalry to England. Of course, it has long been understood that there were subsequent developments; that heraldry took shape during the course of the twelfth century, for example, and that the number of actual knights declined from the mid-thirteenth century onwards. Nonetheless, the role of the knight in English medieval society has tended to be seen in relatively static terms. This sense of stability has been reinforced by an inclination to draw over-much upon manuals of chivalry and upon romance literature in order to discover the actual content of contemporary knighthood.

Advances in historical research, however, have brought the traditional interpretation of knighthood in England increasingly into question. This is particularly true of scholarship on the Continent where the evolution of knighthood has long been recognized as a complex matter; knighthood meant different things at different times, and different things at the same time. In its origins it was by no means synonymous with gentility. The existence of non-noble knights almost everywhere in the eleventh century has inevitably led to central questions being asked about the social position and role of the knights who participated in the Norman Conquest and who functioned in Anglo-Norman England, compounding older questions over continuity with the Anglo-Saxon past.

If chivalric knighthood, as the Pastons and their contemporaries understood it, was not brought into England at the Norman Conquest, when and how did it evolve? What precisely was the relationship between knighthood and lordship, and between knighthood and gentility, and how had these changed over time? These and similar questions are the subject of this book. Its aim is to discover the actual position, role and image of the knight within English society from the eleventh century to the beginning of the fifteenth. It will begin by examining the position of the knight in late Saxon and Anglo-Norman England and place this firmly within its European context. It will then turn to the complex, and in some respects peculiar, role of the knight in England between the middle of the twelfth century and the mid-thirteenth. It will argue that knighthood was at that time a widely shared social distinction, and it will attempt to explain the decline in the number of knights and the changing characteristics of knighthood during the second half of this crucial period. From there it will move to a detailed examination of the rise of a more exclusive, chivalric knighthood and its manifestations, including heraldic display. The various social functions of this knighthood will be considered, together with its role in the diffusion of values within society. Finally, it will turn to literature, where the emphasis will be upon the wide dissemination of ideas about the role of the knight. Having discussed the impact of romance, *Piers Plowman* and the *Gest of Robin Hood* will be used together with Chaucer in order to explore how knights and knighthood were perceived in the late fourteenth century. It will then be possible to understand just how far knighthood had been transformed during these centuries and to comprehend precisely what was to be bequeathed to the English society of the future.

This book is intended both as a work of synthesis and as an essay in interpretation. I have drawn upon the works of many scholars and have relied heavily upon their expertise in specific areas. In all cases, they have been fully cited. As the book is designed to be fully accessible to the general reader, as well as to the professional scholar, I have confined my citations as far as possible to works that are available in print, both primary and secondary sources. With few exceptions, therefore, I have avoided citing unpublished theses and the like. However, although the work is not intended as a bibliography of all that has been written on and around the subject, I have indicated where I think there are significant gaps in our knowledge and where I believe further work needs to be done. With this in mind let us turn to the problem of understanding the knight in eleventh-century England.

TWO

The Origins of Knighthood in England

Sir Frank Stenton once observed that the 'application of the English word *cniht* to the French mounted soldiers who had formed the principal element in the Conqueror's army . . . forms a most remarkable exception to the general prevalence of French nomenclature in England'. And, he added, 'it has a wider interest, for it affords a clue as to the way in which the native English population regarded the professional mounted soldiers of eleventh-century France'.[1] Besides provoking the immediate response that these societies cannot, therefore, have been so very different as scholars have sometimes supposed, this transference of terminology prompts us to ask just what were the characteristics of the English *cniht* and the Norman *miles*, both translatable into modern English as knight. What, in other words, was the role and status of the knight in eleventh-century society?

In order to answer this question it is clearly necessary to understand the society from whence the Normans came as well as that of late Anglo-Saxon England. It will then be possible to examine the contours of knighthood during the Anglo-Norman period which followed and to offer a full explanation of the origins of knighthood in this country. We must begin, however, by understanding the Continental context within which knighthood evolved.

Although his roots can be traced further back in time, the knight is essentially a product of the militarization of society which began in the tenth century and accelerated through the eleventh. He is associated with the advent of feudalism, a form of society distinguished by the decentralization of authority, by the growth of ties of personal dependence between man and man (vassalage), by the physical domination of the rural populace by lords in order to live off their labour, by the rise of the castle and the castellan (lord or holder of a castle), and by the diffusion of the ban (or power of command) which involved the capacity to tax the population.[2] Within this world the old nobility turned itself increasingly into a military aristocracy. Moreover, in order to survive, all rulers, whether lay or churchmen, required armed retinues, garrisons, and agents of various kinds. Those who provided them came increasingly to be called knights. In origin the word *miles* (plural *milites*) meant soldier. During this period it came to be used in preference to denote the mounted warrior so characteristic of the age. However, it had other meanings too; principally it was used in the sense of vassal. Indeed the word *miles* tended increasingly to supplant terms like *vassallus* and *fidelis* from the late tenth century on.

It has to be admitted that the origins of knighthood present considerable problems for the historian, not least because the interpretation of sources, and most specifically their terminology, is fraught with difficulty. There were naturally immense differences between regions, and indeed within regions, and the pace of change varied considerably.[3] Two features do, however, stand out: an increasing use of the word *miles*, and a rise in the status of the *milites* during the course of the eleventh century, accelerating with the approach of the twelfth century. The frequency of the use of the term *miles* in narrative writings, for example, has been shown to have doubled after 1050, quadrupling in the works of the historians of the crusades at the end of the eleventh and the early years of the twelfth century.[4] The same is true of charters. In the Mâconnais in Burgundy those charters which mention the *milites* represent only 20 per cent in the tenth century. This proportion reaches 53 per cent between 1000 and 1030 and culminates in 70 per cent between 1030 and 1060 (after which it slips back to 50 per cent between 1060 and 1090). Although the pace of change varied, everywhere we look we witness the social promotion of the *milites* during the course of this century. As yet, however, this rise had its limits.

By a curious quirk of fate, the Mâconnais, long considered as the model of an eleventh-century society, now appears to have been exceptional.[5] There knighthood and nobility fused as early as the second half of the eleventh century. From 1075 *miles* and *nobilis* became interchangeable. Elsewhere, however, the rise of the *miles* was much slower. In general, though, it occurred more rapidly in the areas towards and around the Mediterranean than it did in the north. The term *miles* could certainly be applied to members of aristocratic families, but in such cases adjectives denoting nobility were often added to it, so that they could not be thought of as members of a social group of *milites*. Qualifications such as *nobilissimus miles* indicate, in fact, that *nobilis* and *miles* were not interchangeable. When used in this way they seem, in fact, to have preserved a profoundly different significance: *nobilis* describes a family condition linked to ancestry while *miles* describes a function. A good witness to this can be cited. In the Chartrain (the area around Chartres) during the middle of the eleventh century a certain Raher enumerated his personal characteristics – his origins, his economic level, his profession, age, social or legal condition, and mode of life. He says he originates from Chartres, he is rich in goods, young in age, a *miles* by profession, but noble in condition, and agreeable in his style of life.[6] Even in those instances where *miles* is used, unadorned, as a title in the eleventh century, as powerful lords wished to underline the military aspect of their power, they were still not identifying themselves with the *milites* as a collective group. In fact, when used in the plural the word describes, even in the southern regions, warriors derived from very humble backgrounds. They are almost always of peasant origins, from which they manage to divorce themselves very gradually. Henceforth they are to be found at the side of those who exercise the ban and no longer among those who suffer it. But they remain as yet at a level lower than those who exercise authority; they are their executive agents.

A brief glance at some of the areas that have been studied closely will make the situation clearer. In Poitou, for example, the descendants of the old Carolingian aristocracy become independent castellans in the eleventh century. They are sometimes called nobles to distinguish them from the *milites*. In the Gâtine the word *miles* described whoever fought on horseback but it was also used for those who were dependents or vassals of the nobles and who fought for them. Here the *miles* is a sort of armed serviteur or bodyguard who accompanies his lord, witnesses his charters, protects him and accomplishes military tasks for him. Those who lived in castle garrisons would more likely have been of peasant origin while those in the villages would approach the *petit noblesse*, as was also the case in Burgundy.

By contrast, in Catalonia at the end of the eleventh century the simple mounted combatants, of obscure extraction, had acquired a respectability sufficient for entry into the *noblesse*. However, their position remained very subordinate. They lent their services to the castellans and, with war having become an affair of specialists, they aspired to enter the *noblesse*. This was achieved, but with some difficulty. The older *nobiles*, proud of their ancestry and imbued with a sense of superiority, did not open their ranks of their own free will to what Pierre Bonnassie calls, 'this crowd of *parvenus de la guerre* who had hardly washed off their rustic origins who constituted the bands of mounted warriors.'[7]

In the ecclesiastical province of Narbonne the *milites* are more numerous in the texts of the eleventh century than they had been in the tenth, especially by its end. From the witness lists to charters it is evident that at the close of the eleventh century the *milites* are for the most part persons of very humble social level, not assimilated to the nobility. From the peasant class, they are attached to the guard of a powerful person, of a castle, or of a city. In 1090, however, they figure among those present at the assembly of the men of Narbonne; but after the *nobiles*, the principal citizens and even the citizens themselves. Here, then, they formed an urban militia rather than a *noblesse*.

Almost wherever we look, the mounted warriors were approaching the nobility by the end of the eleventh century, but so far they had failed to join them. Certainly the rise of the militia is a very real phenomenon and the vocabulary in the second half of the eleventh century is witness to it. But the difference between the *milites* and the nobles is carefully distinguished. Indeed a frontier still separates them. The functionalization of the aristocracy had not yet created a homogeneous military class. On the contrary, the group was not homogeneous in any domain: neither economic, nor social, nor yet cultural. What they shared were attitudes and common techniques in war rather than style of life. They remained separate in birth, social rank and authority – some of them gave orders, and others obeyed. In the halls of castles social differences must have remained acute. Little by little, however, they forged a common mentality. They enjoyed the same violent pleasures: hunting, for example, and martial exercises, especially those designed to produce efficiency in mounted combat. This must have become increasingly necessary as the cavalry tactic of shock combat developed in the late eleventh century, to be shown to such good effect at the Battle of Hastings.[8] Beyond a doubt it was the realization that a body of cavalry with lances couched under the arm could deliver a heavy blow against the enemy that provided the

A hunting scene of the late eleventh century, from the priory church of Goult (Orne), Normandy. Hunting was among the violent pleasures widely shared by members of the military class

•stimulus to the specialized military training which gave rise to the tournament. Perhaps it was here above all that a common mentality was forged.[9] •Physical power and military ability were glorified in the tournament, and this provided a means by which the *milites* of modest rank could show their worth in the eyes of the powerful who employed them and gain higher rank, favours and gifts from them.•It also gave the opportunity to talk with them in the presence of the ladies, for marriage could already lead to social promotion for a simple *miles*.

Normandy was not an exception to the general rule.[10]   As is the case elsewhere, an understanding of the status of knights is dependent upon the usage of the word *miles* in the documents. The different writing offices (*scriptoria*) tended to use different terminology, and some failed to employ the term *miles* at all. On the whole, though, •the Norman nobility was clearly distinguished from the knights. The majority of the knights who appear in the charters of the abbey of Fécamp, for example, are from humble ranks, except where a supplementary adjective indicating high status (*egregius, liber, ingenuus*) is employed. Interestingly, there appears to have been a change in Norman usage over time. Whereas before the middle of the eleventh century it tended to be used more of individuals, from the late 1040s onwards its usage in the collective sense increases significantly. Nevertheless, the most frequent employment of the word

Shock combat at the Battle of Hastings. The Bayeux Tapestry provides an early depiction of the new cavalry tactic that developed during the late eleventh century

refers to individuals; not, however, to describe their status, but to indicate their dependence upon another. A man is the knight of a lord, lay or ecclesiastic, or even of a saint: 'X the knight of Y'. Dukes have their knights, as do bishops, abbots and lesser lords. This meaning is reinforced when it is used together with *fidelis* or *homo*, as, for example, 'a certain knight, the man of Roger the Constable (*quidam miles homo Rogerii conestabuli*)'. Very often there is an insistence on the fidelity of the knight, accentuating the bond between the *miles* and the lord. It is used in this sense in the dukes' own charters, where some elevated persons are so described. In interpreting this, however, the sense of vassalage must be borne in mind; and, once again, it is qualified in some cases by additional words indicating noble status.[11]

Miles, then, tends to mean the personal dependant of someone else, with the implication of 'soldier'. He appears close to his lord, witnessing his acts. Otherwise knights appear as holders of land and rights, and it is often clearly the case that they hold very mediocre possessions. The insignificant social position of some of the knights is indicated, moreover, by their appearance in charters alongside peasants, as appurtenances of manors, with other resources like woodlands, churches and mills. It seems probable that the majority of knights did not as yet hold fiefs, that is land granted to them from which they should provide their own military equipment, although some held land by other tenures. Many were, in consequence, dependent upon the support of their lords, in their households or on their estates. Most were known only by their first names or by their first name followed by their patronym.[12] In short, the term *miles* remained pre-eminently one describing function rather than status.

The status of the knight in Normandy clearly rose during the period from the mid-eleventh century to the mid-twelfth. This advance in social position is indicated by their increasing adoption of a name derived from a place of residence, a *nom de terre*, and this seems to have been connected with the spread of the fief. Moreover, despite the fact that nobility and knighthood failed to fuse it does seem to be the case that the nobility became less disdainful of the term knight and that a shared military ethos was gaining ground here as elsewhere.

Nevertheless the low status of many Norman knights was mirrored in their settlement in England, as was shown by Domesday Book in 1086. In Sally Harvey's famous discussion of the Domesday knight he is revealed as a rather lowly figure.[13] The normal landed base of the 500 or so nameless knights in Domesday Book was about $1\frac{1}{2}$ hides (a hide being notionally 120 acres) giving an income of between 30s. and £2 per annum; it was enough to sustain a knight, as she says, but

The fully equipped mounted warrior was an international phenomenon. This famous early twelfth-century portrayal of an episode from the Arthurian legend (the abduction and rescue of Queen Guinevere) is from the archivolt of the Porta della Pescheria, Modena Cathedral

not nobly. Over a third of them had no more than $^3/_4$ to $1^1/_2$ hides, while another quarter of them had even less than this. Units larger than $3^1/_2$ hides were a rarity. (Holdings in Kent and in the northern counties tended to be larger, though only in the former did this produce units of greater value.) In other words, they were hardly any better off than the more prosperous peasants. Domesday Book also includes a few knights who did not possess their own holdings at all but were among the personnel of the estate. Doubtless there were many others who were being maintained within their lord's household.

These Domesday knights, then, did not enjoy whole manors but small units appurtenant to manors or geographically distinct holdings (berewicks). These berewicks often belonged to their lords' main estates. There is other evidence which supports this picture. Lanfranc, the Conqueror's archbishop of Canterbury, wrote of the hamlets which he had granted as fiefs to some of his knights, while a charter of enfeoffment by Gilbert Crispin, the abbot of Westminster, gave William Baynard a berewick of the township of Westminster called 'Totenhala' to house him and to be held for life by the service of one knight.[14] These outlying berewicks that were given to knights were often described as 'land of the villeins', with the peasants, as Domesday Book says, 'remaining under them'. In other words the knights, and other professional men in the same position, were receiving rents and thereby living off the land without involving themselves directly in agriculture.

It may well be that the foregoing analysis understates the income and wealth of some of these knights. They may have been receiving additional rewards as household knights, for instance, and being anonymous in Domesday Book the same individuals may be appearing more than once. Similarly, a knight who appears anonymously at one point may be appearing as a named tenant (but without the description *miles*) at another. Strictly speaking, 'the statistics reveal not the average size of the entire landholdings of each individual whom Domesday calls *miles* at one point or another, but the average size of parcels for each occasion on which the word *miles* is used'.[15] Nevertheless, the overwhelming impression conveyed by Domesday Book is that the knights it records were of relatively lowly status, an impression which is confirmed by the documents recording feudal tenures preserved by ecclesiastical lords of the Anglo-Norman era.[16]

But this is not, of course, the whole story. The great chronicler of the Norman invasion, William of Poitiers, has the Conqueror giving instructions first to his greatest followers, and then to 'middling noble knights' (*milites mediae nobilitatis*) and finally to the 'common knights' (*milites gregarios*).[17] Clearly, it is the latter who are represented overwhelmingly by the *milites* of Domesday Book. But, even then, not exclusively so. Robert, count of Eu, William of Braose, Hugh of Montfort and two sheriffs also appear as *milites* there, while other men of high rank figure among the *milites* who are tenants of religious houses – Roger Bigod, for example, and Eudo Dapifer.[18]

As on the Continent, then, it very much looks as though knighthood in England at the time of Domesday Book was essentially a matter of function and that it included men of both noble extraction and those who had been drawn from the ranks of the peasantry. As Sir Frank Stenton recognized many years ago, the knights of the Conqueror's time formed a miscellaneous class. They included both men of high social position, from whom important families would descend and men of a very inferior condition whose names were not even felt to be worth recording.[19]

Domesday Book provides an important point of entry into the question of the origins of knighthood in England, especially when seen in a Continental context and against a Norman background. In order to examine the situation more closely, however, it is necessary to take the inquiry back into England prior to the Conquest and then turn to a deeper analysis of the role of the knight and of knighthood in the post-Conquest Anglo-Norman world which followed. An obvious starting point is with the *cniht*. The word *cniht* itself has a history which mirrors that of other terms which emerged during the early middle ages. From its original meaning of 'boy' it came to mean household retainer.[20] The English texts show that *cniht* was used, in particular, to describe the retainer of some great man. He was to be found either in his lord's household or in his retinue as he toured the country. Whereas Wulfstan's account of the miracles of St Swithin begins with an account of an ealdorman setting out to inspect an estate 'attended by a large mounted company, as is the custom among the Anglo-Saxons', Aelfric's homily on the same saint describes a young mounted retainer expressly as a *cniht*. The service of the *cniht* might require him to fight by his lord's side. He was mounted and equipped for war. But fighting was only one of his duties and the *cnihtas* figure in the texts as servants rather than soldiers. This comes across, for example, in Anglo-Saxon wills: one ealdorman left £5 to be shared between his hired *cnihtas*; a bishop similarly left £40 to some *cnihtas*, under the direction of his stewards. A lady bequeathed a band of gold to four named *cnihtas*, and another left an estate to be divided among her chaplain, a named person, and the *cnihtas* who would serve her best. The connection between the *cniht* and household service is shown in the will of Aethelstan, son of King Aethelred II. At one point he makes a bequest of an estate at Chalton in south Hampshire excepting the 8 hides which he has granted to Aelfmar his *cniht*. At another point he grants 8 hides at Catherington to Aelfmaer his *discthegn* (steward). Catherington was, in fact, part of the manor of Chalton, so that it is quite clear that Aelfmaer the *cniht* and Aelfmaer the *discthegn* were the same man. In Essex, Thurstan son of Wine left his knights the woodland at Ongar, excepting his park and stud. Stenton may well have been right to see in these particular *cnihtas* 'a group of hunt servants quartered by their master's park'.[21]

The effects of such grants to *cnihtas* can be seen in Domesday Book. At Grimley in Worcestershire before the Conquest a subtenancy called Knightwick was responsible for all the service due to the king. The many settlements called Knighton appear to have grown up within existing estates.[22]

The *cniht*, then, was a retainer in the personal service of a nobleman, providing escort, hunting and similar duties. In seems rather surprising, therefore, that Stenton should have maintained that it was primarily their military role which caused the English to identify them with the Norman *milites*. This was presumably because Stenton saw the function of the post-Conquest knight almost exclusively in terms of service in the feudal host. In reality, the range of duties undertaken by the Anglo-Saxon *cniht* and the Norman *miles* may often have been very similar. None the less, the military side was obviously important, and should not be neglected. The Anglo-Saxon Chronicle for 1088 refers to the *cnihtas* of Bishop Odo of Bayeux who formed the garrison of Tonbridge Castle. Moreover, *cniht* was indeed used to signify a soldier in late Saxon England. Abbot Aelfric of Eynsham, for example, in his Treatise on the Old and New Testaments, readily equated *miles*, the traditional word for soldier, with the Anglo-Saxon word *cniht*:

> Soldiers are they who guard our boroughs and also our land, fighting with weapons against the oncoming army; as St. Paul, the teacher of the nations, said in his teaching: Non sine causa portat miles gladium etc – 'The cniht beareth not the sword without cause'.[23]

Aelfric and his contemporary Wulfstan, both writing during the reign of Aethelred II (978–1016), were champions of the tripartite division of society into those who fought, those who worked and those who prayed. They were repeating a classification of society first put forward by King Alfred, which was currently being popularized on the Continent by their contemporaries, Adalbero of Laon and Gerard of Cambrai.[24] Like all such schemes it was a simplification of reality but, as has been pointed out, it is a reminder that Anglo-Saxon England was dominated by a military aristocracy which exploited peasant labour.[25] In this it was little different from the feudal societies of the Continent. For all these ecclesiastical writers the essentially exploitive position of the nobility, here as elsewhere, was justified by their military role; by their protective role, as the churchmen argued it.

If late Anglo-Saxon society is to be understood correctly, and in particular the role of its *cnihtas* and its aristocracy, one can hardly avoid confronting the complex question of the composition of the English army. Hard information on this issue, however, is thin on the ground. The statements of custom from Worcestershire and Berkshire, preserved by Domesday Book, taken together, offer the most substantial evidence. Unfortunately, however, their interpretion is open to considerable doubt and has helped to foster a long history of debate among historians. The central issues are the extent to which service in the *fyrd*, the Anglo-Saxon army, was the duty of peasants as against the obligation of the noblemen, or thegns, and the means by which the army was recruited.[26]

Let us glance at the shire customs in turn. The Worcestershire Custumal tells us that:

> When the king goes against the enemy, should anyone summoned by his edict remain, if he is a man so free that he has his soke and sake [in effect, he holds his own court], and can go with his land to whomever he wishes [i.e. he can choose his own lord], he is in the king's mercy for all of his land. But if the free man of some other lord has stayed away from the host and his lord has led another in his place, he will pay 40s. to his lord who received the summons. But if nobody at all has gone in his place, he himself shall pay his lord 40s., but his lord shall pay the entire amount to the king.

The Worcestershire Custumal, from Domesday Book, provides evidence of how Anglo-Saxon armies were recruited

What this seems to tell us is that there were two distinct levels of *fyrdman*. There were the major landowners who enjoyed rights of lordship over the lands of other freemen and who were the recipients of royal summonses, and there were the lesser freemen who often held their land under the jurisdiction of these great lords. The difference in the penalties they faced for failure to respond to military service appears to indicate the existence of a significant social gulf between them. In some respects the Berkshire Custumal fleshes this out:

If the king sent an army anywhere, only one soldier (*miles*) went from five hides, and for his provision or pay, 4s. were given him from each hide for his two months of service. The money, however, was not sent to the king but given to the soldiers. If anyone summoned to serve in an expedition failed to do so, he forfeited all his land to the king. If anyone for the sake of remaining behind promised to send another in his place, and nevertheless, he who should have been sent remained behind, his lord was freed of obligation by the payment of 50s.

Amalgamating the two custumals, the following conclusions can be drawn. First, important landowners were personally summoned to the *fyrd* and were liable to find their lands confiscated if they failed to attend. Second, other freemen participated, and their lords played a major role in their recruitment. Third, troops were in fact raised on a territorial basis. This was one man per five hides in Berkshire, and, no doubt, this or similar systems operated elsewhere.

In all probability, military service to the king was owed essentially by the landowners. Each of them was required to send a contingent of warriors, the size of this contingent being determined by an assessment of their property, essentially the number of hides.[27] These warriors were their own retainers, and how they were actually recruited was their concern not the king's, providing of course that they were properly equipped soldiers. If they wished, landowners might lease land for one or several lives in return for military and other services, as for example did the bishops of Worcester. Or they might prefer to keep soldiers in their own households. Either way the warriors would tend to be bound to them by hold-oaths, that is to say by vassalage or commendation, as it was termed. This meant, in effect, that the landowners fought for the king while their retainers fought for them. The army produced by such means would naturally be reinforced by the troops of the king's own household and by the hiring of stipendiary soldiers.

The military role of the Anglo-Saxon nobility can also be approached from another direction. Under English law each thegn or man of higher rank was bound to arrange that on his death his military equipment was handed to his lord.[28] This payment was known as heriot, meaning wargear. The law code of King Cnut (1016–35), Aethelred's Danish successor, indicates that the heriot of the ordinary thegn consisted of one horse with its saddle and bridle, a shield and spear/lance, a sword, a helmet and a byrnie or hauberk (coat of mail), that is, the normal equipment of the military élite in Continental societies at this time. This is reinforced by the Bayeux Tapestry which depicts English soldiers throughout the Battle of Hastings as well-armed warriors wearing conical helmets and trousered byrnies, and carrying shields, spears and swords, and sometimes two-handed battle axes. The tapestry was undoubtedly produced in England not long after the Conquest. It is possible that its depiction of the battle may have been influenced by recent changes in fashion; for example, the new kite-shaped shield

The Bayeux Tapestry shows the English army in action. Note their equipment, including the trousered byrnies (coats of mail)

which was more suitable for the mounted warrior is generally given precedence over the old round shield, even among the English despite the fact that they fought on foot.[29] Nonetheless, there is every reason to suppose that, on the whole, the artist/designer of the tapestry has faithfully presented the contemporary army, the army that was recruited on the basis of one man from every five hides.

Cnut's ordinance is particularly revealing in its setting out of the heriots owed to their lord by the various ranks of the nobility. The earl pays a heriot consisting of eight horses and eight spears and shields, but only four helmets, swords and byrnies. Only four of the horses are saddled, suggesting that this represents the military equipment of four fully armed soldiers and four lightly armed attend-ants, the unsaddled horses indicating either pack horses or extra horses to enhance the mobility of the retinue. By contrast, the king's thegn pays four horses, two of which were saddled, one helmet and one byrnie, two swords, four spears and four shields, indicating perhaps one fully armed warrior (the thegn himself), one less well-armed man with saddled horse, sword, spear and shield but no helmet and byrnie, and two attendants taking care of the horses. The ordinary thegn, as we have seen, handed over his horse with its harness and all his weapons. This is when heriots were not paid in cash, as they commonly were, for example, in the Danelaw of northern and eastern England.

The impression gained from Cnut's law is reinforced by the evidence from Anglo-Saxon wills. It indicates that heriots paid by the higher nobility were usu-ally in arms. Moreover, a detailed analysis suggests that Cnut's predecessor, Aethelred II, had altered the heriots to include on a regular basis helmets, byrnies and saddled horses, thereby improving the quality of retinues and hence of royal armies. This makes perfect sense when one thinks of the Danish onslaught upon England which this unfortunate king had to face. There cannot be any doubt that the heriot represents the return to the lord of the wargear that he gave out to men entering his service. It ensured that the kings of England were able to continue to attract sufficient followers of the necessary calibre. Moreover, the sharp difference between the heriot of the king's thegn and that of the ordinary thegn, that is, a thegn of any other lord, shows the comparative strength of the royal following.

The Anglo-Saxon heriot, then, takes us to the roots of aristocratic society. The conferring of arms was by no means confined to England; on the contrary, it was a generally accepted way of cementing the bond between warrior and lord. When the Bayeux Tapestry depicts Harold of England committing himself to the cause of William of Normandy he shows him receiving arms from the duke. The equip-ment involved emphasized the distance that now existed, in England as on the Continent, between the fully armed warrior and the lightly armed peasants who in earlier centuries had been more militarily significant. Taken together, the evi-dence from the heriots and from the Bayeux Tapestry suggests a highly equipped English army dominated by the nobility. The same sense is gained from reading the poem on the Battle of Maldon which has been described as 'an idealized, but essentially accurate, portrayal of an early eleventh-century Anglo-Saxon host'.[30] The poem commemorates the military action against the Danes of the year 991 at Maldon in Essex where Ealdorman Byrhtnoth lost his life. It is, of course, a piece of imaginative literature not a record of the battle as such. It was most probably

The delivery of arms: Harold of England receiving his arms from Duke William of Normandy. The precise significance of this scene from the Bayeux Tapestry has been much debated, but it clearly implies the subordination of one man to the other and a commitment by Harold to William's cause

composed a generation after the battle (perhaps *c.* 1020) to extol certain virtues and may be somewhat backward-looking as a consequence. It seems to breathe the air of the ancient warband. Nevertheless, there seems no real reason to doubt that it is substantially accurate in describing the Anglo-Saxon *fyrd* in action. What is especially striking is that the idea of lordship dominates the entire poem. The ealdorman himself is expressly described as King Aethelred's thegn, fighting for his lord's honour and his land, while each of the fyrdmen that is mentioned is personally linked to Byrhtnoth. Some are members of his household, others seem to be local landowners. All appear to have commended themselves to him. Not surprisingly, after he falls, they fight on to avenge their lord rather than to protect their land:

> So was he lost the army's leader,
> Aethelred's earl. They all saw,
> his hearth-men, that their high-lord was dead.
> Yet still advanced these valiant men;
> fearless warriors, they came forward readily;
> they all wanted one of two things,
> to avenge their lord or lay down their lives.[31]

None of this evidence, however, proves that the English army consisted entirely of thegns. It may well be the case that many of the *milites* who went out from five hides (or other units) were retainers of higher lords, commended to them. Sometimes they may even have held land on conditional tenure from them. But this does not mean that they were all thegns. The Battle of Maldon itself refers to Dunnere 'himself just a ceorl' (churl, i.e. peasant) who acquitted himself well in the battle. All freemen were entitled to carry weapons. The legal text known as *Northleoda Laga*, dating from the time of Aethelred II, felt it necessary to state that the *ceorl* who possessed a helmet, a byrnie and gold-adorned sword but who did not have the requisite five hides of land remained a *ceorl*. Domesday Book itself refers to *liberi homines* (freemen) who died at Hastings. One, for example, was Breme, a 'freeman' of King Edward the Confessor who held 1½ carucates (around 180 acres) worth 60s. in Suffolk. But neither does this mean that the *fyrd* was an army of peasant levies. Men like Breme were far from negligible figures. In fact, he not only had peasant tenants himself, villagers and smallholders, but he also enjoyed the commendation of another 'freeman' who held 11 acres in the same village. Some men of this class were undoubtedly professional warriors. One man who held land at Pirton in Hertfordshire was described as a sokeman (a variety of freeman) before the Conquest but as an English knight (*miles Anglicus*) in later years. He, at least, had made the transition tolerably well.[32] It is still possible that there were additional local peasant levies in English armies. The Bayeux Tapestry depicts some lightly armed warriors late in the battle.[33] On the other hand it could well have been the case, despite what is said in the custumals, that not all troops were as well armed as rulers would have liked. Service, including military service, was an important means of advancement in this society. The word thegn itself had service connotations. Its meaning shifted over time from young man to servant to denoting high social status. Royal charters of the tenth and eleventh centuries speak interchangeably of king's minister or king's knight (*minister regis* or *miles regis*), to translate the English term king's thegn. Whether drawn from peasant ranks or not, men performing faithful service to lords were a significant and essential element in society.

In short, the study of the Anglo-Saxon army reaffirms the impression gained from the word *cniht* and its service connotations. This society was very little different from that which prevailed in France. It is true that pre-Conquest England had very few castles and that its warriors, although they generally rode to battle, dismounted to fight. Nevertheless, both societies were characterized by warriors in service and by a militarized nobility.

Given the strong service connotations of both *cniht* and *miles*, it is by focussing first on the retinue that we can begin to appreciate the similarity, if not the continuity, between late Saxon and Anglo-Norman England. It is hardly surprising, in the circumstances of the time, that the great Norman lords who dominated England after 1066 should have found it highly desirable to maintain large military households. 'Clattering and jingling contingents of mounted knights, with gonfalons and shields displayed, must have been a familiar sight in rural England as they rode upon the business of their lords, and lorded it over the countryside.'[34] Looking back over the Conqueror's reign the chroniclers leave us in no doubt here. William of

Malmesbury tells how William fitz Osbern, earl of Hereford, kept a multitude of knights and how he paid them generously, and how Wulfstan, bishop of Worcester, adopted the Norman fashion in this respect. The abbots of Ely and Abingdon, and presumably other churchmen, maintained knights in their own households in order to discharge their obligations to the king. Orderic Vitalis tells how Hugh d'Avranches, lord of the marcher earldom of Chester, kept so many knights about him that he moved about the country with an army rather than a household, adding:

He loved the world and all its pomps, which he regarded as the chief part of human happiness. He was an active soldier, an extravagant giver, and took great pleasure in gaming and debauchery, and in jesters, horses and hounds, and such other vanities. An enormous household, which resounded with the noise of a crowd of youths, both noble and common, was always in attendance upon him. Some good men, clerks as well as knights, also lived with him, and he gladly gave them a share in both his labours and his wealth. In his chapel was Gerold, a clerk from Avranches, honest, religious and well-educated . . . who tried hard to improve the conduct of the courtiers by setting before them the example of their ancestors. In many of them he perceived, and censured, carnal lust, and he deplored the utter negligence that some showed in the worship of God. He uttered salutary warnings to the chief barons, the simple knights and the noble youths, and made a large collection of stories from the Old Testament and more recent Christian histories of the campaigns of holy knights, in order to serve them as models. He recited excellently the struggles of Demetrius and of George, of Theodore and of Sebastian, of Duke Maurice and the Thebean legion, and of Eustace, the general officer, and his men, all of whom by their martyrdom earned a crown in heaven. And he also told of the holy warrior William, who, after many campaigns, renounced the world, and under the monastic rule fought gloriously for the Lord.[35]

An eleventh-century retinue in action. This scene from the Bayeux Tapestry depicts Earl Harold and his knights hunting en route to the coast

Other post-Conquest lords kept large numbers of landless *milites*, if not exactly in their households, at least close at hand. Abbot Baldwin, for example, maintained some thirty-four 'French and English milites' within the town of Bury St Edmunds. Similarly, Gilbert Crispin, abbot of St Peter's of Westminster, set aside twenty-five houses near the monastery for his resident 'milites and his other men [homines]'.[36] Others no doubt did the same. The need for a sizeable armed escort will have been particularly acute in Anglo-Norman England. It was, after all, an occupied land where in addition to resentment against the intruders the fact of invasion and occupation must have caused much social disruption and unleashed considerable violence and turbulence. But, equally, one should be wary of exaggerating the insecurity of post-Conquest society as compared to that which went before. We know a lot about how arrogant members of the warrior class intruded themselves into estates, especially ecclesiastical estates, during the aftermath of the Norman victory at Hastings. But such things had already occurred in the late Saxon state. The records of the bishopric of Worcester afford us a particularly graphic example. It concerns one Sigmund, whom Domesday Book tells us held five hides of the bishop at Crowle in the time of King Edward the Confessor (1042–66). According to Heming (looking back from post-Conquest times) Sigmund was a Danish *miles* of earl Leofric, who held half of the township of Crowle. The other half belonged to the church. Sigmund, however, wanted this half too and, having failed to persuade the monks to give it to him, he took it by force. As a result Crowle was devastated, and the parties came to court. Earl Leofric intervened and this resulted in a compromise. Sigmund gained a life-interest in the church's half of Crowle on condition that he performed military service for the church. Heming records that, in fact, he kept to his promise.[37] This situation was often mirrored in Norman England. Furthermore, freemen had been putting themselves increasingly under the protection of lords, becoming their vassals. More and more, the organs of public justice were passing into private hands. English lords were accustomed to riding around with armed escorts. If there were differences in these respects between then and later, they were differences only in degree.

The household that we know most about, naturally, is that of the king. William the Conqueror, no doubt, maintained a considerable body of knights attached to the court. This, of course, was nothing new. The kings of England since Cnut had employed their housecarls, as indeed had the Anglo-Danish magnates, and earlier English kings had been surrounded by their warrior companions. Many of the Conqueror's knights will have become settled on the land as the country was pacified, again as the housecarls had tended to be. But this last point should not blind us to the fact that the military household of the Anglo-Norman kings was a permanent institution. In recent years that of Henry I (1100–35) has been subjected to close scrutiny. It provided, in fact, 'a professional corps of young knights' who 'formed the shock-troops of Henry's armies, around whom the bands of mercenaries and those fighting to fulfil their feudal duties gathered.'[38] They were numbered in their hundreds and, according to a contemporary observer, Walter Map, they received an annual fee of £5 in addition to receiving wages of up to 1s. a day when on the king's service.[39] Highly trained and extremely mobile, their activities were vital to the Anglo-Norman state. In fact, by far the greater part of their military action was undertaken in Normandy, where they were on a permanent war-footing.[40] They provided the garrisons (up to a hundred strong) of the numerous royal castles, often far in excess it seems of the size of castle garrisons in England. They dominated some of the battles; Brémule, for example, in 1119 against the French king, and Bourgthéroulde in 1124, an engagement that has been described as a fight between a small party of rebel knights and the king's military household.

The composition of this military household can be studied in the pages of the English-born Norman chronicler, Orderic Vitalis. Some of its members were clearly of noble origin, both heirs apparent and younger sons. Henry de Pomeroy, for example, was the heir of Joscelin, lord of Berry Pomeroy in Devon. His father was probably still alive when he joined the household. Later he succeeded to his father's honour, became a royal constable and married one of the king's bastard daughters. Two of the king's natural sons appear as leading the household troops. Younger sons of the nobility include William de Grandcourt, whose father was the count of Eu. Others were equally clearly from lower social strata. Among them were men known by nicknames rather than family names, men like Bertrand Rumex (meaning sorrel) and Odo Borleng (meaning spear's length), drawn probably from families of modest fortune 'with just enough resources to provide themselves with the training and equipment of a knight'.[41]

The chroniclers tell us a good deal about the Battle of Bourgthéroulde, which put an end to the revolt of Waleran of Meulan and Amaury of Montfort. John of Worcester describes the royal forces here as *milites regis*, while the Anglo-Saxon chronicler calls them 'the king's knights from all the castles round about'. Orderic tells us that there were 300 *milites* in all and that two of the commanders were none other than Henry de Pomeroy and Odo Borleng. He puts imaginary speeches into the mouths of the protagonists. Odo Borleng urges his men on: 'If we lack the courage to resist, how shall we ever dare to face the king again? We shall rightly forfeit our wages and our honour, and shall never again deserve to eat the king's bread.'[42] The sentiments are not far distant from those expressed in *The Battle of Maldon.*

In addition to these household troops who served for wages, Henry I occasionally used mercenaries of another type, hired in large numbers for a limited period, during the major campaigns of the first half of his reign. Later, William of Malmesbury wrote in his *Historia Novella* after the death of Henry I that the mercenaries, especially those from Flanders and Brittany, who flocked to serve under Stephen, had 'hated King Henry's peace because under it they had had but a scanty livelihood'.

The household and the hired soldier, however, provide only part of the picture. As is well known, in the wake of the Norman Conquest knights were given fiefs, that is to say they were enfeoffed with land in return for service. The entire land of England was forfeit to the king, because the English had rebelled against him in offering the Crown to Harold. The Conqueror gave land to his followers and they in their turn created subtenancies. Service quotas of knights for the royal host were imposed upon the Crown's direct tenants (the tenants-in-chief) on a decimal basis.[43] In the case of the ecclesiastical tenants, who had held their lands of course before the Conquest, this seems to have been done by 1070–2. With regard to the lay tenants, however, it was much more complicated given that they can rarely have acquired all their lands at one moment and that these lands were subject to extension and to regrouping for various reasons. The process was, therefore, a more gradual one but one very largely completed by the early years of Henry I. After that time it was much more difficult to renegotiate because sub-infeudation had proceeded very far with specific service having been imposed upon subtenants.

However, the military role of the service quotas has been much diminished by historians in recent years. It is now abundantly clear that the Norman kings relied very largely upon those who served for pay and other rewards, and the service quotas played a relatively minor role.[44] The assignment of quotas reaffirmed that the land was held of the king by service and gave him a guarantee that those who received their land from him would play their part in maintaining the Conquest. As has been aptly said, 'it was a simple, rough and ready response to the hazards of conquest'.[45] It seems probable that, in reality, when the Anglo-Norman kings asked for the military service that their tenants-in-chief owed, they turned up not with a precise quota but with a reasonable showing, sufficient to satisfy the king and his marshal. When a later king inquired of his tenants-in-chief, in 1166, as to the enfeoffments that had been made, a considerable number of them were actually ignorant of their service quota and had to make inquiry, sometimes of the aged men of their fee, to ascertain the answer.[46]

The service quota, however, was only one stimulus to enfeoffment. Men were greedy for land. Relatives and major followers of tenants-in-chief were among the natural recipients. By means of enfeoffment, moreover, a lord would increase his personal power and influence. Military tenancy involved the performance of homage and the swearing of fealty. The aspirations of many household knights must have been to acquire their own land. It is hardly surprising that many lords came to enfeoff more knights than they owed to the royal host. Religious houses could increase their security by accepting powerful tenants. In reality they often had no choice but to do so. In some cases we know that the king himself imposed knightly tenants upon them. In one famous case, a knight in the service of the abbot of Abingdon who had not yet received any land was attacked by pirates on a journey from the Continent and suffered the loss of his hands. He appealed to the king who, pitying the knight, ordered the abbot to provide him with enough land to support him as long as he lived.[47] The traditions of Ely and Abingdon tell us that the disruptive behaviour of the resident knights, by which they originally ful-filled their obligation to the king, caused the monks to turn to the alternative of giving the knights land to support themselves. But it is equally the case that by doing so they could satisfy other demands upon them.

Any close examination of the records of enfeoffment reaffirms the Domesday perspective that knights settled on the land were of very unequal endowment. Although, to be sure, the Domesday testament should not be taken entirely at face value, it nevertheless remains the case that there were enfeoffed knights whose land was no more extensive than is depicted there.[48] Knights were differently endowed by the same tenant-in-chief. The well-studied records of ecclesiastical

A land grant of the year 1085. The recipient, Roger son of Walter, will serve the bishop of Hereford with two knights, just as his father had done

tenants-in-chief reveal many cases where small estates or subtenancies jointly owed the service of one knight.

As yet, however, we have not mentioned the influential tenant, sometimes called the feudal middleman, who was responsible for providing a quota of knights towards his lord's service to the king. The records of the abbey of Bury St Edmunds recall that these men received their land 'that they should be able to ride in the Saint's service' and 'that they should find knights for the Saint's service'.[49] Such men, when they in turn enfeoffed knights, were hardly obliged to share it out equally; on the contrary, to a degree they must have been able to make their own bargains with them.[50] However, we ought to be wary of placing too much weight upon this factor alone. There are a variety of reasons underscoring unequal endowment, and they are the product of a complex social situation. As one can well imagine, the advantaged did very well and others had to be content, even grateful, for whatever opportunities came their way. In his response to Henry II's inquiries in 1166 Alexander de Alno replied, 'My father gave to his brother, Hugh de Alno, a small amount of land from his demesne, so that, if it became necessary, he could do the service of one knight to answer for the whole of my father's land. And that grant was made to him and his heirs in the time of King William.'[51] It must also be borne in mind that endowment was not a once and for all situation. Some knights must undoubtedly have been able to improve the profitability of their lands. Some made further acquisitions. A recent study of one lay honour (a baron's estate) has indicated a surprising degree of volatility among the lands of its subtenants during the Anglo-Norman period.[52]

As to how many knights there were in Anglo-Norman England, it is simply not possible to offer an authoritative answer. The latest estimate of the number of knights' fees created suggests a total of 7,525 fees held by the barons in 1166, of which about 5,300 were owed to the royal host. Of these the great majority (all but 7.5 per cent) were created before 1135, by which time opportunities for the creation of new fees must have been much reduced.[53] But the number of knights' fees is not the number of knights. The holders of knights' fees were not necessarily knights themselves. Neither were all the knights fee-holders.[54] Although fractional fees existed from the outset, many more developed in the course of time, as for example when fees were divided among female heirs and where vassals themselves created subtenancies. For various reasons the holders of fees often ceased to be knights. This was encouraged by the institution of scutage or shield-money, by which the Crown took cash in place of knight-service. Although its early history is rather uncertain and complex, scutage was already in place in some form by 1100. It helped with the hiring of mercenaries and general financing of the king's wars.

It has been suggested, too, that the landed provision for knights often proved insufficient by the twelfth century to meet their costs. As far as the Anglo-Norman period is concerned, however, this argument is rather difficult to sustain. It cannot be doubted that full knightly equipment was expensive, but there is nothing to suggest that the expense can have increased much during this period. There were no serious developments in armour until the late twelfth and early thirteenth centuries when horse armour and the pot helm came in. It is possible, however, that by the early twelfth century there was a greater insistence that a knight should always be fully equipped with lance and sword, shield, helmet and hauberk than there had been before, although there is no proof of this. St Anselm, archbishop of Canterbury, listed the essential equipment of a knight. First of all came the horse, 'which is so necessary for him that it could rightly be described as his faithful companion. For with his horse he both charges and puts to flight the enemy, or, if need arise, escapes from his own pursuers.' The trappings of the horse were bridle and saddle; at this date the horse had no armour. The knight himself had hauberk, helmet and shield to protect him, and lance and sword for attack. According to Anselm, 'He cannot properly be called a true knight if he lacks any one of these.'[55]

On the other hand, there can be no doubt that many holders of fractional fees continued to be knights. A list of the knights' fees of Shaftesbury Abbey (that is nine full fees and ten fractions), written in English and dating from around 1100, begins with the statement: 'These will be the estates of those knights who owe, up to their worth, military field service with the king, with their horses and their gear, for the church of Shaftesbury', and concludes by saying that all these knights owe homage.[56] The contemporary *Descriptio Militum* of Peterborough Abbey shows that the abbey was still, in Henry I's time, concerned to put an army in the field, even though its military use to the Crown may be doubted.[57] Peterborough's military tenants, moreover, were among the less well endowed; necessarily so as the abbey, a centre of resistance to the Normans, had had a punitive service quota of sixty knights imposed upon it. Fees held jointly often provided a knight for the host by means of a rotational system, through which one

A list of the knights' fees of Shaftesbury Abbey, written in English and dating from c. *1100. It illustrates the variation in the endowment of Anglo–Norman knights* tenant rendered service and the others paid his expenses. On some baronies, fractional fee-holders were called on to perform military service in proportion to the amount of knight service due from their fee. For example, Nicholas of Stafford, a baron of William II (1087–1100), freed a vassal holding half a knight's fee from all castleguard obligations while requiring him to perform a full knight's service in the host. In contrast, Faritius, abbot of Abingdon (1100–17), enjoined the holder of half a knight's fee to remain on expeditions and castleguard for three weeks instead of the usual six-week period demanded from those who had a whole fee.[58]

But once again it must be stressed that it was not just a matter of fees and military obligations. The circumstances of the Norman Conquest were peculiar, to be sure, but Anglo-Norman society remained a lawless and insecure one, in which great men still required escort, protection and a vigorous household. The household knight was for long a characteristic feature of feudal society. There must still have been employment enough for those with a strong right arm. There were castles still to be guarded, several hundred in fact, and even wars to be fought.

Castleguard must have been an almost universal obligation upon the enfeoffed knight, either in a baronial castle or in one of the royal castles whose guard was provided by combining the services of knights from a number of baronies.[59] Commutation of this service into money payments seems not to have got seriously under way before the reign of Henry II (1154–89), despite the fact that Henry I occasionally released religious houses from these duties. Moreover, the latter's arrangements often serve at the same time to indicate the continuing vital importance of castleguard. In 1130, for example, he released the knights of the bishop of Ely from castleguard at Norwich so that they could perform it in the Isle of Ely, and similarly around 1133 he allowed the bishop of Lincoln to withdraw one-third of his knights from duty at Lincoln in favour of his castle at Newark.[60] In practice, however, even a rigidly enforced castleguard rota system must have failed to provide an adequate garrison, notwithstanding the fact that they were bolstered by non-knights holding land by what was known as sergeanty tenure.[61] In times of peace, in particular, many barons must have been reliant on their household knights. As one historian put it: 'The average baron must have been forced to entrust the peacetime defence of his castle to the porter, the watchman, and one or two household knights while his tenants were bound to supply a more adequate force in time of war.'[62]

Although, in retrospect, Henry I was held to have brought an unusual degree of peace to the land, the civil war which followed during the reign of King Stephen can hardly have encouraged men to lay down their arms. Nor can it be doubted that there remained considerable advantages in belonging to the profession of arms, even in its lower reaches. It may well be true to say that the knights depicted in Domesday Book did not live nobly and that their income was hardly above that of the well-to-do free tenants. Nevertheless, they lived without setting their hands to the plough. On the contrary, they lived off rents, off the toil of peasant tenants. Sometimes historians use the term 'peasant knighthood' as opposed to 'noble knighthood'. This is acceptable insofar as it refers to the fact of peasant origin. However, in terms of how their income was derived and even, to some extent, in terms of their lifestyle and associations – especially those who

The motte and bailey castle at Elsdon, Northumberland. Many Anglo-Norman knights must have owed castleguard at structures like this

spent time in great men's households – all those who fought belonged essentially to seignorial society.

In short, there may well have been some diminution in the number of knights in society as the twelfth century progressed. But this should not be exaggerated. There can be no doubt that the knights of mid-twelfth-century England were still numbered in thousands; perhaps four or five thousand, maybe more, maybe less. And if there had been some losses at the lower end, there is no doubt either of the continued existence of those poorer knights who are revealed in Domesday Book. Although knighthood must have carried some status, it remained primarily a matter of function.[63] It may well be the case that some of the *milites* were comparatively lightly armed but there is no real evidence to support the view that the Domesday *milites* were not real knights, as opposed to those noble knights or chevaliers of whom Domesday Book is largely silent.[64] Knighthood embraced a range of wealth and a variety of conditions.

In common with the Continent, England both before and after the Norman Conquest was ruled by a warrior aristocracy, its subordinates and associates. The first stirrings of a more exclusive attitude towards knighthood can be detected during the late eleventh and early twelfth centuries, and this was bound to magnify differences in status and to create tensions. It is in this context that the frequent references by the chroniclers to rustic knights or *milites gregarii* should be viewed. As we have seen, William of Poitiers, when describing the Conqueror's

St George portrayed as a knight, complete with banner, in the church of St George, Fordington, in Dorset, c. 1100. It probably alludes to the miracle of St George at the Siege of Antioch in 1098 and is, therefore, a product of the First Crusade. St George is striking his Saracen foes on the right, while Christian knights are depicted praying on the left. The banner probably indicates high rank as well as command in the field

preparations for his invasion of England, distinguished between noble knights and common or rustic knights. This distinction is found quite commonly in the works of the chroniclers of the Anglo-Norman period. For example, when in 1101 Henry I was challenged by Duke Robert of Normandy, Florence of Worcester reports that many of the 'English' nobles went over to Robert, but the bishops, *milites gregarii*, and the English remained loyal. Reporting on the revolt of Robert of Belesme in the following year, Orderic gives a remarkable debate. The barons, he said, debated among themselves on the danger of making Henry too strong; it would be better, they felt, to negotiate peace than to overthrow the king's enemies. Hearing this, 3,000 knights of the countryside (*tria millia pagensium militum*) shouted out in protest. They warned the king against the policy being advocated by the lords.[65]

The distinction is still commonly found in the reign of King Stephen (1135–54). In the chronicle known as the *Gesta Stephani* rustic knights are sometimes to be found alongside hired knights. These differences are sometimes alluded to in descriptions of particular knights. Robert of Bampton, a castellan in Devon, for example, is introduced as a knight 'not indeed of the lowest birth, nor of small landed estate'.[66] Sometimes, moreover, rustic knight was used in a deliberately pejorative sense. Orderic Vitalis has the high-born rebel, Waleran of Meulan, exclaim as he saw his enemies preparing for the battle of Bourgthéroulde, 'Far be it from us to fear these *gregarii et pagenses*'.[67] This hardly betokens a perception of a social group in decline, as has sometimes been supposed; on the contrary, it argues for its continued existence.

THREE

Angevin Knighthood and its Transformation *c*. 1150–*c*. 1250

The period from the mid-twelfth to the mid-thirteenth century is an extremely important one in the history of knighthood in England. The exact status of the knight, however, within the society of mid-twelfth century England is not easy to discern. William of Malmesbury, in his *Historia Novella*, tells a story about a local knight (*quidam provincialium militum*) who was proud of his luxuriant hair, long hair being very much the fashion. One night he dreamt that someone strangled him with his own hair; so he promptly had it cut short. This haircut came to set a new fashion throughout England, so that nearly all the knights took to wearing short hair. However, those who considered themselves to be courtiers (*curiales*) went back to wearing long hair, presumably to distinguish themselves from the *milites provinciales*, and even wore wigs if their natural hair was not long enough. William, of course, strongly disapproved.[1] The story is interesting for two reasons: one is that it illustrates the élitist pull which tended to draw the better placed away from the lesser knights in the shires, and perhaps the difficulties they were encountering in making would-be distinctions effective; and, secondly, it indicates that local knights could be sufficiently conscious of themselves as a group to want to follow a common fashion.[2]

Seen from the vantage point of the great lord, however, the world of the knight (and of the enfeoffed knight in particular) was bounded by the lordship or honour and by its honour court to which the lord's tenants owed suit (that is, duty of attendance), or by the lord's household. Status in this world tended to be determined to a large extent by relationship to a lord. The private written instruments of the lords are often addressed to their barons and men, their barons and free or faithful men or to their ministers, barons and free men. Baron, in this context, may mean a man who holds his land directly from a lord and the term is sometimes used together with vavasour (meaning strictly the vassal of a vassal or vassals) denoting a man holding his land at one remove from the lord. It is found in this sense in contemporary legal treatises, such as the so-called Laws of Henry I (*Leges Henrici Primi*).[3] Among those who are expected to be present at the county courts, we are told, are earls, barons, vavasours and all other lords of lands. Otherwise, however, baron seems to indicate closeness to a lord and encompasses his trusted household officers in addition to those of his greater tenants whom he most trusted and whose counsel he most valued.[4]

It is comparatively rare that a lord's knights are mentioned explicitly in their private instruments. On occasion, however, this does occur. Richard fitz Gilbert II, earl of Hertford, for example, made a confirmation to Stoke by Clare priory between 1124 and 1136 'at the petition of my barons, knights and freemen'.[5] The usage is tautologous in that the barons must generally have been knights themselves, so that by knights we should read something like mere knights. Somewhat later, between 1145 and 1154, Walchelin Maminot made restitution of the land of Lee to the monks of Shrewsbury, the men of Ellesmere having declared before him and his knights that his uncle William Peverel had unjustly taken it from them.[6] This declaration was made, of course, in Walchelin's own court.

However, honours should not be thought of as entirely enclosed worlds. Military tenants often held of more than one lord, for example, and in any case their relationship with one another must have been determined by the factor of neighbourhood as well as by the factor of lordship.[7] In a writ of 1109–11 King Henry I had pronounced that in any plea arising over land, if it was between two of his barons it should be decided in the royal court. If it was between vavasours of one of his barons then it should be dealt with in that lord's court. If, however, it was between vavasours of two different lords, then it should be dealt within the county court. In the *Leges Henrici Primi* a man intending to hold a court is advised to summon his peers and neighbours to strengthen the court to avoid the possibility of its judgements being challenged subsequently. Notions of neighbourhood and district must always have retained some strength, and with them some sense of who had status within a localized community.

It is undoubtedly the case, therefore, that being a knight carried some status in its own right within local society, partly because it denoted membership within or relationship to the seignorial world, but over and above this because of the dignity attached to the bearing of arms. In 1150 Hugh fitz Richard reached an agreement with the monks of Reading over pasture rights at Rowington in Warwickshire. In his charter he lets it be known that 'in the year when earl Ranulf of Chester caught me hunting' he had assembled freemen, namely knights, clerics and freeholders (*francos, scilicet milites, clericos et frankelengos*) in order to recognize by oath the common pasture which ought to exist between them in the woods of Shrewley and Aspley.[8] We have, then, a threefold division of men with knowledge of, and an interest and status within, the locality; a threefold division which is headed by the knights.

What made knighthood particularly distinctive, however, in the England of the second half of the twelfth century were the civilian duties borne by the knights. These have to be seen against the background of the Angevin revolution in legal procedure, inaugurated during the reign of Henry II. But, just as these legal

developments built upon Anglo-Norman and ultimately upon Anglo-Saxon foun-
dations, so the role played by the knight within them is partly determined by the
knight's pre-existing status within society. What, then, was the role of the knight
within the Angevin legal system? The most spectacular aspect was his role within
the procedure known as the grand assize. This may be considered the culmination
of Henry II's judicial reforms. Introduced in 1179, the procedure is explained in the
treatise on the laws and customs of England attributed (probably wrongly) to the
king's justiciar, Ranulf de Glanville, and written 1187–9. Glanville calls the grand
assize 'a royal benefit granted to the people by the goodness of the king acting on
the advice of his magnates'. By its means, he explains, all men may preserve the
rights which they have in any free tenement, while avoiding the outcome of trial by
battle, until now the standard means of defending the right to land. In this way they
could avoid 'the greatest of all punishments, unexpected and untimely death, or at
least the reproach of the perpetual disgrace which follows that distressed and
shameful word which sounds so dishonourably from the mouth of the vanquished'.
The grand assize, where it was appropriate, simply substituted the verdict of a jury
of twelve knights for the hazards of trial by battle. In its favour Glanville argues that
just as the testimony of several witnesses in judicial proceedings outweighs that of
one man, so this procedure requires the oaths of at least twelve men as against the
testimony in effect of only one witness in the case of battle.

The procedure was as follows: the defendant faced with a writ of right could
defend himself in the old way, by battle, if he chose; or, he could elect for the
grand assize. The sheriff now received a new writ directing him to summon four
law-worthy knights from the neighbourhood in question to come before the royal
justices. These knights were to elect on oath twelve law-worthy knights, also from
the same neighbourhood, 'who best know the truth of the matter'. These twelve
were then sent to view, that is to say examine, the disputed property and then to
declare on oath whether the plaintiff or the defendant, had the greater right to it.[9]

It was a very solemn procedure; one which was deemed to require the status of
knights. Knights were also necessary to convey to the royal court the record of a
plea determined in a county court, should this be required. Similarly the king
required a record from knights should an agreement (known as a final concord)
which terminated a case held before the travelling justices be subsequently challenged. In these contexts they are referred to as law-worthy knights or as discreet
knights of the county.[10]

Legal proceedings at this time were subject to a well-regulated system of lawful
excuses (or essoins) for non-attendance in court and hence delays. One of these
was the essoin of bed-sickness. If the party in question failed to appear at the
third summons the sheriff received a writ ordering him to send four lawful
knights of the county to discover whether or not the person was seriously ill. In
the case of bed-sickness they would direct him to appear in court one year and
one day from the time they examined him. Should they find the illness to be less
serious, that is house-sickness rather than bed-sickness, they would assign him a
nearer day on which he should appear or send a representative to answer the case.
It is to be assumed that if they found him to be shamming they would order him
to court forthwith.[11]

The survival of plea rolls from the central courts from the 1190s onwards allows the role played by local knights to be seen more fully. There are occasions on record of the specific use of knights rather than freemen for juries other than those of the grand assize; in cases of novel disseisin, for example, the earliest of the possessory assizes which was instituted in 1166 for swiftness of justice. The sheriff could be directed to choose only knights when the king's interests were involved. They had other duties too. In the case of trial by battle, which was by no means entirely superseded by the grand assize, it was they who kept the field and acted as umpires. On one occasion they had to go to Westminster to answer a complaint that when one of the champions was on the ground one of the knights entered the ring and hit the other duellist on the head.[12] Before the fight itself the record of the wager of the duel (the giving of security by both parties that they intend to proceed with the fight) had to be made at Westminster by four knights. Less spectacular but commoner was the survey and valuation of land in dispute, a duty regularly undertaken by knights. In these and other duties they were acting under the direction of the justices and in association with the sheriff and the county court.

They were often called upon in the criminal sphere too. Their testimony might be sought, or offenders might be committed to their custody. They could be sent to inspect the scene of a crime or examine the wounds of a victim of assault. From 1194, when the office was instituted, they could be called upon to be coroners, who gathered information and kept the record of serious crime prior to trial before the royal justices.[13]

For the most part, the legal records of this period give only a terse account of the contexts in which the procedures were invoked. Monastic sources, however, sometimes give more detailed, albeit one-sided, descriptions of lawsuits. One such, which illustrates the role of knights in legal procedures, is the protracted case between the abbot of Crowland on the one hand and the prior of Spalding and the men of Holland on the other, over the marshland between the two religious houses in south Lincolnshire.[14] The dispute began, according to the Crowland source, during the last year of King Henry II (1189) when the prior of Spalding and four prominent lay landowners led most of the powerful folk of Elloe wapentake (an administrative division of the county) in a conspiracy to deny the abbot his right to the marshland. On 12 May they came with an armed force to prevent the abbot from fencing the marsh and impounding the animals which had strayed into it, as he normally did at this time of year, and proceeded to divide the marsh according to the sites of their villages. The abbot and monks of Crowland complained to one of the royal justices, Geoffrey fitz Peter, who was then at King's Cliff in Northamptonshire. Geoffrey sent six knights from Northamptonshire to view and report fully on the matter. In the meantime Abbot Robert hastened to London to set his case before Hubert Walter, who was then acting for the chief justiciar, Ranulf de Glanville, himself overseas with the king. As a result, formal legal proceedings began and the parties to the dispute were set a day, during the Michaelmas term, to appear before the chief justiciar at Westminster.

Meanwhile, however, Henry II died, Richard I ascended the throne and the justices were changed. This, according to the Crowland account, emboldened the men of Holland. In practice, however, the laymen withdrew from the case and came to terms with the abbot, leaving the prior of Spalding standing alone; or so it seemed. The prior argued that the marsh he was accused of entering with an armed force belonged to the priory of Spalding and was of the fee of William de Roumare, and offered the king 40 marks for a grand assize to prove this. The abbot had no choice but to consent to this, although he feared the outcome. There were two grounds for his fear. The first was that the knights of the county tended to be remote from the marshland area, and the second was because there was scarcely anyone living in Lincolnshire who was not bound in some way to the house of Spalding, to Earl William de Roumare, or to one of those who had begun the claim upon the marsh. On the Crowland side it was clearly believed that the men who had earlier come to terms were nevertheless secretly aiding the prior and his men (with advice and with money), and that the men of Holland were therefore rejoicing at the probable outcome.

The text of a royal writ follows naming the jury of knights chosen by the four knights who had been the electors, and instructing the sheriff of Lincoln to summon them to view the marsh on the Monday before Christmas and to be present there himself with four or six of the more law-worthy knights of the shire. According to the account a number of irregularities then occurred. The sheriff did not turn up in person but sent a representative, Walter de Essartis, who was a supporter of the men of Spalding, and very few of the named knights actually came. Furthermore, at least three of the jury had been dropped, through the judge's favour and without the abbot's agreement. It was quite normal for more than twelve knights to be named as the jury, with the expectation that twelve of them would function in practice. How this was done appears uncertain. It may be that the defendant, who had invoked the grand assize, had the right to object to some of the jurors. Despite the implications of the Crowland account, therefore, it is far from clear as to whether any irregularity, in this respect, had actually occurred. Nonetheless, the view was duly made. When the day set for the verdict approached the abbot fell ill on the journey and essoined. Remaining ill and unable to meet a further day he was now able to essoin of bed-sickness, in accordance with legal procedure. Four knights were sent by the justiciar to view him and set him another day after Easter. However, on Easter eve Abbot Robert died and the abbey passed into the king's hands pending the election of a new abbot. The action, therefore, ceased, at least for the time being.

The case was resumed, however, in 1191, when it became bound up with national politics. The next abbot of Crowland was Henry, brother of William de Longchamps, bishop of Ely and Chancellor of England. When Longchamps fell from power, his enemies turned against the abbot of Crowland. They included William de Roumare and Gerard de Camville, one of the parties to the original action, who was now sheriff of Lincoln. The abbot was summoned to appear at Westminster against the abbot of St Nicholas of Angers, now acting for the priory of Spalding as this was a priory dependent upon the house of Angers, to hear the verdict of the knights who had earlier held a view of the marsh under the procedure of the grand assize. In the circumstances, however, the abbot feared for his safety; at least, according to the monastic account. So, he essoined, again once on account of difficulties met on the journey to court and a second time of bed-sickness. The sheriff, Gerard de Camville, was duly instructed by writ to send four knights to view him. It appears, however, that only one of the knights, Reginald of Bennington, actually turned up to view the abbot, and that he came with some low persons, men of the prior of Spalding. The abbot, it is argued, had expected them not to appear, the implication being that the essoin would not then be registered and that he would therefore lose the case by default, through his non-appearance in court. Even though he was not fully recovered, the abbot left for one of his manors in Cambridgeshire which was on his way to the court, and arrived on the appointed day. Meanwhile, Reginald of Bennington had arrived to view him, even though his fellow knights were not with him. He ascertained that the abbot was not there (that is to say that he had risen from his bed without licence), and announced a further day for him to appear before the justices.

When he reached London the abbot found his enemies ranged against him. He was alone in court, it was said, but for three monks and two very modest knights (*militibus mediocribus*), for no one else dared stand with him. Despite this the abbot was able to produce charters which strongly supported his case. However, he lost possession of the marsh because he was judged to have arisen from his bed-sickness without licence. When the four knights were called for, there appeared in their place four low persons, apparently hired for the occasion and named as Geoffrey of Thurlby, William son of Alfred, Walter Rufus of Hamby and Gilbert son of Justi of Bennington. They were not knights, it was emphasized, nor did they hold knights' fees. In vain the abbot argued that they were not the knights named, and that neither they nor the others had come to view him. The account adds, in order to further emphasize his point, that most of those present in court thought that the abbot would win because those who claimed to have been the viewers were not of the military order nor girt with the sword (*de militari ordine nec cincti gladio*); one of them, furthermore, did not know how to speak French!

The abbot of Crowland eventually won the case, although it was not until the reign of King John that his house emerged secure in the possession of the marsh-land. However, it is not the verdict or the rights and wrongs of the matter that concern us here, and the glosses that the Crowland account puts upon events may or may not have been valid. What is important in the present context is that the case enables us to see Angevin knights in their legal capacity, functioning in the grand assize under the sheriff's direction and ascertaining the validity of an essoin of bed-sickness. Moreover, the case contains some clues as to the contemporary status attached to knighthood. First, it is quite clear that there were, in fact, differences in status among knights. One hears of modest knights who by implication possessed little influence. One hears also of knights who are among the more law-worthy of the shire; although this ought not perhaps to be taken too literally, it does at least suggest that contemporaries were able to conceive of knights of inferior status. Most important of all is the insistence that the knights of the essoin and of the grand assize should be real knights, and not nominal knights, as it were, to satisfy the procedures. Although some anomalies occurred,

the awareness among litigants that infringement on this score would invalidate
the procedures and that this could be used to advantage makes it certain that in
the great majority of cases the men employed were indeed knights.[15] Such men
would have some status in the community, as indicated by the suggestion that they
were expected to be able to speak French. They should be part of the military order, to be belted knights girt with the sword.

    Who then were the knights of the grand assize? Surviving rolls from the cen-
tral courts and from the visitations of the king's travelling justices become more
frequent and fuller as the thirteenth century progresses, and these regularly
record the names of knights. They are the only records that consistently do so
before the 1240s, when the charters recording property transactions began to give
the status of knightly witnesses on a regular basis. To take one example, the roll of
the travelling justices who visited Worcestershire in 1221 records a case brought
by Nicholas de Foley against Richard de Foley for land described as a half a
knight's fee at Little (or Lower) Wolverton near Stoulton, to the south-east of
Worcester.[16] The defendant put himself on the grand assize. Four knights were
summoned to elect a jury of twelve, and they duly did so. In the event, Nicholas
surrendered his right to the property to Richard and a formal agreement (a final
concord) was drawn up to record this. As is normal in these laconic records, no
more of the case is told than this. The names of the knights, however, are recorded. The electors chose, in fact, a total of sixteen knights, including two of themselves, from whom the jury would be formed. This, as has been seen, was normal
procedure, to ensure a jury and to allow perhaps for possible objections from the
parties. According to the writ that began the procedure, the knights should be
from the same neighbourhood as the property in dispute. The great majority can
indeed be shown to have held property within an eight-mile radius of the

*An extract from the roll of the travelling justices visiting Worcestershire in 1221, dealing with
the grand assize over property at Little Wolverton*

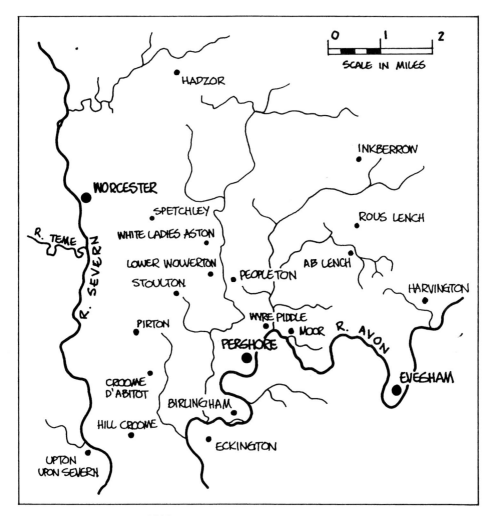

Estates of knightly jurors, 1221

settlement concerned, south or east of Worcester. Some, in fact, held property within a four-mile radius. Robert de Spetchley held land at the neighbouring village of Peopleton as well as being lord of the manor of Spetchley itself, a little to the north. Richard de Bruille held some property at White Ladies Aston, between Spetchley and Little Wolverton.[17] Roger le Poer held Pirton just to the south, among his various properties. Also on the south side, a little further out, lay the manors of Hill Croome that Eudes de Beauchamp had acquired from an indebted landowner, Upton upon Severn held by Peter de Saltmarsh, Birlingham – one of the manors of Geoffrey d'Abitot, and Eckington where Herbert Mucegros, one of the electors who nominated himself as juror, had a manor. To the east of Little Wolverton lay Rous Lench and Ab Lench where Roger de Lench, who later became indebted to the Jews, held his property. William fitz Warin, who was later to be sheriff of the county, also held property on the east side, at Wyre Piddle, Moor and Ab Lench, as well as Hadzor to the north. Osbert d'Abitot held more than one property within the radius, including Inkberrow to the east and Croome d'Abitot to the south. The rather minor figure, Thomas Rupe, held some property on the edge of this radius at Harvington, to the east.

A few of the knights, however, held their main estates well beyond this radius. Peter of Staunton came from Staunton, now in Gloucestershire, way down to the south-west. William de Washbourne came from Little Washbourne, also in the south and now just over the border in Gloucestershire. However, we cannot positively say that these men did not possess some property closer to Little Wolverton. William de Talton had his main estates at Talton in Tredington, now in Warwickshire, and at Alvechurch in the north of the county. Nevertheless, his family had originated in Fladbury, well within the eight-mile radius, and he may well have retained an interest there.

It becomes immediately apparent when we examine the knights of the grand assize that they were variously endowed with property. Some are lords of several manors; some of only one. In many cases their ancestors had taken the name of their chief estate or residence as a surname, as an expression of their status. Some were the successors of families that had done so. Others, on the other hand, were comparatively minor figures, or at least they seem to have possessed little land. Richard de Bruille had but one hide at White Ladies Aston, for example, and Thomas Rupe held a little property at Harvington. Richard de Wyleye, whose land in the county has not been traced, was a forest official (a verderer) of Feckenham Forest.[18] The interest of William son of Philip, the other elector who nominated himself juror, has also not been traced.[19] In order to understand the contours of late twelfth- and early thirteenth-century knighthood more roundly we need a much fuller list of knights.

Such a list has been compiled for neighbouring Warwickshire. Taking the rolls for the king's travelling justices in Warwickshire during the years 1221/2 and 1232 (the eyre rolls, as they are called), together with the rolls of the courts operating at Westminster, the names of about a hundred knights active between 1220 and 1232 can be recovered.[20] The majority of these were holding recognizable manors whose descent has been worked out in the county histories; they were the ancestors, in many cases, of the Warwickshire gentry of later centuries. Some of them became biologically extinct during the course of the century, while others experienced economic hardship and social decline. A minority, however, did not have a solid base within the county. What is surprising is that almost a third of these knights can be placed broadly within this category.

Some seem to be totally obscure. In many other instances only a minor interest can be discerned. How can we explain this? One possibility is clearly that they could be insignificant figures as far as Warwickshire is concerned, but of more consequence elsewhere. Knights were expected to hold some interest in the county in order to properly participate in the assize.[21] But their main estate could conceivably lie beyond the county's borders. A few knights do come into this category, but in actual fact very few. It does not appear to be a significant factor. Two other features, often linked together, appear to have been more prominent. One is the phenomenon of younger sons. The second is the prevalence of minor interests acquired through marriage. Yet another significant feature is that of service. William de Flamville was one-time steward of William de Hastings, while William de Wilmcote was a steward of the earl of Warwick. In all probability these were not isolated cases. William Huse, for instance, handed over a sum of 14s. on behalf of Robert Marmion in 1221, and was very likely in his service. This William, in fact, may have combined all three features: he was probably a younger son, he was in service, and he acquired a minor interest in property through marriage. Figures like William Huse cannot have been uncommon. There were others, too, who may be regarded as ministers. Richard de Wyleye, who figured also in neighbouring Worcestershire, as has been seen, was a verderer of Feckenham forest. Two of the Warwickshire knights were royal falconers by profession. In other words, it was not simply as conventional lords of manors but by a whole variety of means that Warwickshire's minor knights and holders of minor interests were supporting their knighthood.

However, a degree of caution needs to be introduced. The fact that an interest is classified as minor does not necessarily prove that the knight holding it had a limited income. Some of these men may have had other sources of wealth. Their overall income level may not have been very different from other knights holding small manors. The situation is far too complex to think in terms of two classes of knights. Similarly, despite the fact that a significant ministerial element among the knights has been discovered, they cannot be divided into two clear groups on these grounds either. It has recently been suggested that the knights who functioned in the grand assize and in related procedures were not necessarily belted knights but only 'nominal knights', akin to the 'knights of the shire' who attended parliament in later centuries.[22] This view, however, is not correct. Although it is possible that a few non-knights may have been employed from time to time, the pressure for correct procedure on the part of the courts and litigants ensured that in the great majority of cases, at least, the electors and jurors of the grand assize were indeed knights. Contemporary legal opinion insisted that they should be knights, while in 1207 a judge fined the electors for choosing men other than knights for the assize.[23] Also indicative was the concern expressed during the 1250s that a shortage of knights was causing difficulty in holding the grand assize at all in some counties.[24]

Moreover, the lesser knights do not appear on the whole to have been more involved in the grand assize than their fellows. The opposite is, in fact, the case. Taking the 1221/2 eyre with its sixteen grand assizes there are twelve men who are involved in eight or more of the cases. Of these, only three come into the classification of 'minor knights', and one of them, William de Wilmcote, had been, in the past at least, a baronial steward, indicating perhaps a higher status in the community than most. An examination of the electors rather than the jurors reveals the situation even more clearly. Seven men figure more than twice. Again, only William de Wilmcote is from the sample of minor knights.

An analysis of the 1232 eyre yields similar results. Those knights who are most active in the community are a mixed group in terms of their property stake in the county. Some can be classified as minor knights, but the majority are clearly solidly based. It is largely men of this latter type, moreover, who were called upon by the government in other capacities: as judges for the assizes and for delivering gaols, for example, and as coroners. Take John de Ladbroke, for example, lord of the village from which he derived his name. He functioned as a justice for taking assizes and for gaol delivery, but over and above that he was appointed a commissioner for assessing and collecting taxes on moveable goods (the fortieth of 1232 and the thirtieth of 1237), he was appointed to take control of the king's escheats and wards (that is, the lands and heirs that had passed into the hands of the king), and, with the sheriff, he was appointed to inspect the castles in the county and to report to the government on any defects found in them.[25] As to why substantial local landowners wished to undertake these tasks, it was partly, it would seem, a matter of status, and partly a matter of disposition. The great legal historian Frederick William Maitland saw them as 'business-loving gentlemen'. If this is not quite accurate, it is nevertheless closer than the idea of nominal knights.[26] The truth of the matter, however, is that contemporary knights were neither amateurs in a strict sense nor professionals. They were semi-professional, because service was part of the knightly ethos, part of what conferred status. This was more obviously the case where service to great men was concerned.

A great lord might still at this date refer to a knightly member of his household or following as *miles meus* (my knight) or as my bachelor, a term implying both knighthood and household service. Those knights who functioned as stewards to great lords covered the whole spectrum of local knights, just as did the knights of the grand assize. They too could be the heads of established, even of quite illustrious, county families, or they could be younger sons or collaterals of established families, or they could be lowly figures who owed their status to their service alone.[27] Although their cultural level may not have been particularly high, many of them will have been functionally literate at the beginning of the thirteenth century, and probably increasingly so as the century wore on. When chroniclers speak of the *miles literatus* as a comparative rarity, they are talking of the learned or cultivated knight and not of the knight who was able to read. In fact, 'most knights were at least pragmatic readers, functional literates in today's terms, capable of handling simple Latin as a tool in their many tasks of government'.[28]

The surviving records allow this type of analysis to be taken just a little further back, to the beginning of the thirteenth century. The evidence for Warwickshire consists of thirteen panels of four knights, electors to the grand assize, ranging in date from 1200 to 1214. Altogether the panels yield the names of forty-one knights. Of these, eighteen come under the broad category of obscure knights or knights with minor interests in the county as defined above; that is to say not a third this time, but virtually half of the sample. This is one among several indications that the further we go back in time the larger the pool was from which knights of the grand assize and such like could be chosen.

One of the minor knights of this earlier period was Henry de Shuckburgh. He is undoubtedly the same Henry de Shuckburgh who brought a case against Robert son of Warin for 4 virgates (about 120 acres) of land at Shuckburgh. Robert put himself on the grand assize.[29] Unusually, the roll gives not merely the verdict but also the jurors' account of the history of the Shuckburgh family and its property. And an interesting story it is, too. A certain knight called Warin of Walcote, who was a doughty and itinerant knight (or knight errant), fighting in the civil war of King Stephen's reign, came to the house of Robert de Shuckburgh. This Robert had a daughter named Isabella whom Warin loved and took. He sought her hand but was prevented from having her by both Robert, her father, and by William, her brother, who was also a knight. However, William was also an itinerant knight, and he was later killed in the war. Warin now appeared with a large number of men and took Isabella away by force. He took her without her father's consent, the jurors said, and held her for some time. At length, after the death of King Stephen when peace had been restored by the new king, Henry II, Warin returned; but he fell into poverty because he could not rob as he had done before. Nevertheless he could not refrain from violence and attempted to carry on in the way that he had been used to do. Eventually he was captured, ambushed in fact, and led before the king at Northampton. Henry, wishing to make an example, had him put into the stocks, and there he died. After his death Isabella returned to her father's home and was taken back by him because she had not left willingly.

The present case had arisen because Isabella had subsequently married and had been given the land in question as her marriage portion. Henry de Shuckburgh, the plaintiff, was the fruit of this marriage. Isabella, however, had already had a son by Warin, out of wedlock. Warin son of Warin had been given a half-virgate of land by Isabella and her husband in order to sustain him. Warin the younger's son, Robert, was the defendant in the case. Presumably he had acquired the land after Isabella and her husband had died. Henry de Shuckburgh and Robert son of Warin were brought into agreement 'by licence of the justices for God's sake because they are poor'. Henry was to have the land less the half-virgate which Isabella and her husband had given Warin son of Warin. Henry was described as poor, meaning that he had no cash with which to pay. Nevertheless, he must have had an income of some sort, or at least some means of sustaining knighthood.

Another significant case is that of the knight, Warin de Coundon, who flourished at the very beginning of the thirteenth century in the locality of Coventry. He first appears in a charter recording a matter between two local free tenants which was witnessed by Warin, together with John Dive and John Benet, all three knights, followed by William the Huntsman and four others. Warin's land was sold off by the next generation, both the third which passed to his widow as dower and the remainder held by Warin son of Warin. All of this had occurred by the early 1220s at the latest. From the transactions it is clear that Warin de Coundon's property was not very extensive, that some of it, at least, was tenant land, and that when the king asked for scutage or shield-money it was assessed as one tenth of a knight's fee. Warin the knight may nonetheless have lived in some style, as perhaps is indicated by his vivary (private fishpond), which naturally implies a residence. He was also the possessor of urban property in Coventry.

Warin's family disappears from view.[30] The descendants of his fellow knights, however, remained on the land. None of them ever appear to have been knights. But they do figure as local freeholders in the area. The Benet interest was particularly persistent. A later John Benet was said, in 1279, to be holding of John de

Hastings at Coundon and Allesley, land that was assessed at a tenth part of a knight's fee, precisely the level at which Warin was assessed at the beginning of the century and a further indication that they were of similar standing.

It seems likely that all three knights were associated with the Hastings lordship. It is surely significant that in the charter they witness together, their names are followed by William the Huntsman, suggesting that he, too, was in service. It is probable, then, that they belonged to the Hastings retinue and should be thought of as within the category of household knights. Of course, they were not landless. However, too great a distinction has been made by historians in the past between the enfeoffed knight and the household knight. A recent study of the household of Roger de Quincy, earl of Winchester (1235–64) has shown at least one landless knight being rewarded with a *fief-rente* (money granted as a knight's fee), with another receiving rent from property under the earl's control.[31] Little is known about how household knights were rewarded at this date, except, of course, that they received their board and lodgings for at least part of the time. It would seem probable, however, that they received additional rewards, in cash or otherwise, from time to time. There was nothing to prevent them from investing, especially in small parcels of land. They did not necessarily have to wait to be enfeoffed by their lord. In fact, for household knights, rent income – including that from urban property – was probably extremely useful as it required little management to maintain and could be regarded as an investment for the time when they retired from service.

It is possible, then, that the three local knights were directly supported in addition to holding minor property, and that they sustained their knighthood by the combination of these means. It is, however, in the witnessing of a local charter that they have come to light. They were not functioning here as part of their overlord's retinue, but were witnessing a property transaction as men of standing in the community. In other words they enjoyed some status and some stake in society. Warin de Coundon and his fellows do not figure in the surviving legal records, but some of the knights of the grand assize were undoubtedly of similar position to them.[32] It is worth recalling that knights were required to possess some property in a county to be eligible to be called upon for the Angevin legal procedures. Interesting in this context is a case from Herefordshire in 1220, when Robert Vernay was disqualified from acting as one of the knights sent to view a litigant who had essoined of bed-sickness because he was of a household and did not have any land.[33] No doubt some of our minor and seemingly obscure knights were indeed household knights, but if so they should also have possessed some land and rent.

Lest too much attention be given to the minor knights it should be added that no less than twenty-three of the forty-one knights from Warwickshire who figure in the legal cases between 1200 and 1214 were more solidly based figures of the later 'gentry' type. Looking across the whole period from 1200 to 1232, the knights of the grand assize range from very substantial figures in the county to knights of very modest fortune or social significance. The baronage was not represented. No earl of Warwick is found, nor lesser barons like the Marmions of Tamworth or the Montforts of Beaudessert, nor indeed figures who are closely associated with the royal court like Gilbert de Segrave, justiciar of England, or Geoffrey de Langley, one of Henry III's most notorious justices of the forest. But with that proviso, a cross-section of the knighthood of Warwickshire is undoubtedly represented. What it indicates is the size of the pool from which the knights of the grand assize were drawn; with a clear suggestion that the further one goes back the greater is the number of knights and the higher the proportion who are not the heads of what would later be called county families. Knighthood was a widely-shared status, but there were clearly very considerable differences within it. Minor knights (or *milituli*) remained an important feature of English society in the early thirteenth century, while knighthood itself was a complex phenomenon involving the profession of arms, service and status conferred either by lordship itself or by service to the great.

It is hardly surprising that there should have been tension around the issue of knighthood. There are several indications that contemporaries perceived and expressed differences. From the late 1190s, if not before, the royal writ which began the solemn procedure of the grand assize called for the election of knights from among the 'more law-worthy' of the locality in question, and it was not the only twelfth-century source to include this concept.[34] One can only surmise as to what made a knight more or less law-worthy, but it may be readily supposed that it involved a stake in the community, that is to say essentially the possession of property or, perhaps, the holding of an important office. When Robert Vernay was disqualified from acting as one of the four knights to check on a litigant who had essoined of bed-sickness in 1220, on the grounds that he was from a household and did not hold any land, this may well be a clue as to what was meant by being less law-worthy.[35] Phrases denoting rustic knights, *milites gregarii* and *milites rustici*, were often used by chroniclers during the first half of the century, sometimes to distinguish them from noble and finely equipped knights, and sometimes with prejorative intent. The idea was still current when the chronicler, Robert de Torigny, told how Henry II preferred not to burden the country knights (*agrarios milites*) with his campaign in Toulouse in 1159.[36] These distinctions, like the concept of more law-worthy, might well indicate not so much the decline of the *militulus* but rather his continuing presence. It ought not to be assumed that such distinctions ceased to apply during the second half of the twelfth century. A hint of the sense of social exclusion involved has been detected in the *Dialogue of the Exchequer*, completed in 1179, when the author distinguishes between two types of knight in cases of debt, the belted knight who should have a trained horse left to him 'lest a man who is entitled by his rank to ride, should be compelled to go on foot', and the active knight whose armour and necessary horses should be free from distraint 'so that when need arises he can be employed on the business of the King and the realm, fully equipped'.[37] A sharper example is the famous retort by the justiciar Richard de Lucy to Gilbert de Balliol that 'it was not formally the custom for every petty knight (*militulus*) to have a seal, which befits kings and great personages'.[38]

The distinction between the noble or courtly knight on the one hand, and the *militulus* or rustic knight on the other was not, however, the only one felt by contemporaries. There was a further distinction between those who actually fought and those who rarely, if ever, did so. This seems to be the central message of the passage in the *Dialogue of the Exchequer* just discussed. The insolvent debtor who has been knighted should retain a horse suitable to his rank. If, however, he is the kind of knight who 'keeps his armour bright and loves to use it', then all of his equipment may be free from distraint. Should such a knight hide himself away, without excuse, when his country needs him, he will forfeit this right and 'must share the common lot and be thankful to keep the single horse due to his station'. The last point probably reflects the royal minister's concern for the military pre-paredness of the nation, but the existence not only of knights who do not fight but also of knights who merely profess to fight is strongly suggested. Moreover, some of the active knights themselves may well have felt contempt for the purely honorific knights. As Nigel de Longchamp of Canterbury stated around 1192: 'there are many knights without skill and practice in arms, who for that reason are called "Holy Mary's knights" by the others'.[39]

During the latter part of the twelfth century the number of knights who rarely fought probably increased, notwithstanding the Continental campaigns fought by the English kings. Despite Henry II's great inquiry into knights' fees in 1166, it is doubtful whether he ever demanded the full service due from his tenants-in-chief.[40] In 1157 Henry asked for one-third of the total service and two years later preferred to take scutage (shield-money) in lieu of service from the majority of his tenants-in-chief. By the reign of King John, if not before, the king had to be satis-fied with men coming on campaign accompanied by a retinue that they felt was appropriate to their status, rather than with their full service quota. On all sides men were demanding a reduction in service, both subtenants and tenants-in-chief. Many of those who ceased to serve were undoubtedly among the least endowed and holders of fractional fiefs, a situation certainly aggravated by sales, partitions and sub-infeudations (the creation of subtenancies). Only in extreme circumstances would the body of England's knighthood be called upon to fight for their king, as in the famous instance of 1189 when the justiciar was sent back to England to call upon its knights 'even the poor and diminished'. There was, in fact, a progressive reduction in the old feudal quotas, a process that was virtually completed by the time of Henry III's Welsh campaign of 1245. By this date it was possible to send two mounted sergeants in lieu of one knight. In his 1277 army Edward I had a total feudal service of only 228 knights and 294 sergeants.

What, however, of those other two scenes of knightly employment, the castle and the household? Castles certainly needed to be garrisoned in Angevin England. For the first century or so after the Norman Conquest the system of castleguard attached to the tenure of land seems to have continued in full rigour.[41] Gradually, however, both king and barons found the obligations more difficult to enforce in times of peace. The commutation of castleguard into money seems to have begun during the reign of Henry II, and evidence for it becomes stronger towards the end of the century. The rate of commutation, however, varied as lords made the best bargains they could with their tenants. Since there was little danger attached to it in times of peace, it seems that tenants were often able to drive a hard bargain and that the level of commutation tended to be low in consequence, often well below the cost of hiring replacement knights. In fact, Article 29 of

Magna Carta suggests that even as late as 1215 there were knights who preferred to perform the service in person rather than be forced to hand over their cash:

> No constable shall compel any knight to give money in lieu of castleguard when he is willing to perform it in his own person, or (if he cannot do it from any reasonable cause) then by another responsible man.

By and large, though, it would seem that castles were garrisoned by a small number of stipendiary knights and sergeants in times of peace and that these were paid for essentially by commutation of castleguard obligations. In times of war those who owed castleguard service would continue to serve, although there is every reason to suppose that the professional garrisons would also have remained. The records of the royal Exchequer, the Pipe Rolls, illustrate the system of payment to garrison knights from early in the reign of Henry II, although for obvious reasons their use greatly increased during times of particular difficulty, such as the baronial rebellion of 1173–4.[42] Some of the mercenary knights were from the Continent, Flemings for example, but others no doubt were from England. In times of war certainly, but in times of peace too, household knights will also have continued to play a role.

The size of the royal knightly household can be seen clearly during the minority of Henry III. There survive three lists of household knights summoned for campaigns during the 1220s.[43] The first was drawn up before 1227, probably during 1226–7 when the war with France was resumed. It gives a total of 123 household knights. The remaining two lists date from 1228 and 1229 and name seventy and sixty-seven household knights respectively. But this reveals only part of the picture. Lists of the men actually summoned to military service in 1225–6 and 1229 indicate that many of the household knights brought their own retinues. In 1225–6 fifty-one of the knights brought their own knights giving the young king a total force of 211 knights. In 1229 the number was similarly boosted to 116 knights.[44] The evidence from his father's reign is patchy, but a recent study has indicated that King John could certainly mobilize a royal household comprising more than fifty knights. Moreover, it was clearly the case at this date, too, that some at least of the household knights brought their own retinues with them on campaign.[45] Additionally, John employed large numbers of stipendiary knights. The muster roll for 1215 lists forty-seven household knights and a further 375 ordinary knights, the majority of whom seem to have come from the Low Countries.[46]

By contrast, baronial retinues at this period appear to have been rather small. Eighteen men have been identified as long-standing household knights of Earl William Marshal, with seven to ten knights regularly in attendance.[47] The known household knights of Roger de Quincy, earl of Winchester, in the years between 1219 and 1264 come to twenty-eight.[48] In the case of Earl David of Huntingdon (d. 1219) only a handful of household knights can be named.[49]

Nevertheless, if relatively few knights from England were fighting in the Continental wars of Henry II and his sons, there was still some additional military employment to be found in baronial retinues in Wales and Ireland. It would seem that most knights of this period found the greater part of their employment either in the king's civilian duties or as members of household retinues, or in some cases in both. Knighthood in Angevin England carried social status, but it did so without entirely displacing the earlier ideas of knighthood as a function and as a particular form of service.

As yet, however, we have left the question of chivalry out of account. What role did it play in the development of knighthood in England? The development and diffusion of a chivalric mentality is extremely difficult to chart. As Jean Flori has so aptly said, 'chivalric ideology was forged slowly, obscurely, like a cobweb in the gloom of a crypt'.[50] One problem is the extent to which reliance has to be placed upon chroniclers and other ecclesiastical writers and, more particularly, upon nuances contained in their work. Their relationship to the secular world and to secular attitudes was inevitably a complex one. A great deal of weight is often placed upon the legitimation of knighthood by the church, but this can be misleading if taken out of context. It can offer no easy explanation.

Since at least the early eleventh century the church had been attempting to direct and control the profession of arms. In the course of time this was to give rise to the idea of knights directly serving the international church and ultimately to the crusades. When Pope Urban II preached the First Crusade at Clermont in 1095 he called upon men to leave the knighthood of the world (*militia saecularis*) and to become Christ's own knights wearing a hauberk marked with a cross. Many flocked to the banner and the crusade was a great success. Jerusalem itself was taken in 1099. But it is not at all easy to gauge the effects of the crusade upon contemporary knighthood. The needs of the Holy Land led to the formation of new orders: the Hospitallers and the Templars.[51] Half-monk, half-knight, these were men who were acknowledged to be the *militia Christi*. When St Bernard wrote his eulogy of the new knighthood (*De laude novae militiae*) in 1130 he was not only referring explicitly to the Templars but directly contrasting them with the knights who lived in this world, contrasting *militia* with *malitia* (wickedness). Certainly, the struggle against the Saracens must have had some effect upon contemporary perceptions of knighthood outside the church as the earlier epics known as the *chansons de geste* and their Christian knights would seem to suggest. But for some time the chroniclers were as likely as not to write of the essential iniquity of contemporary knighthood. In England, for example, William of Malmesbury described the knights as a class full of greed and violence. Something of a breakthrough may be seen in the work of John of Salisbury, the scholar who wrote his *Policraticus* in 1159 when chancellor to archbishop Thomas à Becket. For him the primary purpose of knighthood is service to the prince chosen by God. Knighthood is, therefore, willed and instituted by God himself and is necessary for human well-being. Like St Bernard he contrasts *militia* and *malitia* but the sense is now different. Knighthood is a necessary, even a worthy profession; he attacks only its unworthy members. As to the qualities a knight should possess these are, above all, obedience, and then physical strength, endurance, courage, and sobriety and frugality of life.

The Templars as drawn by Matthew Paris in the thirteenth century, indicating the simplicity and ascetic ideal of the order

This validation of knighthood solely in terms of service to a prince may be seen, to some extent, as a failure on the part of the church. As Maurice Keen puts it,

> Church ceremony and ecclesiastical teaching could enlarge and refine ideas of the range and meaning of knighthood's functions and could add a measure of general obligation to their original particularity; but they could never, even in an age of the crusade, effectively shake the hold of the principle of loyalty to secular lordship by interposing the church's own authority between the knight and his lord.[52]

It also indicates that the explanation for the rise and maturation of chivalry has to

Twelfth-century knights were often portrayed as worldly and sinful. This depiction of the Last Judgement, from the west portal lintel, Ste Foy, Conques (Aveyron), France, shows a mailclad knight (on the left) being pitchforked into hell

be found essentially within secular society itself. Between the lord and the serving knight there was an immense gulf, even in the early twelfth century, which had to be bridged.

One feature which played an important role in reducing some of the consequences of social distance, arguably, was the tournament. Here, on the training ground for war rather than in war itself, warriors of high and low birth came together on more equal terms.[53] It can hardly be doubted that the origins of the tournament are closely connected with the new cavalry tactic of shock combat which becomes evident in the sources towards the end of the eleventh century.[54] It came to be realised that a body of cavalry with lances couched under the arm could deliver a heavy blow against an enemy. The Bayeux Tapestry depicts this way of using a spear among various others at the Battle of Hastings and it seems highly likely that the tactic was born around this time. It was greeted with great surprise in the East, where it was remarked that by such means a Western horseman could drive a hole through the walls of Babylon. This tactic led naturally on to a new type of single combat between heavily armed horsemen, as depicted in the early twelfth-century epic, the *Chanson de Roland*. Such a method of warfare, which included the use of a heavier, longer lance would obviously require some very specific training and it is surely no accident that the first references to

Training in knightly skills began at an early age. A fourteenth-century manuscript shows the initial stages in the development of the necessary techniques

tournaments occur around this time. The tournament was, in fact, condemned by a council of the church in 1130 in terms which suggest that it was then a relatively new phenomenon, despite the fact that chroniclers tend to project it further back in time.[55]

   •During the first half of the twelfth century a chivalric code of honour was gradually taking shape. Incidents and opinions offered by the chroniclers begin to indicate this, even though the world is being seen through the eyes of the monks. Orderic Vitalis shows knights reluctant to kill fellow knights, pitying knightly prisoners and allowing them free on parole. He applauds largesse. He sees in the good knights not only obedient and courageous warriors but protectors of priests and monks, of the weak and of pilgrims.[56] Explaining the few casualties at the battle of Brémule, Orderic wrote: 'I have been told that in the battle of the two kings,

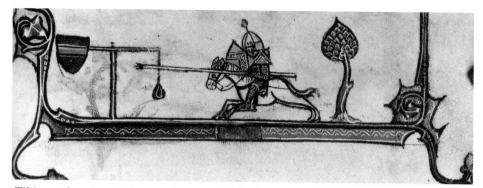

Tilting at the quintain (fourteenth century). Effective mounted combat required continual practice

in which about nine hundred knights were engaged, only three were killed. They were all clad in mail and spared each other on both sides, out of fear of God and fellowship in arms; they wished rather to capture than to kill those they had routed.' Prisoners were particularly valuable as a source of ransom, but one should not neglect the collective self-interest which lay behind these sentiments. The internationality of knightly arms produced what one historian has called 'A kind of freemasonry of knighthood'.[57] Another sees the knighthood of this period as a sort of corporation, with grand masters and masters who commanded the troops, companions (knights) and apprentices (squires); it had its professional code, its rites and its patron saints.[58] In England, chroniclers of the troubled reign of Stephen refer occasionally to knightly acts considered appropriate or inappropriate.[59] By this time, moreover, the *chansons de geste* are beginning to talk of the qualities of person and behaviour defining a knight.[60] A primitive chivalry was beginning to crystallize.

During the second half of the twelfth century, however, chivalry was transformed through its adoption as an ideology by the high aristocracy of northern France. Romance literature points to the development of a clearer class consciousness within aristocratic circles towards the end of the twelfth century, investing knighthood with strong and exclusive moral and social values. The works of Chrétien de Troyes, produced around the 1170s and early 1180s, are especially significant here.[61] In these romances the knights of *la Table Ronde* are invested with a mission which is at once political and social, moral and religious. It was decidedly aristocratic and exclusive, violently antipathetic towards the peasantry and towards townsmen, it was anti-*vilain* and anti-bourgeois. Flori calls the affirmation of chivalric virtues in the romances 'almost spell-binding'. For both Chrétien de Troyes and his contemporary, Etienne de Fougères, author of *Le Livre des Manieres*, chivalry was now an 'order'. 'The order of chivalry', says Chrétien, 'is the highest order God has willed and made.'[62] As has been pointed out 'The very word "order" of knighthood implies duties with a wider frame of reference than those imposed by entry into a war band or a vassal-group'.[63]

These new developments have been seen as betokening a fusion of the aristocracy. In the words of the famous French historian Georges Duby, 'What happened on the eve of the thirteenth century – more exactly sometime between 1180 and 1220 to 1230 – was that the dividing line between these two ranks of the aristocracy seems to have vanished somewhat abruptly. Castellans and simple knights were no longer separate groups; they fused and became one.'[64] The evidence for this includes an increased significance attached to knighthood on the part of the greater men, with particular stress upon the ceremony of dubbing, and on the part of lesser men the use of the hitherto reserved title *dominus* in charters, the construction of fortified manor houses and the adoption of armorial bearings. For this process of fusion a variety, almost a plethora, of causes have been adduced. There was the rise in the power of the regional principalities and of the royal house and a corresponding and resultant decrease in the power of the castellans. This rebounded to the advantage of the simple knight and the distance between him and the castellan was reduced. Secondly, there was the continuing elevation of knighthood itself around which the class consciousness of the French aristocracy crystallized, a process in which, Duby believes, the aristocratic youth, the *juvenes*, played a very significant role. Thirdly, there appears to have been a fear of upward social mobility from below, aggravated both by the prospect that the princes would take those of *vilain* descent into service and by the nobility's own indebtedness. In his most recent statement on the subject, Duby has laid particular stress on yet another factor pushing the aristocracy towards fusion – the threat to their station posed by the rise of the mercenary soldier.[65] Noble indebtedness, due largely to increasing expenditure and 'a tendency to prodigality' as an expression of noble status, began to involve the sale of land, and to result in a retreat from knighthood as many ceased to be able to afford the elaborate knighting ceremonies for their sons that had now become necessary.

Whether fusion of the aristocracy is quite the best way to perceive these developments is open to doubt, at least as far as England is concerned.[66] What seems clear is that the elaboration of knighthood as an expression of status by the higher nobility not only led directly to a thinning of knightly ranks at the lower end but also threatened the viability of knighthood as it had been traditionally understood. As a result, knighthood itself was transformed. It may well be the case that in attempting to explain the full flowering of chivalry overmuch attention has been focussed on aspirations of lesser knights and insufficient attention paid to the higher reaches of the aristocracy. That the milieu in which the mysterious Chrétien worked was highly aristocratic is beyond doubt. He tells us that both Marie, countess of Champagne, and Philip of Alsace, count of Flanders, commissioned romances from him.[67] Towards the end of the century the family chronicler of the counts of Guines looked back over the career of Arnold, son and heir of Count Baldwin. As a youth he was entrusted to the care of Philip of Flanders, the crusader and patron of Chrétien, who educated him in knightly ways. At Pentecost 1181, with four of his close friends, Arnold was ceremoniously knighted by his father in a great court. A knight was was no longer merely a warrior; he was a practitioner of courtly culture, of *courteoisie*.[68] Lambert's contemporary, Gislebert of Mons, the chronicler of Hainault, reveals the same values among the high aristocracy within his own county. Great personages were frequently designated knights and were undoubtedly keen that it should be so. Knighthood is also projected backwards in time, among their illustrious ancestry. The same was true in the chronicles of Anjou by Breton d'Amboise (writing as early as 1155) and Jean of Marmoutier and in the works of Henry II's court poets, the Jerseyman Wace and Benoît de Sainte-Maure, in their celebration of his Norman ancestry.[69]

It is from Anjou that we get our first full description of the knighting ceremony. Jean of Marmoutier, writing in about 1180, gives what purports to be the details of the knighting of Geoffrey V, count of Anjou, at Whitsun 1128.[70] Clearly it is seen through the eyes of a later generation. After a ritual bath, Geoffrey is clothed sumptuously and brought to the king (Henry I of England). 'He left his privy chamber and paraded in public, accompanied by his noble retinue . . .'. His armour is described in loving detail, including a sword from the royal treasure said to have been forged by the great armourer, Wayland. His shield was decorated with painted lions. Thirty other young men were knighted with him. 'In this way our armed champion, new in knighthood, but the promise of the future, leaped on his horse with marvellous agility, without using stirrups for the sake of speed'.[71] Tournament and festivities followed, after which Geoffrey left for the borders of Flanders and far-away lands to win praise. Similar celebrations surrounded the knighting of Emperor Frederick Barbarossa's two sons at Mainz in 1184.[72] In fact, a close relationship between the tournament and the knighting ceremony is observable from the late twelfth century on. Tournaments called round tables followed the knighting of Baldwin and Balian Ibelin in Cyprus in 1223 and, to take a later example from England, the knighting of the three sons of Roger Mortimer at Kenilworth in 1279. In other cases aristocratic young knights and their fellows left immediately for the tourneying circuit upon receipt of knighthood. Baldwin of Hainault, for example, did so in 1168, and Arnold of Ardres in 1181–2.[73] The tournament and the knighting ceremony became twin expressions of the higher nobility's adoption of knighthood as a means, conscious or otherwise, of articulating their sense of superiority within military and pseudo-military society.

Given that the knighting ceremony is one of the clearest expressions of the rise of chivalric knighthood, it warrants close attention. The history of dubbing is, however, a difficult and controversial subject.[74] There can be no doubt, however, that the ceremony is derived from the formal delivery of arms to emperors, kings and princes either at their annointing or at the moment they began to exercise their function. It recognized, often publically, the right to govern. Not surprisingly, the formal delivery of arms, with precisely these connotations, travelled downwards in the feudal France of the eleventh century from princes to counts to châtelains, to those, that is, who actually exercised power, to those who laid claim to be the protectors of the weak in society and of the Church. The delivery of arms figured also in another context; when lords formally armed their vassals with the military equipment with which they were to serve them. Its origins lie deep in the Germanic past, signifying the warrior's entry into the warband.[75] In the feudal context, however, it signifies the formation of a bond between those men who command (in effect, the nobles) and those who serve them by their arms: the *milites* who aid them in the exercise of their power. The most famous of all eleventh-century conferring of arms contains a clear vassalic element. 'Here', reads the commentary on the Bayeux Tapestry, 'William gave Harold arms (HIC WILLELM DEDIT HAROLDO ARMA).' Harold thereby became William's man. It is possible, however, that the scene has another dimension. Harold, the Norman sources insist, swore to advance William's cause in England; to become, in effect, his substitute while King Edward lived. We may have in this delivery of arms, then, another symbol of the transfer of power.

During the early twelfth century dubbing seems to have meant, as yet, hardly more than the delivery of arms without any ceremonial character, and the verb *adouber* no more than equipping a man with arms. The continuation of the Anglo-Saxon Chronicle, looking back from the late 1120s, describes William the Conqueror's 'knighting' of his youngest son, the future Henry I, in 1086, in the following terms: 'he . . . dubbade his sunu Henric to ridere', anglicizing, as it were, a contemporary French term. Orderic Vitalis, a decade later, has the honours performed by Archbishop Lanfranc who dressed Henry in a suit of mail, put a helmet on his head (just as William is seen to be doing in the arming of Harold) and girded him with the belt of knighthood (*militiae cingulum*). Even such a solemn and significant event as this, undertaken 'for the defence of the realm' and 'in the name of the Lord' is depicted without lavish ceremony.[76] Although Henry was not about to become a ruler, the ceremony probably signified his capacity to rule and in the minds of the chroniclers it probably prefigured his coronation. It should not be forgotten that the king was then seriously at odds with his eldest son, Robert, who was to succeed in Normandy.[77] It can hardly be doubted that the many other knightings mentioned by Orderic in or nearer his own day (some of them, as later, on the field of battle) consisted of no more than the delivery of arms.[78]

By the end of the twelfth century the rise of chivalry had transformed this simple act into an honorific and ostentatious festival of initiation, charged with symbolism and mystique. When the twelfth-century writers tell us of knightings, however, they are very elevated affairs, occasions for princes and other members of the high aristocracy. From these we can learn much of the attendant ritual, and even more from the proliferation of accounts in the romances towards the end of the century.[79]

What, then, of the effects of all this in England? Let us look first at the tournament and then at the impact of the crusades. The role of the tournament for English knighthood during this period is difficult to ascertain. In a famous passage written in 1198 the chronicler William of Newburgh maintained that the tournament was formally introduced into England by Richard I in 1194. He explained that both Henry I and Henry II had prohibited tournaments so that those knights who wished to take part in them were obliged to go abroad. This tends to be borne out by a famous charter of Osbert of Arden, lord of Kingsbury in north Warwickshire, in which he gave land to Turchil Fundus for the service of carrying his painted lances from London or Northampton and attending him when he wished to tourney overseas.[80] The charter belongs to the latter part of the reign of Henry I, or to the early years of King Stephen. There is evidence that tournaments in fact occurred in England during Stephen's troubled reign, as William of Newburgh also acknowledged, and indeed they seem not to have been totally unknown in the England of Henry II, but there can be no doubt of the essential truth of William of Newburgh's assertion. According to William of Malmesbury, King Stephen's knights attempted to joust with the enemy before the Battle of Lincoln in 1141, but had to abandon the idea because their opponents were fighting 'not with lances at a distance, but with swords at close quarters'.[81] Northern France and the Low Countries contained the regular tourneying grounds. The English chronicler Matthew Paris was later to call tournaments Gallic fights (*conflictus gallici*) and it is undoubtedly true that they originated in France.

As has been seen, the tournament had been condemned by a council of the church in 1130. It was condemned in more precise terms by the Third Lateran Council of 1179, by which time it had become immensely popular. According to the biography of the greatest twelfth-century exponent of this art, William Marshal, there was one almost every fortnight in northern France and the Low Countries during the 1170s and 1180s. They were now compulsory ingredients in aristocratic literature, pre-eminently of course in the romances of Chrétien de Troyes. Notwithstanding the disapproval of the church, the tournament was flourishing right across western Europe, from Ireland to Germany and beyond. As a recent historian of the tournament has written, 'Tourneying was an entrenched habit among the knights of western Europe – a habit that they took with them and established in the lands of the east where crusade or simple aggrandisement led them.'[82]

But who actually participated? There can be no doubt that the highest nobility were by this time heavily involved. All of Henry II's own sons were tourneyers. Both Henry the Young King and his brother, Geoffrey of Brittany, were allowed to take large companies of young men from England and their continental possessions on tournament tours. King Richard was naturally heavily involved also, jousting *en route* to the Holy Land. On his return he issued his famous writ, in 1194, which fully sanctioned the tournament on English soil. Tournaments were allowed under licence at five named locations. Each participant was required to pay a fee, namely 20 marks for an earl, 10 marks for a baron, 4 marks for a landed knight and 2 marks for a landless knight. These stipulations were taken very seriously by the Crown, with fines exacted for holding tournaments without licence. From hereon, and throughout the period covered by this book, the aristocracy were heavily involved in the tournament in England. In fact, notwithstanding the pro-tourneying attitudes of Richard I and his licensing system, for several generations after him the tournament in England was essentially a baronial affair. Indeed, it tended to be feared by less martial kings as a possible focus for political opposition since it brought the magnates and their retinues together under arms. Not surprisingly, therefore, royal prohibitions featured strongly under John and Henry III, as they were to do again later under Edward II. Despite the haphazard nature of the evidence, it is not difficult to point to high-born families whose members can be seen attending tournaments in generation after generation, the Clares, the Beauchamps and the Bohuns, for example, and the various families

Tournaments were condemned by the Church. This fourteenth-century manuscript shows the tournament as a major inducement to sin

Tournaments led to homicide. Devils are shown here seizing the soul of a knight at a tournament (fourteenth century)

that successively held the earldom of Pembroke.[83] Soon chroniclers were devoting much space to reporting them. Matthew Paris, the famous St Albans chronicler of the reign of Henry III, was acutely interested in them; among his reports of them is a story of the ghostly tourneyers sighted in Yorkshire.

It seems probable that the high-born dominated the tournament by the 1170s and 1180s, if not earlier. The verse life of William the Marshal, the incomparable source book for the later twelfth-century tournament, tells us how Henry the Young King retained the best of the youthful tourneyers available and how other lords emulated him in this.[84] It seems probable that most of the landless knights who participated, and whose presence is acknowledged by Richard I's writ, did so as members of retinues. In many cases they were very probably heirs to fortunes who had not yet inherited, and younger sons and brothers of the wealthy, the *juvenes* of the courts of whom the French historian Georges Duby has written so eloquently. Sure enough, a true devotee like William Marshal, and perhaps Osbert of Arden before him, actively sought out tournaments and attached themselves to retinues and parties as best they could. But in all probability there were relatively few knights of the type of Warin of Coundon tourneying, and where they did occur it was rarely in an independent capacity. The tournament was probably a fairly élitist affair by the time of William Marshal, if indeed it had not been since its inception.

In important respects so, too, was the crusade. Participation from England in the Second Crusade of 1147–8, as in the First, was comparatively slight. However, some important and influential figures did go, and the country can hardly have been immune from such influences. Anything that had a palpable effect within the aristocratic world must have percolated through society.

A scene from the chronicle of Matthew Paris: Richard Marshal unhorses Baldwin of Guisnes at a tournament in 1233

However, it was not until the Third Crusade of 1189–92 and the leading role played by England's warrior-king, Richard I, the Lion Heart, that the English became a crusading nation. When a future heir to the throne, the young Edward I, followed in his footsteps in 1271, one contemporary was led to exclaim, 'Behold he shines like a new Richard'.[85] After Richard I the crusade became a more prominent feature of English society. Ascertaining the numbers of crusaders is a high risk business, and by the nature of things, more is known about crusaders the higher up the social scale they tended to be. There certainly were many crusade participants who were not knights, but increasingly the crusade preaching was aimed at the military classes. Other folk were expected to participate in other ways, primarily financially. What becomes clear is that England's crusade contribution is largely built around the household and retinue. The Pipe Rolls (the Exchequer records) from the years 1190–2 list fifty-nine crusaders by name who were exempted, as participants, from the crusade tax of 1188. They were drawn essentially from the knightly class, and were clearly just a fraction of the actual number of crusaders. Interestingly, the records sometimes group them under baronies, for example the knights of Richard, earl of Clare, or the knights of the honour of Peverel. The names of individuals, however, are often omitted. Sometimes the record simply names the lord and says that his followers are also exempt. This applied, for example, to the followers of Robert de Lacy in Yorkshire, Richard fitz William in Sussex and Richard Basset in Northamptonshire. Others were given under counties.[86] Matters such as geography and kinship must have played a part

From the time of King Richard I, the Lionheart, the English Crown became closely identified with the Crusades. The thirteenth-century Chertsey Tiles show Richard triumphing in single combat with Saladin

in recruitment, but lordship was the chief organizing principle lying behind knightly participation in the Third Crusade. Knights going to the Holy Land largely did so in increasingly well-organized and properly financed parties.

Thereafter the crusade mentality permeated England. There was some response from the English military classes to every crusade to the Holy Land that was declared during the thirteenth century.[87] Within aristocratic circles, tournaments were closely connected with the promotion and preparation of crusades. Many prominent English crusaders were also keen tourneyers. In 1234 Henry III prohibited seventeen earls and barons from tourneying at Northampton and Cambridge. No less than fourteen of them either went on crusade between 1239 and 1241, or took crusading vows. Earl Gilbert Marshal died at the Hertford tournament of 1241 on the very eve of departing on crusade.[88] Unseated in combat, he was dragged to death by his horse, a common cause of fatalities at tournaments.

The crusade mirrored the tournament in another respect too. After Richard I, it was a matter of aristocratic rather than royal leadership, even though the king strongly influenced whether the great lords could actually go or not, and this remained the case until the crusade of the future Edward I in 1270–2.[89] The leading figures who left England during the years 1218 to 1221 for the Fifth Crusade, for example, comprised Earl Ranulf of Chester, William de Ferrers, earl of Derby, William d'Aubigny, earl of Arundel, Saher de Quincy, earl of Winchester, Henry de Bohun, earl of Cornwall, Henry fitz Count, claimant to the earldom of Cornwall, and numerous powerful barons, including Robert fitz Walter, John de Lacy, Brian de l'Isle and Geoffrey de Lucy. Where they led, lesser men followed. As with the Third Crusade, so throughout the thirteenth century, when all the

The Westminster Psalter depicts a crusading knight from c. *1250. It may well have been intended to denote King Henry III, who had taken crusading vows*

various relationships that encouraged men to participate have been analysed, as Simon Lloyd stresses, the ties of lordship were paramount. In other words, knights went as members of aristocratic retinues.

Direct participation reinforced the indoctrination contained in the literature of the crusades, the *chansons de croisade*. It was undoubtedly in this context that the *miles Christi* overtones of knighthood began to seriously penetrate English society. As time went on this was further reinforced by the effects of family tradition. Men were proud of the crusading ventures of their ancestors and often felt the need to emulate them. Some traditions went back to the twelfth century, particularly of course to the Third Crusade. Gerard de Furnivall, for example, went with Richard I. His son, Gerard II, died on the Fifth Crusade. His sons in turn, Gerard and Thomas, went as bannerets of Simon de Montfort in 1240. Traditions in other families extended over centuries. It can hardly be doubted, then, that the crusade deeply affected aristocratic mentality, in this country as elsewhere. But it had another effect too. Crusade and tournament together are likely to have played a major part in the development of a more exclusive attitude towards knighthood in England. It is most likely that this crystallized in aristocratic circles and around the retinue. To put the matter in Georges Duby's terms, this is where the fusion of knightly values between high nobility and lesser brethren was primarily forged.

It is against this background that the thinning of knightly ranks which is perceived clearly in England during the first half of the thirteenth century must be understood.[90] The strongest evidence for this decline in the number of knights comes from the Crown's policy of compulsory knighthood, distraint of knighthood as it is known, from the few surviving sheriffs' returns to the government's request for names and from the resultant fines for respite from individuals wishing to avoid knighthood. Distraint of knighthood has been closely studied, and the main developments are fairly clear. The age of distraints seems to have begun on 10 November 1224 with an order to the sheriffs that every layman of full age who holds one or more knight's fees, and is not a knight, is to take up arms and be made a knight by the Sunday after Easter. This measure was clearly part of the preparations for the expedition to Gascony of 1225. The timing of this and subsequent distraints makes it certain that their primary purpose was military: to enable the king to mount foreign campaigns and, more broadly, to increase the military preparedness of the nation.[91] Distraints were ordered for the campaigns of 1230, 1242/3 and 1253/4, while that of 1256 was connected with the king's attempt to construct a force sufficient for his projected invasion of Sicily.

In total, twenty-six writs were issued during the reign of Henry III ordering 'distraint of knighthood'. These writs also make it clear that the bearing of knightly arms was the matter of prime importance, not just that there should be sufficient men of knightly status in the community. According to the chronicler, Matthew Paris, the intention of the 1256 distraint was to strengthen the knighthood (*militia*) of England. From the late 1240s onwards the king increasingly gave practical help, in the form of equipment and dress, to favoured individuals who were about to become knights. Distraint of knighthood, moreover, was not the only measure concerned with the military resources of the nation. The *Assize of Arms*, obliging all freemen to carry arms in defence of the realm, was reissued on

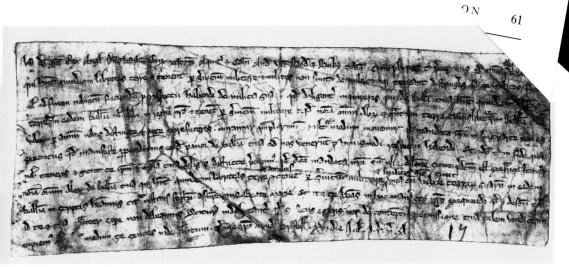

A writ ordering distraint of knighthood (that is, compulsory knighthood), 1256

a number of occasions beginning in 1230. In 1242 a new and heavier burden was placed on the wealthier freemen, a development that coincided with an important extension of the distraint of knighthood. Hitherto it had been directed only at those who held a full knight's fee, and with the probable exception of the first distraint of 1224, had applied to tenants-in-chief only and not to subtenants. It was now decided that land yielding £20 per annum should be regarded as equivalent to a knight's fee, so that all those who held such land, whether or not they held directly of the Crown, should be ordered to take on knighthood. Henceforth this was to become the norm, so that the whole basis on which distraint of knighthood functioned was effectively transformed. It was an obligation centred solely upon the possession of land of sufficient value.

By this time, the Crown seems to have realized that there was a serious decline in the number of knights. In 1246 there began a new visitation of the king's travelling justices, the general eyre as it was known. The articles of the eyre, the items on which the judges were to gain information from local juries, now included distraint of knighthood. From now on two new headings were added to the inquiries, viz. whether sheriffs or other bailiffs had taken bribes from those seeking to avoid knighthood, and whether there were *valetti* who held a full knight's fee or £20 worth of land and who were of full age but had not been knighted. A further development took place in the 1250s when on two occasions, in 1253 and 1256, the king specifically offered to receive fines in place of knighthood. An increased volume of fines followed, though even at this date the financial motive may have been secondary to the military one. In any case, respites were given for a limited period only. Everything suggests that this was the point when knighthood reached its nadir in England. The policy of distraint appears, however, to have achieved a measure of success. It hardly reversed the process, but it did at least stem the decline in the number of knights.

The evidence of the distraints, however, gives only a partial picture of the thinning of knightly ranks. As has been seen from the evidence of the legal records of the first three decades of the thirteenth century, there are strong indications that there were more knights in existence the further one goes back in time. If the Warwickshire evidence is anything to go by, there is a lower level of duplication in the names of knights employed as electors and jurors in the grand assize as the inquiry is taken back towards 1200 and an increase in the number of minor or, at least, less well-endowed knights. The fact that the distraints set the level at £20 worth of land meant that the erstwhile lesser knights escaped the net. Indeed, in all probability, most men of this type had already given up the expectation of being knights, so that distraint was actually operating at something like a realistic income level. There were simply many fewer knights of the type of Warin of Coundon around.

But what was the cause of this decline in the number of knights? Three basic reasons have been suggested: cost, a decline in military service, and the burden of administrative duties imposed upon the knight. The first of these appears to hold the key. It is difficult to see military matters as the primary cause. It is certainly true that the Crown faced problems in trying to enforce feudal military service, either in the form of the original service owed or in the form of quotas. There can be no doubt that military service in France was decidedly unpopular and considered something of a burden. Factors such as division of fees between heiresses, the sale of land, difficulties encountered in the baronial courts in enforcing service, and the problems arising out of long campaigns abroad, all tended to reduce the amount of service the Crown could call upon. But none of these factors necessarily decreased the number of knights in society. As has been seen, the status of the early thirteenth-century knight was a complex one involving a certain lifestyle, a degree of standing in the community and service of various kinds. It was not necessarily dependent upon the active exercise of a military calling, as the author of the *Dialogue of the Exchequer* and others make clear. It is also difficult to believe that the grand assize and activities arising out of the county court, so much a feature of the local knight's life since the time of Glanville, can have suddenly become so burdensome as to lead to a decline in the number of knights. Certainly, the number and incidence of these activities tended to increase, but it is hard to see how they alone could have reversed the attraction of knighthood.

All of this leaves the question of cost – that is to say, the cost of increasingly elaborate equipment and the cost of the ceremony involved in becoming a knight. There were technical advances in armour during the latter half of the twelfth century. Experimentation with new forms of helmet gave rise to the face-concealing great helm. The sleeves of the hauberks were extended to form mittens with leather palms. These were slit to enable them to be thrown back when not required. The surcoat or coat armour, a long fabric garment worn over the mail, became increasingly popular, while the introduction of the cloth trapper announced the beginnings of horse armour. Both tended to be decorated elaborately, indeed armorially.[92] The most costly item of equipment, however, was undoubtedly the horse itself. The great warhorse, the destrier, needed to be specifically bred for the purpose.[93] An active knight, moreover, would require more than one warhorse not to mention horses for other purposes, and a squire to look after them.

This knight, from the north-west tower of Wells Cathedral (c. 1230s), shows the face-concealing great helm which was in wide use by the early thirteenth century

The seal of William de Roumare, earl of Lincoln (mid-twelfth century). His armour should be compared with that of John de Warenne (right)

As far as the knighting ceremony is concerned, much obscurity still surrounds the question of how far down the social scale of knighthood it was to be found. When the twelfth-century writers tell us of knightings, they are very elevated affairs, occasions for princes and other members of the high aristocracy. From these, and even more from the proliferation of accounts in the romances towards the end of the century, we learn a good deal about the ritual attendant upon knighthood. Sources from this side of the channel indicate clearly enough that twelfth-century barons here also underwent a ceremony of knighthood. As early as 1130 the first surviving Pipe Roll of the Exchequer shows knighthood being associated with the coming of age of male heirs among landed families.[94] Glanville tells us that English lords could levy an aid from their tenants to defray the cost of knighting their eldest son, while Magna Carta reaffirmed this was the case both for the king himself and for his vassals. Henceforth such aids were to be limited to what was considered reasonable.[95] It is below this level that the question becomes particularly difficult. How exalted the belted and indebted knight of the *Dialogue of the Exchequer* is intended to be is not at all clear, though it seems unlikely that the author had only the highest ranks in mind. In short, whether the knight of mere local importance went through any ceremony of knighting in the twelfth or early thirteenth centuries is unknown for sure.

The seal of John de Warenne, earl of Surrey (mid-thirteenth century). Note, in particular, the helm with the vizor down, the armoured horse and the prick spurs. Both man and horse carry the Warenne arms, checky or and azure

It seems probable, though, that local knights did experience a *rite de passage*. Michael Powicke has described this, appropriately , as 'mere dubbing'.[96] There is every reason to suppose, however, that 'mere dubbing' would have ceased to be considered sufficient in the thirteenth century. An indication of the cost of knighting in the twelfth century is given by a rare entry on the Pipe Rolls for 1158 which speaks of £5 being spent on the arms and equipment for making a knight.[97] A growing fashion for a more elaborate ceremony is likely to have escalated costs, and to have added to the problems faced by less well-endowed knights.

It seems certain that the development of more self-consciously élitist witness lists to charters is an important symptom of the drive towards an exclusive knighthood. This practice had begun to spread during the mid- to late 1230s to become common around 1240. Although there are serious difficulties involved in locating the social origins of this change, it does seem likely that the full chivalric witness list emanated from the aristocracy and from others of high status such as courtiers. It does not appear, however, to have come from the court as such, and certainly seems to have had no effect on royal documents emanating from the Chancery. On the whole it seems very probable that the inspiration for its adoption and diffusion emanates from within the aristocracy, perhaps following the Continental example. The appearance of rolls of arms and the emergence of the science of heraldry are further symptoms of the arrival of a more élitist attitude towards knighthood.[98]

When we look at the behaviour of the Crown more closely it looks as though it was reacting to changes in society, at least in the first instance, rather than promoting them. For one thing, the decline in the number of knights was real and, as has been seen, it was already under way during the first two decades of the century. For another, when the knighting ceremony is first encountered on the Chancery Rolls the king is clearly helping favoured individuals to defray the expenses incurred in their knighthood, but without being directly involved. For example, in 1227 Reginald de Mohun was granted a letter of request to his knights and free tenants suggesting that they contribute an effective aid towards his knighting.[99] Lesser men than he were also finding the act of becoming a knight a financial burden. In 1233 Nicholas de Wicheford was similarly granted a letter to his tenants asking for an aid; this time it was to discharge the debts he had incurred through being knighted. At the highest levels, at least, the knighting ceremony involved a feast. In the same year as Nicholas de Wicheford was knighted, the king granted his kinsman, William Longespée, nine deer from his various forests for venison for his knighting feast, and in the following year Gilbert Marshal received twenty deer for the same purpose. It is only with the evidence

A knighting ceremony of the mid-thirteenth century

from direct royal involvement in knighting from the 1240s onwards that the luxurious display involved can be seen more clearly. For the knighting feast of William de Valence on St Edward's day, 1247, the king supplied twelve plain, white goblets each with a shield engraved at the bottom. During the next year the king sent from Marlborough for the following: a silk robe, two other robes, a cape, a couch, and the other necessary items for the making of a knight. It is important, however, that the king's involvement is correctly understood. There are few references on the Chancery Rolls to knightings by him before 1247–8, and they are essentially cases where men are to be treated like his own *valetti*. In the case of Oliver de Chaleys who was to be knighted by the king at Christmas 1245, he was clearly responsible for holding his own knighting feast. The king gave him wine for this purpose.

The 'mass knighting' which took place with William de Valence may have been something of a turning point. From 1248 onwards the granting of military equipment to those about to be knighted by the king became relatively common; while in Gascony in 1254 the king entered into bonds with individuals in the same situation for them to acquire their own equipment and to be reimbursed later. In short, it is clear that royal influence and involvement was strong from the late 1240s; it is equally clear that the ceremony was becoming elaborate and the whole business fairly costly, at least in some circles, well before this. This suggests that knighthood was already beginning to take on a more exclusive character.

The importance of the comparison between the sorts of gifts made by the king from the late 1240s and the evidence of the Pipe Roll of 1158, thin though it is, is obvious enough. It may well be that the king, in his encouragement of ceremony and elaboration of dress, actually contributed to the growing spirit of exclusivity and hence to the increasing cost of taking on knighthood. Ironically, royal policy may have exacerbated the underlying problem which the Crown was trying to solve. Be that as it may, there must have been many among those who maintained their knighthood who had some difficulty in facing the costs. As has been seen, one Nicholas de Wicheford got himself into debt through this cause as early as 1233. Moreover, there is a clear example of the cost of knighting being offered as a major cause of indebtedness to the Jews. The knight in question was John de Carun of Sherington, Buckinghamshire, who was knighted in 1243. Having used his land to guarantee the loan, he found himself in severe difficulties when it came to repayment.[100] There can be little doubt that the increasing cost of knighthood caused considerable problems for those who wished to keep up with the higher fashion. Many clearly did not do so, preferring to relinquish knighthood. For those who stayed the course the best proposition was probably to gain help, if they could, from a patron. The mass knightings offered by the court from time to time should be seen in this context, and may even have arisen to some degree from pressure from below for help as much as from royal initiative. The idea was widely disseminated due to its strong presence in chivalric literature, and there is no reason to doubt that it was practised also by other great lords from time to time.

There were, then, special factors affecting the cost of knighthood. However, the general price rise must also have played an important part. Inflationary pressure

Mass knightings occurred in reality from time to time, as depicted in this thirteenth-century manuscript

reduced the real incomes of those living off rents and in some instances (for example, urban rents) made their collection and management more problematic. Around the turn of the twelfth and thirteenth centuries many landlords were turning away from leasing in favour of direct management of their estates, cashing in on the growing demand for food and unwilling to see the profits going to their lessees. Not all estates, however, were of sufficient size or well-enough endowed with demesne land to allow much additional benefit to their lords.[101] Many of the lesser knights were finding it increasingly difficult to sustain knighthood as it and its attendant lifestyle became costlier. Better endowed families must have found it harder now to sustain more than one adult member at a time in knighthood. Even the household knight may have found problems, as his support became more of a total drain on the lord. Perhaps this is why thirteenth-century retinues came to consist partly of *valetti*, forerunners of the esquires, rather than knights.

It is important, however, not to see cost solely as an external factor acting upon knighthood. The factors causing the price rise itself were partly at least on the demand side. The economic growth of the twelfth century no doubt helped to sustain more knights; it also led to increased standards of consumption which had the effect of pushing up prices. Beyond doubt aristocratic and, by emulation, knightly lifestyles led the way. The rise of chivalric fashions should perhaps be seen as developing from this. The crusades alone must have sharpened exotic tastes. But it caused difficulties for those less able to pay. In this context, it was easy for a move towards a more exclusive knighthood to get seriously under way. It can hardly be doubted that the insistence upon more elaborate knighting ceremonies was a manifestation of a growing tendency towards social exclusion. As a result of these developments local knights were unable, perhaps even unwilling, to keep up. There reached a point where the decline in numbers became generally noticeable. An effect rather than cause of the decline was that those activities such as the grand assize, which traditionally relied exclusively on knights, devolved now upon the few, some of whom had no particular interest therein. As a result these duties became something of a burden and may have become, at a critical point, a further factor reducing the numbers. If this diagnosis of the situation is broadly correct, the question must then be when did the decline in numbers actually begin? Twelfth-century evidence is extremely difficult to come by. However, if indebtedness is a symptom, then by the 1180s there may already have been a perceived problem. As has been seen, the *Dialogue of the Exchequer* was much concerned with the problem of the insolvent knight, while the almost contemporary *Assize of Arms* was equally concerned lest the stock of knightly equipment should be reduced by falling into the hands of the Jews. Perhaps this evidence ought not to be taken too far. Indebtedness was already a feature of noble life, and in any case the ruined knight was only a problem, in national terms, if he was not replaced. Nevertheless, it does look as though the thinning of numbers began during the last decades of the twelfth century and extended into the second quarter of the thirteenth.

To fully understand the decline in the number of knights it is necessary to look beyond the evidence of the distraints themselves. When, in the writ of 1241, the Crown extended it to all holders of £20 land, it effectively defined the limits of the pool from which knights could be drawn. As would have been thought, the type of men who were caught by the distraint were very largely drawn from outside the ranks of those obsure and minor knights that have been found in the Warwickshire eyres and the *Curia Regis Rolls*. The decline in knighthood had already progressed well beyond these. The records reveal the names of seventeen Warwickshire knights who were fined for respite of knighthood following the distraint of April 1256. Eleven of these are descendants of knights who are found in the Eyre and Curia Regis Rolls, but they are from among the better endowed 'county knights'. Some of them possessed only one major estate and most of them were experiencing or had experienced a period of some difficulty. Their preference for avoiding knighthood was doubtless determined very largely by this. The action by the Crown was intended to reverse their decision and by doing so to stem the tide of decline.

Estimating the number of knights must always be a risky business. As far as the first half of the thirteenth cenury is concerned, one is dealing with a moving target. Using grand assize juries from the eyre rolls, Jeremy Quick arrived at a figure of 1,539 knights in twenty-seven out of the thirty-nine counties, and suggested a figure of around 2,000 knights in England at any one time during the thirteenth century as a whole. However, the eyres range in date from 1202 to 1269, during most of which time the number of knights was fairly constantly in decline. The true figure for 1200 must have been at least half as many again.[102] Going back no further than the 1220s, by which time a decline in the number of knights had already set in, there were then eighty-nine knights active in civilian work in Buckinghamshire, seventy-one in Oxfordshire and ninety-seven (between 1221 and 1232) in Warwickshire.[103]

In numerical terms, knighthood had probably reached its nadir during the middle decades of the thirteenth century. An attempted roll-call of the knights who fought for or against the Crown during the Barons' War of 1264–5 yielded barely four hundred names.[104] The evidence from the grand assize, although extremely problematic, points in the same direction. In Shropshire, for example, while forty-one knights participated in the grand assize (on seven cases) in 1221, only seventeen did so (on six cases) in 1256. In Warwickshire, forty-seven knights participated (in twelve cases) in 1232, but twenty-nine (in eight cases, though only six yield juries as well as electors) in 1262. In Bedfordshire thirty-five participated (on five cases) in 1247, whereas only sixteen did so in 1262.[105]

There appears, however, to have been a partial recovery in numbers from the 1270s onwards, although the pace of that recovery remains uncertain. Some of the men who paid fines rather than take on knighthood during the 1250s, or their descendants, later came back on board.[106] In the end, the system of distraint probably did have an effect in stabilizing the situation. So, perhaps, did the attitude of the Crown more generally. Henry III had an interest in heraldry, or at least in its decorative possibilities. In Edward I, however, England was to have a king with a strong interest in chivalric knighthood. His early participation in tournaments and, more particularly, his crusade of 1270–2 set the tone for his reign. The main factor, however, was undoubtedly a social one. As has been seen the primary cause of the change in the character of knighthood had been a drive towards social exclusion. For long it was unclear as to how far down the social scale this would apply. A crisis of confidence in knighthood may well have resulted within the counties. Once it became evident that knighthood was still viable as an aspiration, but at a more elevated level, and that it was not to be confined to an aristocratic milieu in the narrow sense, then the county élites came to retain, or readopt, it. Although there has been much study of avoidance of knighthood, and attempts to explain it, there has been less interest in exploring its attraction. There certainly were those who strove to retain it, even to the point of becoming indebted as has been seen. Some certainly wished to remain within or to become part of an increasingly restrictive world. It is in this context that one should view the action of Ingram de Oldcotes who, during the 1270s, agreed to hand over his entire land to Roger d'Arcy in return for his agreeing to make him a knight.[107] By this time chivalric knighthood was approaching its full maturity in England.

FOUR

The Triumph of Chivalry in England

It is unlikely to be accidental that the very time when the more exclusive knighthood becomes fully evident in England is also the time when the knightly effigy begins to appear in churches and when the first purposeful recording of coats of arms proclaims that heraldry had come of age.

As one would expect, aristocratic personages figure among the earliest effigies.[1] William Marshal, earl of Pembroke, is thought to be represented by one of the figures in the Temple Church, London, for instance, and William Longespée, earl of Salisbury, by the effigy in Salisbury Cathedral which has been dated to as early as 1230–40. The great majority, however, are of more local figures. From the middle of the thirteenth century they become increasingly common in churches throughout southern and middle England. Once knighthood took on a more exclusive character it became increasingly something to celebrate and to advertize socially in its own right. The more it became confined to substantial landowners the more its depiction could be used to indicate social dominance within a locality. The knightly effigy in the parish church must have helped to reinforce that sense of association with a specific place which had become so important to noble landowners and which had led to the increasing adoption of toponymic surnames during the twelfth century.

One of the most striking features of these effigies is the worldly rather than spiritual atmosphere that pervades them. In many cases they display an obvious, indeed deliberate, martial valour, but combined with a sense of comfort, of social ease. They very quickly lost their rather statuesque quality in favour of natural expression of both body and garments. Styles were diffused from two centres, one being the west country and the other London. Each of these 'schools' developed its own features, although there was clearly some overlap and cross-fertilization between them. The cross-legged knight, for example, seems to have spread from the west country. The romantic notion that this style was reserved for crusaders has now been largely discarded. Early effigies display a considerable variety of treatment. By the last quarter of the thirteenth century, however, the sword-handling, cross-legged knight was becoming something of a national model.

One of the earliest knightly effigies: William Longespée I, earl of Salisbury (d. 1226), in Salisbury Cathedral

A good example of a knight about to draw his sword is a mid-thirteenth-century effigy from Worcester Cathedral. Others, including the knight at Rushton, Northamptonshire, show a more elaborate, sword-handling action. Note also the crossed legs and the flowing surcoats. The figure at Pitchford, Shropshire, is unusual for the thirteenth century in being of wood, although this was to become commoner later, while the knightly figure at Pershore is also a forester, carrying both sword and horn, a late reminder perhaps of the service connotations of knighthood.

The emergence of the knightly effigy is roughly contemporary with the first listing of arms. To the 1240s and 1250s belong both the Matthew Paris Shields and Glover's Roll, the earliest of our rolls of arms.[2] The St Albans chronicler, Matthew Paris, illustrated his works with paintings in the margin, the great majority of them in all probability his own work. Many of these are shields charged with the arms of persons referred to in the texts. Some are placed upside down, when the death of their owner is being recorded. In his Book of Additions there is one sheet with painted and unpainted shields and another with twenty-seven roughly sketched shields. The former belongs to *c.* 1244. Its

A mid-thirteenth-century effigy of a knight about to draw his sword, in Worcester Cathedral

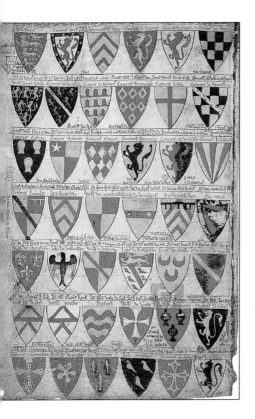

Thirteenth-century shields: this collection of heraldic shields was painted by the St Albans chronicler Matthew Paris c. 1244. The prominence of heraldry in this monk's works indicates the social significance which coats of arms had attained by his day

A fifteenth-century copy of the Dering Roll: dating from the 1270s,, this is one of the earliest rolls of arms. Consisting mainly of the arms of knights from Kent and Sussex, it was much copied during succeeding centuries

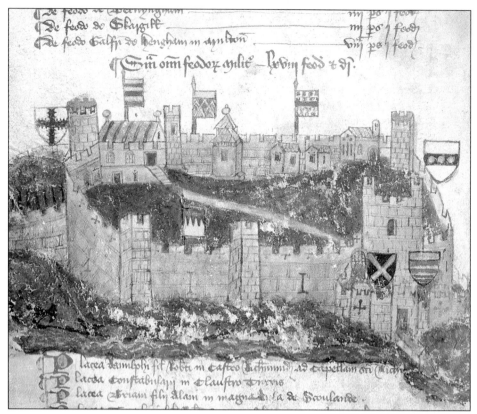

Richmond Castle, Yorkshire: the list below the castle gives the names of eight knights who owed castleguard service, while the stations at which they served are shown pictorially along the battlements themselves

Markenfield Hall, Yorkshire: built by a royal servant, this was the home of a knightly family of the fourteenth century. The hall is on the first floor at the centre of the picture. Internally, the solar, chapel and private chamber can still be seen at right angles to it

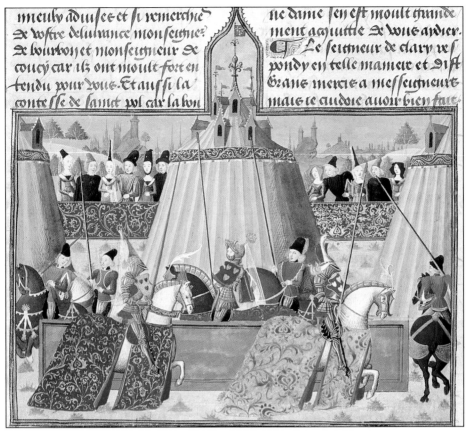

The jousts of St Inglevert (near Calais), 1390: organized by Jean de Boucicaut, Marshal of France, this lavish event was an occasion for the individual jousting which had become fashionable by this time

High-born knights: the clerestory windows in the choir of Tewkesbury Abbey portray its patrons as fully-clad knights. The north window displays the Clare and Despenser arms, flanked by those (supposedly) of the abbey's early twelfth-century founders

A battle outside the gates of a city: this actually denotes Troy, but the scene is typical of the Hundred Years' War with its many sieges

Walter Helyon, Franklin, of Much Marcle, Herefordshire: this wooden figure bears an uncanny resemblance to Chaucer's Franklin with his beard, anlaas (dagger) and gipscr (purse). By the late fourteenth century minor members of the gentry were being commemorated in their parish churches

The Langley glass: the chapel of the Langleys at Siddington, Gloucestershire, was an example of a private mausoleum within a parish church. It contained, in addition to effigies, a fine series of glass commemorating members of the family from the thirteenth and fourteenth centuries

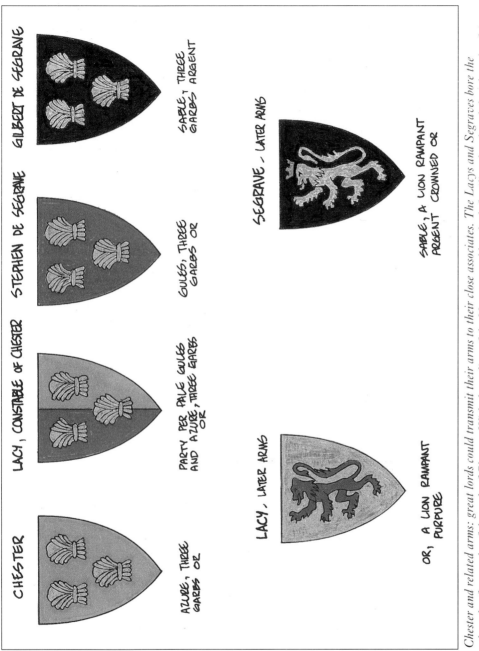

CHESTER

AZURE, THREE
GARBS OR

LACY, CONSTABLE OF CHESTER

PARTY PER PALE GULES
AND AZURE, THREE GARBS
OR

STEPHEN DE SEGRAVE

GULES, THREE
GARBS OR

GILBERT DE SEGRAVE

SABLE, THREE
GARBS ARGENT

LACY, LATER ARMS

OR, A LION RAMPANT
PURPURE

SEGRAVE, LATER ARMS

SABLE, A LION RAMPANT
ARGENT CROWNED OR

Chester and related arms: great lords could transmit their arms to their close associates. The Lacys and Segraves bore the wheatsheafs or garbs of the earls of Chester. With the ending of the Norman earldom both families abandoned the wheatsheafs in favour of the lion rampant

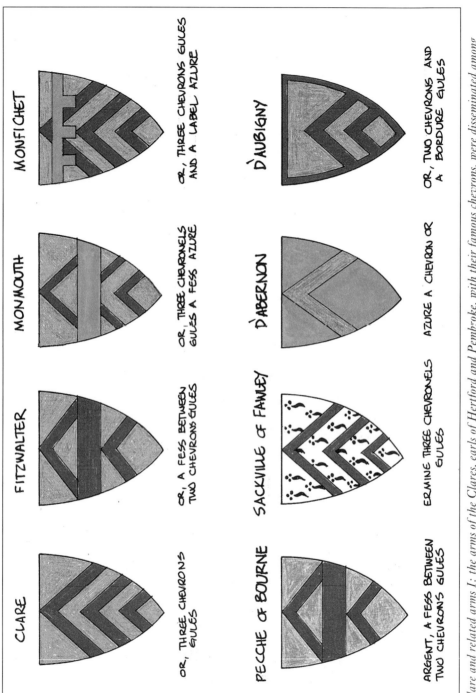

CLARE

OR, THREE CHEVRONS
GULES

FITZWALTER

OR, A FESS BETWEEN
TWO CHEVRONS GULES

MONMOUTH

OR, THREE CHEVRONELS
GULES A FESS AZURE

MONFICHET

OR, THREE CHEVRONS GULES
AND A LABEL AZURE

PECCHE of BOURNE

ARGENT, A FESS BETWEEN
TWO CHEVRONS GULES

SACKVILLE of FAWLEY

ERMINE THREE CHEVRONELS
GULES

D'ABERNON

AZURE A CHEVRON OR

D'AUBIGNY

OR, TWO CHEVRONS AND
A BORDURE GULES

Clare and related arms 1: the arms of the Clares, earls of Hertford and Pembroke, with their famous chevrons, were disseminated among related families

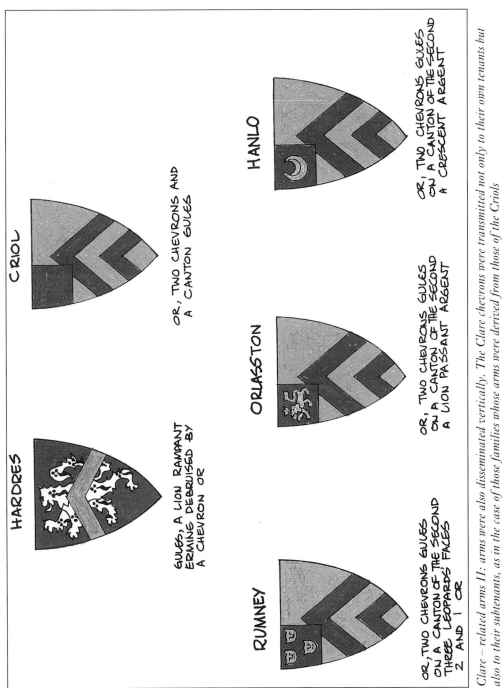

CRIOL

OR, TWO CHEVRONS AND
A CANTON GULES

HARDRES

GULES, A LION RAMPANT
ERMINE DEBRUISED BY
A CHEVRON OR

RUMNEY

OR, TWO CHEVRONS GULES
ON A CANTON OF THE SECOND
THREE LEOPARDS' FACES
2 AND 1 OR

HANLO

OR, TWO CHEVRONS GULES
ON A CANTON OF THE SECOND
A CRESCENT ARGENT

ORLASSTON

OR, TWO CHEVRONS GULES
ON A CANTON OF THE SECOND
A LION PASSANT ARGENT

Clare – related arms II: arms were also disseminated vertically. The Clare chevrons were transmitted not only to their own tenants but also to their subtenants, as in the case of those families whose arms were derived from those of the Criols

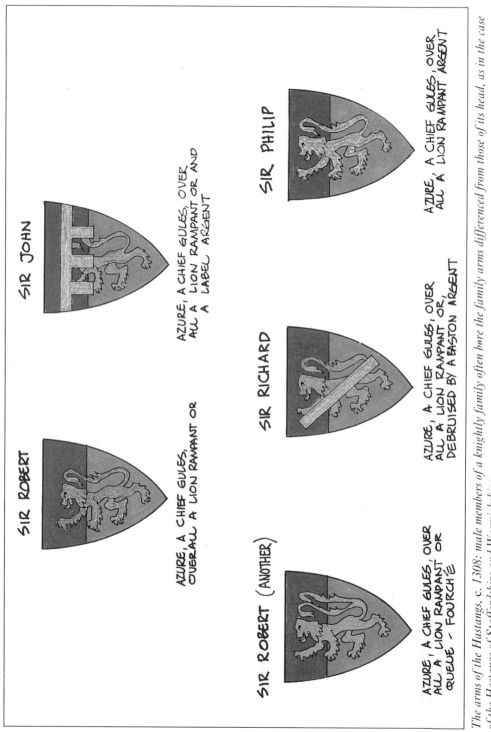

SIR ROBERT

AZURE, A CHIEF GULES,
OVERALL A LION RAMPANT OR

SIR ROBERT (ANOTHER)

AZURE, A CHIEF GULES, OVER
ALL A LION RAMPANT OR
QUEUE - FOURCHÉ

SIR JOHN

AZURE, A CHIEF GULES, OVER
ALL A LION RAMPANT OR AND
A LABEL ARGENT

SIR RICHARD

AZURE, A CHIEF GULES, OVER
ALL A LION RAMPANT OR,
DEBRUISED BY A BASTON ARGENT

SIR PHILIP

AZURE, A CHIEF GULES, OVER
ALL A' LION RAMPANT ARGENT

The arms of the Hastangs, c. 1308: male members of a knightly family often bore the family arms differenced from those of its head, as in the case
of the Hastangs of Staffordshire and Warwickshire

An effigy of a knight from Rushton, Northamptonshire, illustrating the developed sword-handling action. Note also the crossed legs and flowing surcoat

A wooden effigy of a knight from Pitchford, Gloucestershire

purpose is uncertain, but it may have been intended as a reference for the arms Matthew was to draw in the margin of his histories. The same may be true of the rough drawings which belong to the same or possibly a slightly earlier date. His various histories themselves were compiled from *c*. 1245 until Matthew's death in 1259. Altogether, there are 143 different coats for about 400 persons. Seventy-two of the coats are British. The arms of nearly all the most important lay magnates of the time are included, together with the arms of foreign rulers such as the Holy Roman Emperor and the kings of France, Jerusalem and Norway. However, the arms of men of lesser importance also figure, such as Gerard and William de Odingseles of Maxstoke, Warwickshire, and Robert Herring of Kent, as well as courtiers like John de Lexington and Paulinus Peyvre.

Coats of arms, then, were widely diffused among the knightly class of Matthew's day. Matthew himself was a monkish chronicler, observing heraldry from the outside. He appears to have collected his knowledge of arms, like so much else in his chronicles, from information gathered from visitors to the abbey and

An effigy of a knight-forester, from Pershore, Worcestershire

from his travels. What his work indicates, therefore, is the wide social significance that arms had already attained in his day.

The evidence of Glover's Roll, appearing hard on the heels of Matthew Paris,
points in the same direction. It is known only from later copies. The original contained 215 blazons, beginning with those of the king and his eldest son. These
were followed by 20 English earls and then 193 lords and knights. They include
men from nearly all counties, but the recent editor concludes that it is 'impossible
to detect any logical principle either in the choice of men or in the order in which
they are presented. The roll, indeed, seems to be the personal collection of someone who set down names and arms as they occurred to him. Again and again one

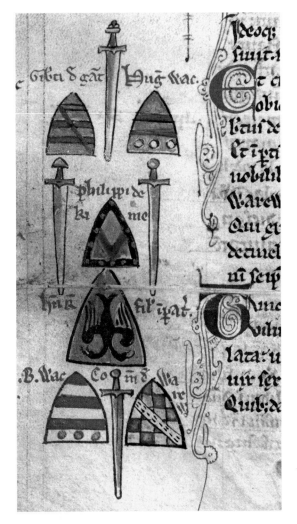

The chronicle of Matthew Paris is an important source for early thirteenth-century heraldry. In this case he has painted the shields of deceased knights upside down in the margin close to where their deaths are recorded in the text

can see how the compiler's mind was led from one item to the next, nearly half the entries being linked in one way or another.'³ There are family groups and groups of neighbours. In many cases kinship or alliance seems to provide the explanation; but in other cases it is similarity in the arms themselves that caused the compiler to link them.

Whether this means that Glover's Roll, and Walford's Roll with which it has been recently edited, are the work of heralds, or at least of men involved professionally in the subject, as argued by Sir Anthony Wagner, Garter King of Arms, is less certain. It is undoubtedly suggested by the use of blazon, the technical language of heraldry. Both Glover's Roll and its exact contemporary, the northern French roll known as the Armorial Bigot, show blazon at an early stage of development. 'Conventional forms and terminology had been attained, but these were in some ways fluid and still primitive compared with what we find fifty years later.'⁴

The date of Glover's Roll appears to be *c.* 1253. However, it seems to contain some slightly earlier material and it may well be that the compiler used a previous collection which he incorporated into his roll. This seems to have belonged to 1240–2, and is now known as the 1240 collection. Material taken directly from the latter appears also to have found its way into a roll known as Grimaldi's Roll in the fourteenth century. There is also a version of Glover's Roll containing only fifty-eight painted shields which has been dated to soon after 1258. This, it has been suggested, may have been intended as a textbook on heraldry.

The evidence, then, is overwhelming that there was widespread interest in heraldry by the middle of the thirteenth century and that it was by then becoming a science, albeit one that was still some way from full realization. Moreover, those who recorded arms during the 1250s drew on material going back a generation. Some of Matthew Paris's shields are of men who died during the 1220s and 1230s or even earlier in the century.

How, then, should we understand these developments? Heraldry has been defined as 'the systematic use of hereditary devices centred on the shield'.[5] In outline at least, the origins and development of this system seem clear enough.[6] The Bayeux Tapestry shows clear use of shields painted with devices, while the Song of Roland similarly refers to shields with cognisances (*connoisances*). What precisely was the significance of these at this date remains uncertain but it seems highly probable that the purpose shifted at some point from mere decoration to recognition, and there can be little doubt that the rise of the tournament and advances in armour that concealed the individual participant's features played a major part in this development. A famous instance in Chrétien de Troyes' Lancelot or *Le Chevalier de la Charette* where tourneying knights are being identified by their arms for Queen Guinevere and her ladies indicates this clearly enough. Here, and in other twelfth-century depictions, there appears to be a preference for the depiction of birds and animals, including mythical ones.

The tournament and the origins of heraldry are intimately connected. A manuscript of the romance of Lancelot shows how the knights might be identified through their arms, not only by the participants themselves but also by the ladies looking on

How fast the tendency towards hereditary employment of such devices developed is unclear. How far, for example, should we trust John of Marmoutier's depiction of the knighting of the young Geoffrey of Anjou in 1128, when a blue shield with golden lioncels is said to have been hung about his neck? By the time we get into the second half of the century, however, the lion had certainly become a family emblem.[7] A hereditary tendency can be discerned in some instances in the use of armorial devices upon aristocratic seals from the 1130s and 1140s. As it is equally true that there were families that used more than one device or that changed the devices pictured on their shields it is necessary to be cautious over the inferences drawn from particular examples. However, it does appear to be the case that 'from somewhere around 1140 on we are moving into a world of heraldic usage in the strict sense'.[8]

As is often stressed, the simpler a coat of arms is, the older it is likely to be. In many cases more complex arms can be seen to have derived from straightforward ones. The mode of dissemination of armorial bearings appears to have been collaterally, that is to say among kin, in the first instance. One group of arms, for example, has been shown to have derived from those borne by Geoffrey de Mandeville, first earl of Essex, who died in 1144.[9] The Mandevilles bore *quarterly or and gules* (that is, gold in the first and fourth quarters, red in the second and third). The Veres (descended from Geoffrey de Mandeville's brother-in-law, Aubrey de Vere, first earl of Oxford), the descendants of Roger fitz Richard of Warkworth in Northumberland (who had married Geoffrey's sister-in-law), and the Beauchamps of Bedford (descended from Geoffrey's wife through her second marriage), all bore arms that closely resembled, and were derived from, the Mandeville arms. The arms of John de Lacy, earl of Lincoln, who died in 1240 were derived from his grandmother, Alice de Vere, daughter of the sister-in-law of Geoffrey de Mandeville who had married Roger fitz Richard of Warkworth. John de Lacy bore *quarterly or and gules, a bend sable and a label (5) argent*.[10] The thirteenth century saw some further refinements. John fitz Geoffrey, Henry III's justiciar of Ireland, half-brother to two earls of Essex, bore the Mandeville arms with a bordure of vair. When the second of these earls of Essex died, the earldom was conferred on their nephew, Humphrey de Bohun, who placed two small quarterly shields to his seal on either side of his own arms.[11] The evidence that all of these arms are derived from the Geoffrey de Mandeville connection is not strictly contemporary, but comes from the rolls of arms. However it would be extremely difficult, if not impossible, to explain why these families adopted the quarterly coat other than by reference to the time when they all intermarried.[12]

A similar case is that of the Clares, who bore the famous arms *or, three chevrons gules*.[13] In this case the arms are to be seen clearly on seals from the 1140s onwards, when they are borne by the two branches of the Clare family who were the earls of Hertford and Pembroke respectively.[14] Again, a number of related families bore arms that were clearly derived from theirs. That of fitz Walter, lords of Dunmow, descended from Robert fitz Richard de Clare who died in 1136, bore *or, a fess* (a horizontal bar) *between two chevrons gules*. The families of Montfichet and Monmouth, descended from sisters of Richard fitz Gilbert, lord of Clare

(d. 1136) and Gilbert fitz Gilbert, earl of Pembroke (d. 1148) both bore arms similarly derived. The Monmouths bore *or, three chevronels gules* (chevronel being the diminutive of chevron) *a fess azure*, and the Montfichets *gules, three chevrons or and a label azure*. This last may well represent an early example of a label, used as a mark of cadency to denote a junior member of the family, becoming a permanent charge (that is to say it featured for ever upon the shield).[15]

However, arms were also disseminated vertically, to tenants and to dependants. This phenomenon was remarked upon by William Camden centuries ago, and it is one which calls out for systematic study.[16] The family of Berners, for example, who held Roding Berners, Essex, from the Mandevilles bore *quarterly or and vert*, in some instances with a *label gules*.[17] Among tenants of the Clares, the family of Pecche of Bourne bore *argent, a fess between two chevrons gules*, that of Sackville of Fawley *ermine, three chevronels gules*, that of d'Abernon of Stoke D'Abernon *azure, a chevron or*, and that of d'Aubigny of Belvoir *or, two chevrons and a bordure gules (colour plate 11)*.[18] In general the dissemination of arms to tenants is very probably a more recent phenomenon than transmission of arms within kin. The Sackvilles, for example, became tenants of the Clares only in 1189.[19]

The great antiquary, William Camden, much interested in the question of derived arms, made a particular study of Kent. Interestingly, he was able to point to yet more families whose arms appear to have derived from the Clares. The Criols, for example, bore *or, two chevrons and a canton* (diminutive of the quarter) *gules*, and the Hardres family *gules, a lion rampant ermine debruised* (crossed so as to partly cover) *by a chevron or*. Both were Clare tenants of the honour of Tonbridge. This derivation has passed unnoticed in more recent studies. Camden, however, took the matter further, showing how the arms of Kent families were differenced by their own tenants. The families of Hanlo, Orlasston and Rumney (or Romenal) all carried the Criol arms but added on the red canton a *crescent argent*, a *lion passant or* and *three cats' or leopards' faces or (colour plate 12)*. Three other families bore arms derived from the Leyburns' *azure, five lions rampant argent*.[20]

Camden's evidence was taken from the rolls of arms of the reign of Edward I, moving forward somewhat from the period of the origins of heraldic arms. It must be remembered, however, that Matthew Paris and the earliest rolls are incomplete in their coverage and, for that matter, themselves appear rather late in the process of adoption of arms. It is possible that a more systematic study of seals might make the chronology of this process clearer.[21] It does seem though that the adoption of heraldic devices began in the highest social circles and travelled downwards with increasing velocity during the later twelfth and early thirteenth centuries. It may be that there should not be too much emphasis placed on tenancy. Sheer neighbourhood might itself be a factor farther down the social scale. In some instances where arms are derived from a feudal superior the reason might well be a ministerial or familial connection rather than mere tenancy. This would certainly seem to be the case with two families which adopted the garbs or wheatsheafs from the earls of Chester. Earls Hugh II (d. 1181), Ranulf III (d. 1232) and John le Scot (d. 1237) all appear to have borne *azure, three garbs or*. The Lacys, hereditary constables of Chester, bore *party per pale* (that is a shield divided longitudinally) *gules and azure, three garbs or*.[22] Stephen de Segrave, who was ultimately to become justiciar of England, was closely associated with Earl Ranulf III. He bore *gules, three garbs or*.[23] His son, Gilbert de Segrave, bore *sable, three garbs argent*. In the next generation the family broke with this tradition. The earldom of Chester passed to prince Edward in 1254 and hence to the Crown. Gilbert's son, Nicholas de Segrave, was in wardship to the prince. Rolls of Edward's reign give him *sable, a lion argent crowned or*. This change of arms was apparently famous, for the heraldic poem on the Siege of Carlaverock (1300) which mentions the Segrave brothers refers to their valiant father who had abandoned the garbs and assumed the lion. Changes of arms were not unusual in the early days. John de Lacy, earl of Lincoln, seems to have preferred to use arms derived from the Mandevilles[24] rather than the garbs used by his father, although he and his own son continued to used the garbs when sealing as constables of Chester. Henry de Lacy, earl of Lincoln, John's grandson, changed the arms again to *or, a lion rampant purpure (colour plate 10)*.[25]

Means used to difference arms were clearly in use from an early date – changes of tincture, for example, and marks or *brisures* as they were known. These included the bend, the border or bordure and the label. The canton (the diminutive of quarter) was also in use from a relatively early date. There seem to have been no rules whatever governing the use of *brisures* in these days. The same is true of their use to denote younger sons or cadet lines, as marks, that is, of cadency. The label appears to have established itself early as the commonest means of denoting a younger son, but it was not used exclusively in this sense and is found, as has been seen, on derived arms. Much less systematized than it later became, heraldry was nonetheless quite sophisticated even by the mid-thirteenth century. Its coming of age across the later twelfth and early to mid-thirteenth centuries is one further witness to the transformation of knighthood that occurred during this period.

From the 1270s onwards, rolls of arms began to proliferate, to become an established part of chivalric culture. Walford's Roll, the Herald's Roll and the Dering Roll all belong to that decade, while a further twenty-five date from *c*. 1280 to the 1320s. There are three times as many again between then and the end of the fifteenth century.[26] Rolls, moreover, were copied, recopied and extended.[27] Most are either in blazon or in trick (that is to say, shields drawn with the colours indicated by letters). Wagner classifies them as follows: in addition to the few Illustrative Rolls, akin to Matthew Paris's Shields, there are Occasional Rolls, General Rolls, Local Rolls and Ordinaries. Occasional Rolls give the arms of those who were present at a particular occasion, most often a siege or a tournament. Almost all of these were in blazon only. They include, for example, the Falkirk Roll of 1298 and the first and second Dunstable Rolls of 1309 and 1334. The Carlaverock poem commemorating the lords and knights present at Edward I's Siege of Carlaverock in 1300 also belongs to this type, as it gives 106 blazons of their arms. Not all of these rolls, however, belong to such spectacular events. Also included is the obscure Nativity Roll of *c*. 1300, which gives the arms of seventy-nine knights present at some unknown place on the Monday before the feast of the Nativity of Our Lady. The General Rolls constitute the largest group. Most of these are painted. They are variable in content and in quality. Most tend to include foreign rulers and other knights. Then there is the small but significant group of Local Rolls. The earliest of these is the Dering Roll, which consists mainly of knights from Kent and Sussex.[28] The so-called Parliamentary Roll of *c.* 1308 covered the whole of England by counties.[29] It contains 1,110 coats. So popular did it prove that Wagner's catalogue gives twenty-two copies of its original form and a further sixteen of a recension made some sixty years later. Furthermore, some of its sections were made the basis of rolls for individual counties. The County Roll of the reign of Richard II or later contains 696 coats covering ten counties. And, finally, there are Ordinaries in which coats of the same type are grouped together. They were working tools used by professionals, and the earliest date from the reign of Edward III.

Many of the rolls, certainly by the fourteenth century if not before, were the work of heralds. They were responsible, no doubt, for the more polished productions.[30] One should be wary, however, of suggesting too centralized a system. Baronial heralds functioned as well as royal ones, and some of the rolls were probably not the work of professionals at all. The rolls of arms, then, take the inquirer deep into aristocratic culture.

The most outstanding feature of the world of armorial rolls is that it was a relatively small one. Although there was a diffusion downwards of the bearing of heraldic arms during the later twelfth and thirteenth centuries, this was of course coterminous with a thinning of knightly ranks. As a result the rolls of arms record the social status of a relatively small number of families and men. Even the Great Roll of Arms, known misleadingly as the Parliamentary Roll of Arms, contains only 1,110 names, and this probably encompasses a very high proportion of the knights living and functioning at the time. The list begins with the king, thirteen earls and the bishop of Durham, followed by the bannerets (nos. 16–169). A banneret was a senior knight, entitled to carry his own square banner as opposed to the triangular pennon of the ordinary knight and often to be found commanding his own contingent in the field. Then come knights listed on a county basis, up to number 1034. The remainder of the roll, however, contains difficulties, for it includes earls and other great men recently deceased and various additions, in many cases most probably men accidently omitted from the county lists. Even the resultant figure of somewhat under 1,100 knights would, if not qualified, exaggerate the number of knightly families represented. Under Staffordshire, for example, no less than five members of the Hastang family are given, Sir Robert de Hastang bearing *azure, a chief gules, over all a lion rampant or*, and the others the same arms variously differenced. Sir John de Hastang bore them with a *label argent*. Sir Richard's arms were debruised with a *baston argent*. Another Sir Robert had his lion's tail forked, while Sir Philip's lion was argent (colour plate 13). Nor is this an isolated case. The roll gives no less than six Segraves bearing the new family arms of *sable, a lion rampant argent crowned or* and its variants. On the other hand there were also knights omitted from the roll. For example, only a proportion of the 300 who had recently been knighted at the Feast of the Swans was included.

The Great Roll of Arms, as Noel Denholm-Young pointed out, badly needs re-editing; meanwhile he suggested a working figure of around 1,250 knights in

An extract from the Parliamentary Roll of Arms, c. 1308, which gives 1,100 coats of arms in blazon, the language of heraldry

England at this particular time, and this would seem to be of the right order of magnitude.[31] He went on to argue, by means of the data compiled by the Revd Charles Moor[32] and with the aid of some rather tortuous mathematics, that at any one time during the reign of Edward I, there were around 500 fighting knights, 1,250 actual knights and 3,000 potential knights (bearing in mind the broader number of families from which knights could be drawn), and these figures have generally been followed. The king had been able to summon around 960 knights individually for service in Scotland in 1301.[33]

When the sheriffs drew up lists of knights and men-at-arms in their counties for the Crown in 1324 the numbers reached 1,150 and 950 respectively.[34] In many counties there were clearly more knights listed than were given in the Great Roll of Arms. In Warwickshire, for example, there were thirty-one knights listed in the roll (though only twenty-five separate surnames) as against forty-two (forty surnames) in 1324. Both sources undoubtedly contain omissions. The historian using the 1324 lists, moreover, is faced with additional problems. Some men occur in more than one county, for example, while others did not have their residence (or at least their chief residence) in a county for which they are returned. Some of those listed as men-at-arms should have been knights and often were so in future years. Even so, the returns give an indication of numbers of knights with land in particular counties. In Leicestershire forty-eight knights are given, in Staffordshire thirty-seven, in Worcestershire twenty one, in Northamptonshire thirty-four (although some names have been lost in the original), and in Gloucestershire forty-four knights.[35] Much work requires to be done on these sources if we are ever to have an entirely accurate picture; meanwhile, however, it would appear that Denholm-Young's 1,250 actual knights is not too far wide of the mark. Set against a national population of somewhere in the order of 5–6 million, it really was a small élite.

The Feast of the Swans has much to tell us about the social appeal of Edwardian knighthood. It was held at Westminster at Whitsuntide (22 May) 1306, in honour of the knighting of Prince Edward, the king's eldest son and future Edward II. The feast is famous for the vows which the old king and his son took, on the two swans that formed the main dish: the king to take vengeance upon Robert Bruce for the murder of John Comyn and then never more to bear arms against Christian folk but to make for the Holy Land; the prince not to sleep two nights in one place before he reached Scotland. During Easter week, however, the king had sent instructions via the sheriffs inviting those who wished to be knighted with the prince to come to London prior to Whitsun to receive the necessary equipment. This comprised helmet, hauberk, lance, sword and spurs, and the material for making the ceremonial robes, mattress and quilt. According to the chronicles some 297-300 knights answered the call. Of these, the names of 282 can be resurrected.[36] The Swan knights were drawn, as one would expect, almost entirely from the aristocracy and the élite of the shires. The whole occasion was a lavish elaboration of the traditional ceremonial knightings of the past, which had their counterparts, and to some extent their inspiration, in chivalric literature. After vigil and mass the prince was knighted by the king; the young knight then proceeded to dub his fellows, and the banquet followed. But the crafty old king, it is generally agreed, had military and political motives for maintaining the court's role in inspiring knighthood. The royal invitation, it has been aptly said, was 'a glittering bait dangled by a wily old fisherman'.[37] The king's gesture was designed to appeal to the spirit of social exclusion that persisted strongly in the counties. Since the contours of chivalric knighthood had crystalized some time before, it was by now fairly clear as to the social and material level at which knighthood was felt to be appropriate out in the shires.

As a result, it was possible for someone of the relevant social experience to identify a considerable proportion of his contemporaries from their arms. The author of the *Song of Carlaverock* tells how men and women alike marvelled to see two knights, Hugh Poyntz and Brian fitz Alan, wearing the same coat. Many years later, in 1386, when giving evidence during the great Scrope versus Grosvenor controversy in the Court of Chivalry over the right to bear *azure a bend or*, Sir Robert Laton stated that his father had made him write down the arms of all the princes, dukes, earls, barons and knights that he could remember and learn them by heart.[38] What is underlined here is the fact that members of the relatively restricted world of chivalric society could expect to be identified on the basis of the arms they displayed.

A further point to bear in mind is that heraldry, and the developed chivalry of which it was a part, involved its participants in an international culture. The content of many of the rolls themselves indicates this. In some cases up to a third of the blazons are of foreign dignitaries and knights. Interestingly, while those of the highest ranks of the continental nobility are drawn from a geographically wide area, there is a clear preponderance among the mere knights of men drawn from northern France and the Low Countries, the areas with which the English had most frequent contact. The Fitzwilliam version of Herald's Roll, which contains the coats of over two hundred foreign lords and knights, includes the names of a number who participated at the tournament at Chauvency in 1285 and at the chivalric festivities at Le Hem in 1278, both of which were commemorated in contemporary verse narratives.[39] And, of course, the same phenomena as are found in England are to be found equally on the Continent. The Northern French Bigot Roll, as we have seen, is contemporary with the Glover Roll, and France boasts fine examples of all Wagner's classes of rolls except the Ordinaries. *Le Tournoi de Chauvency* and *Le Roman du Hem* are comparable to the *Song of Carlaverock*.[40] There are remarkable productions, too, from both Germany and the Low Countries, including the *Clipearius Teutonicorum*, the *Manesse Kodex*, the Zurich Roll and the Great Roll by Gelre. English knights participated in tournaments in northern France and the Low Countries, just as they had done back in the time of William the Marshal. Present at a tournament at Compiègne in 1278, for example, were the earls of Lincoln and Gloucester, Hugh de Courtenay, Roger de Clifford, Thomas de Molton, Hugh Despenser, Otto de Grandison, William de Say, John de Vesci and John Comyn, while Hugh Despenser and Robert d'Enghien were at Mons in 1310. The *Chronique* written by the Brabancon Jan van Heelu, composed *c.* 1291–2, includes England among the list of chivalric venues with Germany, France, Gascony, Brittany, Poitou, Champagne and Burgundy. It records, moreover, the presence of English knights at the round table

where Jean I, duke of Brabant, was fatally wounded. Edward I had participated in tournaments both at home and on the Continent during his youth and had
won a considerable reputation. This is doubtless why Sarrasin's *Le Roman du
Hem,* which records in verse narrative the chivalric festivities held at Le Hem in
1278, entertains the hope that Edward I and English knights would attend.[41] Nor
was this only a feature of the life and times of Edward I. During the early stages
of the Hundred Years' War, English knights were still attending local tournaments on the Continent, as did Henry de Grosmont when he had leave from his
creditors to quit prison to do so in December 1340. At this time, of course, many
knights from the borderlands between France and the Empire were to be found
fighting alongside the English, men that is from the traditional heartland of tourneying society.[42]

It was not only on shields and horse caparisons, on seals depicting them and on
rolls recording them, that arms were displayed. During the thirteenth century
heraldry spread to horse harnesses, to aspects of dress, and to buckles and belts,
including the belt of knighthood.[43] Illuminated manuscripts, domestic plate and
furniture, including caskets and chests, were adorned with their owners' arms.[44]
The same is true of liturgical vessels and ecclesiastical vestments, proclaiming the
benefactors of churches and monastic houses. Heraldry was not only a matter of
recognition in the field and inclusion in rolls of arms. What it denoted above all
was status; status and family pride. It helped satisfy that urge for social display
that was so much a feature of feudal society.

Heraldry came to adorn buildings. In England Henry III seems to have led the
way, during the middle decades of the thirteenth century, much influenced by his
contemporary St Louis of France. Castle halls were heraldically glazed, as was
Westminster Abbey. Heraldic floor tiles were introduced. Heraldic wall painting
first appeared in the king's painted chamber at Westminster. The greatest surviving monument to the king's interest, however, are the shields carved in the nave of
Westminster Abbey between 1259 and 1264. In addition to the royal arms and
those of other royal houses with which the king was connected by marriage, most
of the important aristocratic families of England were depicted there.[45] The same
phenomenon was to be found in York Minster by the early fourteenth century,
when a great series of stone shields came to adorn the nave. Headed by the arms
of Edward I, Margaret his queen and Edmund his brother, this again included
many of the most significant baronial houses in the land.[46] A fine series of heraldic
glass was introduced into the clerestory of the nave at around the same time, once
again including the arms of prominent English baronial houses.[47] A wealth of further shields in glass and stone were added as time went on. Where kings led,
nobility soon followed. In the fourteenth century armorial glass became prominent throughout England.[48] The east window of Gloucester Cathedral was glazed
in about 1350 to celebrate Edward III's great victory over the French at Crécy. In
monastic houses and in other churches heraldic display indicated, indeed cele-
brated, benefaction. In the clerestory windows of Tewkesbury Abbey, for example, the founders and the more recent patrons of the abbey were portrayed as
knights with their arms. They include the Clares and the Despensers, successively
lords of Tewkesbury. At parish level a coat of arms, displayed in stained glass or

The virtues Largesse *and* Debonereté, *from Stothard's watercolours of the Painted Chamber at Westminster. Note the heraldry in the margins as well as on the displayed shields*

otherwise, indicated primacy in local society. The more knighthood became confined to substantial landowners, the more its depiction could be used to indicate
social dominance of a locality. A church or chapel adorned with one's arms served
this need from the thirteenth century on particularly well.

The records of the Scrope versus Grosvenor dispute in the Court of Chivalry
have much to tell us of chivalric culture in general and of contemporary attitudes
towards the depiction of knightly arms in stained glass in particular. The dispute
began in 1385 when Sir Richard Scrope of Bolton in Yorkshire found Robert
Grosvenor of Cheshire wearing his coat of arms, *azure a bend or*, during a military
expedition to Scotland. A considerable array of notables gave evidence during the
course of the proceedings, and the matter was finally resolved in favour of Scrope
in 1390. William Troy, a canon of Aske, testified that the Scrope arms were in
glass windows and wall paintings in over forty Yorkshire churches. Sir Thomas
Markenfield and Sir John Wade deposed that it was common knowledge that the
Scrope arms could be traced back to the Conquest, while a chronicle provided by
the prior of Bridlington included an illustration of the Scrope arms purporting to
date from the time of William the Conqueror.[49]

Although they were wrong on this last point, the deponents were certainly correct about the display of the arms within churches. Members of the northern
nobility gave evidence in the chapter house of York Minster. The cathedral was
the family burial place for the other branch of the Scrope family, the Scropes of
Masham: Stephen Lord Scrope was buried in St Stephen's Chapel and his son,
Lord Henry Scrope asked to be buried there and left money for an image of himself in armour with his shield bearing a coat of arms. Within the choir of the
church of St Agatha in Easby Abbey the history of the Scropes of Bolton themselves was carved in freestone and alabaster. Their heraldry was displayed around
family tombs, in glass windows, before altars, on panels, abbey vestments, in the
refectory, and on the pavements of the church. Above the choir stood effigies of
the founders, Henry Scrope and William Scrope, with their arms painted on their
shields.[50] They continued to add to this display up to the very eve of the
Reformation. A fine early sixteenth-century wooden parclose screen enclosed
their chapel at Easby Abbey. Depicting the generations of the Scropes and their
arms, it survives today in Wensley Church where it vies with the several pieces of
heraldic glass that persist in the east window. Both glass and screen exhibit *azure
a bend or* quartered with the arms of related families. But it was not only in the
interior of churches that heraldic arms were displayed. The arms both of Scrope
of Bolton and of the prestigious families with whom they were related can still be
seen high on the external walls of the parish church of Wensley, from whence the
Scropes originated, and on the porch of the parish church of Easby, alongside
St Agatha's Abbey.

The arms that one bore, and hence their depiction in glass and elsewhere, could
reveal honorific aspects of family history. One might bear the escallop shells, indicating that an ancestor had been on pilgrimage to the Holy Land, perhaps on crusade, something that continued to attract high prestige within chivalric society
throughout the thirteenth and fourteenth centuries. Crusades, however,
were not only to the Holy Land. The Scrope versus Grosvenor records tell how

Geoffrey le Scrope the younger's faithful esquire, John Ryther, stayed on in Konigsberg after his master's death in 1362 to supervise the installation of a glass panel with the Scrope arms in the church there. Indeed, Maurice Keen tells us that the Teutonic Knights encouraged crusaders to leave a memorial of themselves and their achievement there, 'to judge by the testimony given in the Scrope versus Grosvenor dispute, there must have been a time when a whole history of foreign crusading enterprise could be read in the armorial glass and blazoned memorials of the Marienkirche of Konigsberg.'[51]

Heraldic display in the great churches was more a matter for the higher nobility. Lesser families had often to be content with demonstrating their status in their parish churches. English churches of the fourteenth and fifteenth centuries seem to have been literally festooned with armorial glass and depictions of donors. A wealth of art has been lost from them, as the notes and drawings of antiquaries like Sir William Dugdale, William Wyrley and William Burton make clear.[52] First and foremost, for these local families, heraldic glass notified the world of the relationship between lord, church and parish. A particularly well-known and fine example of the depiction of a manorial lord is that of Sir James Berners at West Horsley, Surrey, shown in late fourteenth-century plate armour and a tabard with his family arms, *quarterly or and vert*.[53] Berners, however, was an elevated figure, a chamber knight of Richard II. In similar style and of similar date is the depiction

From the fourteenth century parish churches were becoming increasingly adorned with armorial glass and portraits of donors. One example is that of the Ruyhales of Birtsmorton, Worcestershire

in the parish church of Birtsmorton in south Worcestershire, of two men of the Ruyhale family, one shown with his wife. The glass is now fragmentary but it is known in more perfect condition from earlier drawings.[54] An earlier example is Sir Simon de Drayton, depicted with a model of his church at Lowick, Northamptonshire, and with his family arms clearly visible.[55] Often specific family chapels existed within the churches, becoming in effect private mausoleums, containing effigies or brasses and sometimes glass. The chapel of the Langleys at Siddington, near Cirencester, is one example of this.[56] Sometimes the glass indicates that the donor as a lord of the manor had the right to present to the living. For example at Carlton Scroop, Lincolnshire, glass of the early fourteenth century shows two donors, one with the Newmarch arms and the other with the arms of the Biddeshall family. John de Newmarch, lord of Carlton, presented William de Biddeshall, chaplain, to the living in 1307, and it is clearly this that is being conveyed in the glass.[57] Similarly at Mancetter, in north Warwickshire, glass of the second quarter of the fourteenth century showed two knights holding their coats of arms. The rector at this date was Ralph de Crophull and the lord of the manor Sir Guy de Mancetter. Ralph appears to have been a relative of Sir John de Crophull, and in all probability it is he who is represented in the glass. The glass itself suggests not just the fact of presentation but also perhaps a close relationship between the families.[58]

Families were concerned not only to indicate their own prominence and their relationship with a specific locality but also to indicate their associations, their

Armorial glass in a parish church might represent both the family of the rector and the lord of the manor who presented to the living, as shown here at Mancetter (from an engraving in Sir William Dugdale's Warwickshire*)*

kinship and affinity with other families. By the fourteenth century the practice of marshalling had been introduced. The union of families by marriage was often indicated by impalement, that is the depiction of the two coats alongside one another on the same shield. If the wife was an heiress, her husband would bear a small shield or escutcheon of pretence at the centre of his shield until she inherited. Their descendants would bear the two coats of arms quartered, the paternal arms being in the first and fourth quarters. As time went on further quarterings might well develop, although it was by no means obligatory to display them all. Sometimes arms were displayed together with those of one's overlord or of a magnate with whom one was connected. The series of shields that were, and sometimes still are, found in parish churches are often to be explained in these ways. A fifteenth-century example makes explicit the thinking behind the juxtaposition of many local coats of arms. The will of John Pympe of Nettlestead, Kent, included the exact words he wished to be placed on his tomb, no less than an account of his lineage stretching back five generations. He further requested that there be inserted into the blank spaces of the windows in the nave the arms of members of the St Leger, Cheyne and Guildford families, 'that a knoleche be sought howe alliaunce of Sellinger, Cheyne and Pympe came first in by mariage' and that this should also be indicated by armorial glass.[59] These families were all, in fact, of greater prominence in the county than were the Pympes, which presumably gave an added stimulus to the desire to be depicted with them.

The depiction of a whole series of armorial shields could indicate something else as well. It suggested that one belonged to a greater community of elevated persons, to a territorial élite, to a nobility. There was much mileage in having one's arms displayed not only among one's peers but also in company with more elevated personages. A good example of this is Sir William de Etchingham's fourteenth-century church in which he had the arms of the royal family depicted in the east window, with his own arms next and those of all the English earls in the chancel, followed by those of fellow east Sussex gentry families in the nave.[60] As has been said, they 'proclaim in the language of visual symbolism the solidarity of all the noble- and gentle-born, the sense of pride, perhaps even of separateness, felt by those of armigerous rank.'[61]

•Heraldry was also increasingly associated with effigies. Indeed, the two could combine to reach new heights of grandeur and opulence, as shown by the sepulchral monument of Edward, the Black Prince in Canterbury Cathedral. The spread of the effigy continued, moreover, unabated. By the beginning of the fourteenth century it was penetrating the northern counties of England. There were new developments, too. Alabaster came in and was increasingly used during the second half of the century. The same is true of the double effigy, depicting husband and wife. The most spectacular development in funeral monuments during the fourteenth century, however, was the diffusion of the monumental brass.[62] The first figure brasses, of the late thirteenth century, had been for ecclesiastical patrons. During the first decade of the new century, however, a workshop was in operation in London, catering for customers wanting secular effigies in brass. The producers were the same Purbeck marblers

*The tomb of the Black Prince in Canterbury Cathedral. During the fourteenth century
sepulchral monuments reached new heights of grandeur and opulence*

who had played such a prominent role in the dissemination of the stone effigy.
Not surprisingly, the styles in the new medium owed a good deal to the styles
in the old. The market was similar at first to that for the stone effigy, although
the brass was to become widely diffused among the middle strata of the nation.
A particular workshop was responsible for what is known as the Camoys style,
after the earliest known example. Knights in this style include Sir Roger de
Trumpington II, of Trumpington in Cambridgeshire and Sir John D'Abernon II,
of Stoke D'Abernon, Surrey, both now thought to have been produced around
1326–7. A variant style is that named after Sir William de Setvans of
Chartham, Kent.[63] Among other differences, the Setvans style is more expressive facially. All three brasses illustrate the use of plate armour to provide extra
protection for the joints. The Trumpington and Setvans arms are examples of
canting arms, arms which allude to the name of the bearer. Thus, Roger de
Trumpington bears trumpets and William de Setvans (that is sept vans) bears
winnowing-fans. The brass of Sir William fitz Ralph of Pebmarsh, Essex,
belonging to the 1330s but basically in the Camoys style, shows the steady
advance of plate armour.

In mid-century the styles changed. The figures became slimmer, the brasses

The exquisite tomb of Lord Edward Despenser, Tewkesbury Abbey

The tomb of Sir John Beauchamp of Holt and Joan, his wife, in Worcester Cathedral. The double effigy became fashionable during the second half of the fourteenth century

more elaborate. As with stone effigies brasses began to show couples, for example that of Sir John and Lady Harsick *c.* 1384. The knight is now in plate armour. One of the most magnificent fourteenth-century brasses, however, is that of Sir Hugh Hastings in his church at Elsing, Norfolk. His soul is being taken up to heaven by angels, and the weepers depicted in the borders are fellow members of the Order of the Garter, including Edward III himself, with their arms.

Heraldic display, however, was somewhat arcane, and deliberately so. Deciphering its meaning was held to be a matter only for the gentle. In the prologue to *The Tale of Beryn*, which tells of the adventures of Chaucer's pilgrims when they reached Canterbury, we find the Pardoner and the Miller hiving off in the cathedral church to examine the glass. They:

> Pyrid fast, & pourid, highe oppon the glase [peered intently & pored]
> Countirfeting gentilmen, the armys for to blase.

Of course, they got it hopelessly wrong. In fact, they read it 'right as would horned rams'.[64]

Moralists naturally disapproved of all this worldly vanity. One of them was the author of the late fourteenth-century poem *Pierce the Ploughman's Crede*[65] who describes a house of the Dominican friars:

The double brass: Sir John and Lady Harsick, of Southacre, Norfolk, c. 1384

A monumental brass in the Camoys style: Sir Roger de Trumpington II, of Trumpington, Cambridgeshire, c. 1326–7. Note the canting arms, alluding to the name of the bearer

The brass of Sir John D'Abernon II, of Stoke D'Abernon, Surrey, also c. 1326–7 in the Camoys style. Note the beginnings of plate armour depicted in these early brasses

*The brass of Sir John de
Cobham, of Cobham, Kent.
By the mid-fourteenth
century brasses were becoming
slimmer and more elaborate*

*The brass of Sir William fitz Ralph, of
Pebmarsh, Essex, dating from the 1330s.
Note the advance of plate armour*

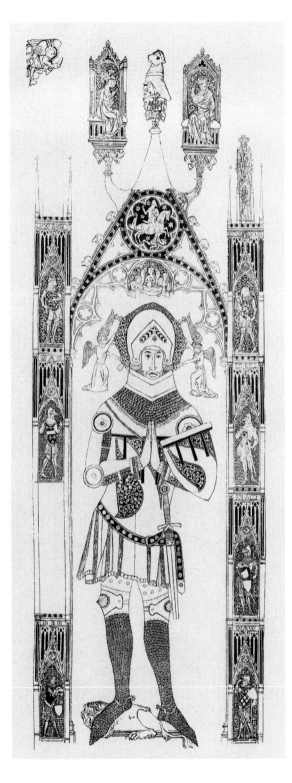

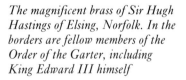

The magnificent brass of Sir Hugh Hastings of Elsing, Norfolk. In the borders are fellow members of the Order of the Garter, including King Edward III himself

The brass of Sir William de Setvans, of Chartham, Kent. A variant on the Camoys style, the Setvans style is more expressive facially

Wyde wyndowes y-wrought y-written full thikke,
Schynen with schapen scheldes to schewen aboute, [shaped]
With merkes of marchauntes y-medled bytwene, [merchants' marks placed]
Mo than twenty and two twyes y-noumbred
Ther is non heraud that hath half swich a rolle, [herald]
Right as a rageman hath rekned hem newe. [roll/counted]
Tombes opon tabernacles tyld opon lofte, [raised]
Housed in hirnes harde set abouten, [corners]
Of armede alabaustre clad for the nones, [for the nonce]
Made upon marbel in many maner wyse,
Knyghtes in her conisantes clad for the nones, [cognisances]
All it semed seyntes y-sacred upon erthe;
And lovely ladies y-wrought leyen by her sydes
In many gay garmentes that weren gold-beten.

(ll. 175–88)

The strictures of the moralists were largely ignored in this regard. The primary function of chivalric knighthood was to proclaim an élite, and the most effective manner of doing so was through the visual image.

FIVE

The Role of Chivalric Knighthood in English Society

'One consequence of the triumph of chivalry was to reinforce the martial implications of knighthood. Once such a clearly articulated expression of élite mentality and solidarity was in existence, based as it was upon the concept of a finely arrayed warrior and led by a warlike aristocracy, then militaristic kings like Edward I and Edward III could expect to call upon the full force of *la chevalerie* to support them in their wars. The new spirit of cooperation between the king and the aristocracy, which characterized the greater part of the reign of Edward I (at least until the last ten years of his reign) and which reappeared after the accession of Edward III, served to reinforce the aristocracy's own taste for war and to provide effective outlets for its martial aspirations. The conquest of Wales and Edward I's early successes in Scotland validated the chivalric idea to such a degree that the number of knights in society seems actually to have risen during these years, as some of the county families came back on board. Neither Edward's ultimate failure in Scotland and the disaster at Bannockburn in 1314 nor the Crown's lack of leadership during the reign of Edward II were sufficient to dent these values, and Edward III was subsequently able to cash in on the prevalent military ethos to lead his aristocracy to even greater military glories against France during the Hundred Years' War. The reigns of the three Edwards must be seen, therefore, as the high water mark of chivalric knighthood in England.

To appreciate the military role of knighthood it is necessary first of all to understand how English armies were brought into operation. Much work has been done on the armies of Edward I in recent years, principally by Michael Prestwich.[1] Prestwich has considerably modified the conventional view that Edward I transformed the English army from an old-fashioned and inefficient feudal force into a professional, paid army recruited by contracts and indentures. In fact, the pace of change was slow and the king's cavalry forces were recruited on very mixed lines. The fullest documentation is for the army that the king took to Scotland in 1300. It indicates that the cavalry was recruited in four ways. First, there was a traditional request for feudal service and the subsequent muster roll shows that the tenants-in-chief provided a total of 40 knights and 366 sergeants performing their forty days' unpaid service. In addition, the wardrobe account book shows that there were about 850 cavalry-men performing paid service, twenty-three of whom held the rank of banneret. However, the muster roll and the wardrobe account tell by no means the whole of the story. This campaign produced the marvellous *Song of Carlaverock* which names 87 bannerets who participated and claims that even this was not the full total. Only three of these men appear in the muster of those doing feudal service and, as has been seen, a further twenty-three figure among the paid cavalry. This means that the great majority, sixty-one, must have served both voluntarily and at their own expense. In a formal sense this indicates that they must have responded to the second half of the writ of summons, which asked that they provide as many men-at-arms as they could in addition to their quotas as tenants of the Crown. Beyond this the king demanded that all those with at least £40 worth of land should come and serve for pay, although the response to this was probably very slight. Altogether a cavalry force of around 2,000 seems to have participated in the 1300 campaign. It was divided into four main battalions, one of which consisted exclusively of men from the royal household.

Each of the elements making up the army must be dealt with in turn, beginning with the royal household. Edward's household, like that of his predecessors, was 'more of a small army than a domestic establishment'.[2] The lists of Edward's household knights show a higher degree of continuity than was the case with magnate retinues. Some were inherited from his youth like the highly favoured Savoyard, Otto de Grandson. Many were there as part of a family tradition. During the Scottish wars of the latter part of the reign, Edward was served by many who were the sons of household knights of his youth. The majority of the knights were English, although he also employed a few Gascons and Spaniards. Each of the household bannerets and knights would have had a small troop of their own retainers, so that the total number of men the household could put into the field was quite considerable. In addition to these, others were paid wages by the household for the duration of a single campaign. Numbers were highest on the Falkirk campaign of 1298, when the horse valuation rolls indicate a household strength of almost 800 together with non-household contingents numbering 564. For the campaign that saw the Siege of Carlaverock, 522 men had their horses valued on the household horse list, while a total of 850 cavalrymen were paid by the wardrobe. During the first years of the fourteenth century the household continued to put appreciable forces into the field but never again on quite the scale of 1298.

The household knights generally served together, forming a coherent military unit. However, some might be detached from the main body and given individual responsibilities. Some, for example, were made constables of castles in Wales and Scotland. Frequently they commanded the chevauchées, or raids, used to harry the Scots. They also held naval commands. During the Welsh wars household knights were often used to help recruit troops and to organize the preparatory stages of campaigns. In 1300 William Felton bought the lances from which five banners were to be flown: two with the arms of England, one with the cross of St George, one with the arms of St Edmund and one with those of St Edward. They might also be used on diplomatic missions and on other matters of state.

Quotas were provided under feudal obligations on five occasions during Edward I's reign and a further four during his successor's. The number of troops produced was not particularly large as, of course, the quotas involved were those renegotiated piecemeal with tenants-in-chief in the thirteenth century. Increasingly, obligations were discharged by sending sergeants-at-arms, two of whom had been regarded since the second quarter of the thirteenth century as equivalent to one knight. In addition there were obligations under sergeanty tenure, that is to say where land was held for very specific services. This could produce its comic turns, for example when Hugo fitz Heyr came to fight in 1300 with a bow and one arrow. He fired this as soon as the Scots were first seen and then left for home. In 1282 another man had appeared at the muster carrying a side of bacon which he ate and then disappeared. Few tenants-in-chief now served in person under this obligation, only twelve doing so, for example, in 1300. The chief advantage to the Crown of this type of summons seems to have been its traditional nature, with many of the great lords treating it as an invitation to participate on campaign with their own troops over and above their limited quotas.

Relatively few of the knights who participated on campaign did so, then, under feudal obligation. For the most part, Edward I's magnates served without pay; indeed, in 1282 they rejected a move on the king's part to take a wholly paid army into Wales. Presumably, it was not only beneath their dignity to accept pay but it also implied, and perhaps would have resulted in, an unacceptable degree of subordination on their part. This appears to have held good throughout Edward's reign. One who did serve for pay was the relatively poor Aymer de Valence. The account book for the 1306–7 campaign, for example, shows that from May to July 1306 he had a squadron of 2 bannerets, 15 knights and 37 men-at-arms. Over the following winter he served under contract with 100 horse for £1,000. During the next reign matters changed and although some of the earls, including Lancaster and Gloucester, held out, the majority seem to have succumbed. In any case the war against the Scots had become an increasingly defensive one with less opportunities for profit through booty.

Knights and other men-at-arms served in retinues. In many cases by this time they served under the conditions stipulated in their indentures for life such as that drawn up between John de Segrave and Roger Bigod, earl of Norfolk and Marshal of England in 1297. Others served under temporary agreements. An early survival is one from 1287 by which Peter Maulay agreed to serve Edmund Stafford with ten men-at-arms for the war in Wales. Although the survival of documents is haphazard, this system was clearly prevalent by the time of Edward I and many a knight saw service on such terms in his day.[3] The rolls of protection reveal a lack of continuity and there was clearly a tendency to serve under different lords in different campaigns.

Contracts, by contrast, were little used by the Crown itself in the time of Edward I except for armies where the king was not present, for example in the winter campaign in Scotland of 1297–8. On this occasion the king contracted with the earls of Surrey, Norfolk, Hereford, Gloucester and Warwick, and Henry Percy to serve for three months with a total of 500 horse in return for £7,691 16s. 8d. Contracts were commonly used for garrison service. Castle constables were often contracted to remain at their posts with a specified number of men in return for a lump sum rather than receive daily wages. For example, on 18 October 1297 an indenture was drawn up with Robert Hastang for the custody of Roxburgh Castle with a force of 18 men-at-arms, 20 crossbowmen and 92 archers until the following spring, for £130. The use of contracts certainly increased during his son's reign, partly no doubt because the king preferred not to campaign personally. It was not until 1337, however, that an entire army was to be recruited by such means. In the words of Michael Prestwich, what was most significant was the fact that 'by the time of the 1327 campaign virtually the whole cavalry force, save for the feudal contingents who were making their last appearance in an English army, were paid'.[4]

In addition to the household troops, the feudal quotas and the additional troops provided by the magnates, both Edward I and Edward II attempted to reach out beyond feudal service and beyond the retinue, whether unpaid or under contract, to the lesser landowners themselves for military service. Distraint of knighthood continued, although this was very largely a fiscal measure. Over and above this, an attempt was made to cajole all those with a certain income in land to join the royal armies. In November 1282 all those with at least £20 worth of land who were not serving in the Welsh war were summoned to appear at Northampton early in the following year, in all probability as an attempt to squeeze more money out of them. In 1295 the treasurer was ordered to make the sheriffs hold inquests into the number of men who held more than £40 worth of land. These were to be ready to set out on campaign at royal wages, with horses and arms, at very short notice. This inquiry seems to have been carried out and to have achieved some success in providing reinforcements in Wales. The order to the £40 landholders was repeated in the following year, while in 1297, planning to take a force to Flanders, the king ordered the sheriffs to draw up lists, this time of £20 landholders, and summoned all such men to muster at London. On this occasion, with the king in any case at odds with the leaders of his baronage, there was very little response.[5]

The idea was again revived in 1300 and again met opposition. Commissions were set up to draw up lists of men holding £40 worth of land and to summon them to serve for wages in Scotland. The lists were duly drawn up but there is nothing to suggest that in practice men were forced to go on campaign. In the following year, in place of the summons of £40 landholders, some 935 men were sent individual summonses. Unlike the writs to magnates these promised pay, but again there is no means of knowing how many of those summoned actually went to Scotland. These experiments were not to be repeated by this king, and in the end the policy proved a failure. It was to be followed up, however, during the next reign, though once again, it would seem, with little success. In 1316 Edward II ordered all £50 landholders to serve against the Scots, actually under threat of confiscation of their lands. In 1322, in addition to the normal feudal summons, sheriffs were instructed to proclaim that all cavalrymen, from bannerets to men-at-arms, who were not retained by others, were to muster at Newcastle. Many were sent individual summonses and the sheriffs were requested to return lists. The surviving lists show considerable variation and in practice it does not appear to have been particularly successful.

For the intended Gascon campaign of 1324 an even more ambitious attempt was made. A summons was issued on 9 May asking all knights to come to Westminster to meet with the king and magnates to discuss affairs of state. The following day a distraint of knighthood was ordered and all who wished to be knighted by the king were asked to come to London by 3 June. The sheriffs drew up lists of all knights and men-at-arms in their counties. Once again the lists are less reliable than the historian would wish. In total there are about 1,150 knights and 950 men-at-arms listed, giving some idea of the country's cavalry resources. It was clearly intended as part of a wholesale reorganization of cavalry service. In the last two years of the reign commissioners of array were ordered to recruit knights and men-at-arms as well as infantry. Such measures proved ineffectual, were deeply resented in the country and were regarded as one element in the tyrannical rule of Edward II and the Despensers. When Edward III tried similar measures in the 1340s he met renewed hostility. The future lay with contract armies.

All in all, it was probably very difficult for knights to avoid at least occasional service and a glance at the (often very stark) biographies that can be constructed of individual knights tends to confirm this. For the most part, however, those landholders who did not take on knighthood seem in practice to have been able to decide whether to serve or not as they saw fit. Compulsion was resisted within the landowning classes. Nevertheless, many men did participate. There were various reasons for this, but not the least, especially among the knights, was the prevailing *mores* and a sense of social obligation; obligation, that is, to rank.

The effects can be seen most clearly during the earlier phases of the Hundred Years' War.[6] Already in 1335 the royal forces in Scotland included 450 knights and some 2,250 men-at-arms. The army that Edward III took to Brittany in 1342 included 330 knights and 1,470 men-at-arms. As many as 927 knights have been identified as serving at Crécy and Calais in 1346–7, while the royal expedition to France in 1359–60 included 870 knights.[7] The government was still trying to force men to serve.[8] Admittedly these were some of the largest armies of the Hundred Years' War and the contract armies led by members of the nobility tended to be smaller. Not all of the knights were English. The army of 1359–60, for example, contained 680 English among the 870 knights. Nor, indeed, were all of the men-at-arms established members of the landed classes. This was the period that saw the emergence of the professional captain; men of the calibre of Hugh Calveley, Robert Knollys, David Hulgreve, Geoffrey Sais and John Norbury.[9] None the less, the extent to which the gentry was involved in the wars was remarkable.[10]

•Something of the socio-military role of knights and others who shared gentility with them is revealed by the few surviving subcontracts made by those providing troops for the aristocratic commanders. Sir Hugh Hastings, for example, contracted to serve with Thomas of Woodstock, earl of Buckingham, on his expedition to Brittany in 1380.[11] He was to provide a retinue of sixty men-at-arms (including himself as banneret and seven knights) and sixty archers. Twenty-four indentures of subcontract survive with twenty-six men. The indentures stipulated that each subcontractor would serve Sir Hugh in war, sufficiently arrayed and mounted, usually for one year. One of these subcontractors was a knight and three others were styled esquires. Seventeen contracted to provide an archer in addition to their own services, while the knight, Sir William Moton, agreed to provide not only an archer but an esquire who would be accompanied by a further archer. Furthermore, one of the number, Jankyn Nowell, was to contribute four other men-at-arms besides himself and five archers. As Nowell received special terms, it seems likely that he was a professional soldier leading a miniature company. All in all Sir Hugh's subcontracts would have covered fifty-three of the retinue he had contracted for (one of the seven knights, thirty of the fifty-two men-at-arms, twenty-two of the sixty archers). He certainly had twenty of the twenty-six subcontractors among the men-at-arms with him in France in August 1380. Nowell was among them, although Sir William Moton was not. In fact, Hastings had only two knights with him rather than the seven he had contracted for; however, there were five more men-at-arms and four more archers than the contract had stipulated.

Certain aspects of the personnel are interesting. Nowell's little company may well have consisted in part or in whole of his relatives. Among Sir Hugh's men-at-arms mustered in France were Richard Nowell the elder, Richard Nowell the younger and Robert Nowell. Some of the other subcontractors, four at least, appear to have been Sir Hugh's own household servants or long-term retainers. One of them was trusted to receive the first instalment of his pay for the retinue from the Exchequer, while three others, according to their contracts, received their food and drink (*bouche de court*).

A most important feature of this type of evidence is that it reveals the commander's dependence upon subcontracting men-at-arms for recruiting archers, in particular, but also for some additional men-at-arms. Professional soldiers like Nowell must have been especially useful in this respect, with their reputation and contacts; but so must knights with their particular status. It has been suggested that this dependence upon lesser men for recruitment helps to explain why magnates were prepared to retain the long-term services of knights and esquires by indenture in war as well as in peace.[12] They were thereby guaranteed a nucleus of dependable subcontractors of suffcient status to attract support and to be able to enter into the financial arrangements involved.

Money matters were clearly spelled out. Not only was the remuneration clearly stipulated, but also the arrangements over the division of the spoils of war. There were profits to be made from the remuneration too. The pay that Sir Hugh offered was usually below the rate he was receiving from the Crown, and it seems highly likely that, equally, the men-at-arms paid their archers at rates lower than those that they had contracted with Sir Hugh. These were among the profits of war.

Sir Hugh Hastings was of quite exalted rank, being a kinsman of John

Hastings, earl of Pembroke, and was a substantial landowner in his own right in Norfolk and Yorkshire. Other knights who contracted with magnates were not quite so elevated as he. A good example is the Cheshire knight, Sir Ralph Mobberley, who embarked on the Black Prince's service in Gascony in September 1355. The Black Prince had formally agreed to serve in Gascony as the king's lieutenant on 10 July 1355, and under the terms of his indenture was to provide a retinue of 433 men-at-arms, 400 mounted archers and 300 foot archers. Mobberley's contingent comprised himself, an esquire and thirty-two mounted archers. A close study of this retinue from the journal of John Henxteworth, the Black Prince's treasurer, shows that most of them were recruited within ten miles of the Mobberley estate in East Cheshire. A few others came from an area in the south of the county where Sir Ralph had additional land and a mistress by whom he had two illegitimate sons. Some can be shown to have been recruited from his own following in the county. Some were kin – Richard and Jenkin Mobberley and the knight's nephew, John Leycester. Others were dependants or neighbours, and dependants of neighbours. A number were clearly kinsmen and younger sons of gentle landowners. In short, Sir Ralph Mobberley's retinue was drawn from local society: they were men who took service with him as a result of his own position within that society.[13]

The retinues of other Cheshire subcontractors, insofar as they can be ascertained, tend to show the same characteristics. John Leycester of Tabley recruited three esquires and eight archers for Thomas de Felton's retinue in 1374. Of the esquires one was Jenkin Mobberley, with whom Leycester had served in Ralph Mobberley's retinue in 1355, and another was a neighbouring landowner, John Mascy of Tatton. At least 25 per cent of the retinues of both Sir David Hulgreve and Sir Hugh Calveley in 1380 were Cheshire men, judging by surname evidence. However, Calveley's retinue also included a small group of Londoners, while Hulgreve's included a company from Weardale, County Durham.[14] Factors other than local ones certainly figured in at least some subcontracted retinues.

This is clearly true in the case of Sir John Strother of Kirknewton, Northumberland . He was the eldest son of Henry Strother, sometime sheriff of that county and lessee of the castle and lordship of Wark-on-Tweed.[15] Sir John contracted with the earl of March to provide a force of thirty men-at-arms and thirty archers for his expedition to Brittany in 1374. Eight subcontracts survive between Sir John Rother and individual men-at-arms. Each indenture stipulates that the man in question had agreed to serve the earl of March for an entire year, mounted at his own expense, and to bring an archer, unarmed but sufficiently well arrayed so that Sir John would incur no reproach at the muster. The terms were carefully stipulated, including once again the division of the profits of war. Assuming that all of Strother's arrangements were of the same order as those in the surviving indenture, he stood to gain £255 out of the deal, irrespective of any windfalls from the spoils of war. It is hardly surprising that shrewd men like him remained enthusiastic over the war in France. Indeed, Strother was clearly making a profession of war, at least until he came fully into his estates. His father was still alive and, although some of the family land had been assigned to him in 1372, he was probably dependent upon this type of additional income to maintain his knightly estate.

Strother's relationship with the earl of March was clearly a temporary one, even though he became part of the lord's household for the term of the contract. March had no landed presence in Northumberland. Similarly, it looks as though Strother's men-at-arms similarly had no personal or geographical links with him. They were not non-entities socially, for four of the eight were styled esquire. However, three of them, at least, were East Anglian and it seems probable that they were recruited not in the provinces but in London. In this instance it would seem to have been Strother's knightly rank and probable military experience that made him valuable as a recruiter, rather than his presence in any local sense.

Men like Strother and the Cheshire captains were making a career out of soldiering. In Strother's case his father's longevity kept him from the major part of his inheritance and this, as well as his own preference perhaps, explains his long-term involvement in war. Mobberley, although the head of an established Cheshire family and well connected, suffered a depleted inheritance as a result of feud and dispute. Others were younger sons, landless or near-landless members of the gentry, or of relatively obscure origin. It has been suggested that those who had achieved advancement and grown rich through war and were not established landowners in their own right by patrimony, may have been 'reluctant or unable to re-enter the local society from which they had sprung' and that consequently they often tended to invest in the land market elsewhere.[16] Among the Cheshire men, for example, John Norbury bought lands in Hertfordshire, while David Hulgreve gravitated towards Herefordshire and Northumberland. Perhaps it was partly for this reason, too, that such men bonded together for their mutual benefit as brothers-in-arms.[17] They provide a strong contrast with those sons of county landowners who joined one or more expeditions in their youth before succeeding to their family estates and their full place in local society. Sir John Hardreshull, for instance, who had risen to prominence in Brittany during the 1340s, retired from war at exactly the time his son, William, appeared on the battlefields of France.[18]

In Cheshire this is graphically illustrated through the Scrope versus Grosvenor dispute in the Court of Chivalry in 1385.[19] Many of the witnesses in favour of the Cheshire knight, Sir Robert Grosvenor, recalled their service with Sir James Audley in the Black Prince's campaign in Poitou in 1369, and a few recalled earlier campaigns. No less than eleven members of the Prince's retinue of 1369, including Grosvenor himself, gave evidence in 1385. What is illustrated here is the existence of a collective memory; what has been called 'a spontaneous demonstration of class unity in Cheshire'.[20] Particularly significant is the 'discordant note' struck by Sir Hugh Browe of Tushingham who said that he could not offer evidence in support of Grosvenor because, although he had been armed for twenty years, he had served in companies and garrisons, not on great expeditions. He had, however, seen Grosvenor armed with *azure a bend or* in Poitou and in the recent expedition to Scotland where the famous dispute had arisen. His was not part of the collective memory. Men like Browe and Claveley, Hulgreve and Norbury were not the norm.

As far as the great campaigns were concerned the leadership of gentry society in peace also provided its leadership in war. There was a difference then between those who served once or twice in their lives and those who served regularly, men like Hulgreve and Norbury who made soldiering a career. Studies of the county gentry of the fourteenth century indicate that the phenomenon of heads of gentry families serving once or twice in their youth was a widespread one.[21] The contrast may perhaps have been stronger in Cheshire than many other counties, given its peculiar prominence during and after the Black Prince's lordship, as a recruiting ground for the soldiery and the captains of the French war.

But one ought not to exaggerate these contrasts. The reasons why men served were various. There were reasons of lordship which took men to war and, over and above that, there was obligation determined by convention. But part of the allure, no doubt, must often have been ransom and booty; and the pay was not bad. The central point to stress, however, is that the knights of fourteenth-century England were a military class, and military experience confirmed, if it did not confer, status. When the commissioners set about finding witnesses in favour of Sir Robert Grosvenor in 1385, they noted the length of each man's military service. As a result, within local society in general, militaristic values were power-fully sanctioned. Whatever may have been the case during the second half of the twelfth century and the first half of the thirteenth century, no longer would it be easy for a knight to avoid, had he wished to do so, the military consequences of belonging to his order. His sense of honour forbade it.

Honour has been defined as: 'the value of a person in his own eyes, but also in the eyes of his society. It is his estimation of his own worth, his claim to pride, but it is also the acknowledgement of that claim, his excellence recognised by society, his right to pride.'[22] Honour, then, would take a knight to war and would largely determine his conduct during the war. Naturally, men's inclinations towards war would have varied considerably as would the balance of their motives. Some actively sought war and spent many years in the field. Others, it seems, were con-tent to have seen some military action during their youth.

It is in war, arguably, that one comes closest to understanding the real content of chivalry, not least because here the behaviour of the knights can be examined collectively. There are, of course, major formulations of chivalry, by representa-tives of the church and in romance. But to what extent the content of these corre-sponded to how the thirteenth- or fourteenth-century county knight actually felt is far from clear. Religious chivalry represents the progressive attempts by the Church to tame and direct the energies of the military classes, going back several centuries. And romance, however much it influenced aspects of behaviour, was essentially the fictive world of the middle ages and not the reality. Arguably, the tracts by fourteenth-century writers on the nature of war and on the rules by which it should be fought reveal rather more. Popularizers like Honoré Bonet and Christine de Pisan discussed the justifications of war, strategy and tactics and matters such as ransoms, safe-conducts, questions of obligation and points of honour. Even these works, however, despite the fact that they draw upon the experience and opinions of individual knights, are ultimately the work of lawyers not combatants. It is only in the chronicles and the few contemporary biographies that one gets really close to what these men actually felt.

Even here there is a heavy concentration upon the greatest figures. Something is revealed of the mentality of Henry of Grosmont, first duke of Lancaster, of the Black Prince, and of faithful and highly successful followers like Sir John Chandos. They tell of extravagant acts of chivalry, such as the Black Prince's freeing of Bertrand du Guesclin, constable of France, and what prompted them. They tell how putting the inhabitants of a city to the sword did not detract from the chivalry of the author of the deed; how, indeed, a sense of honour could determine such an act while at the same time lead to the sparing of the remnant of the valiant but exhausted knightly garrison. They tell most of hard acts of war and of the profits of war, but also of how the effects of war were mitigated for the privileged combatants. Warfare for the knight was no easy matter as, for example, the oft-quoted chivalric treatise of Geoffroi de Charny makes clear, but it was very much more preferable to the world of the footsoldier. The differential treatment accorded to men in battle is well known. The massacre of the London militia by the future Edward I and his forces at the Battle of Lewes in 1264 contrasts sharply with the relatively few fatalities among the knights on either side. The Battle of Evesham of the following year is on the face of it an exception, as Simon de Montfort and his followers were killed; but in actual fact their deaths constituted a deliberate act of policy as the verse chronicler, Robert of Gloucester, makes clear when he calls it 'the murder of Evesham'. That knights should behave courteously towards fellow knights was a matter of self-interest. Part of the motive was ransom, and here warfare borrowed from the tournament, itself in origin a preparation for war. But it was also wider than this. Of the Hundred

Soldiers looting a house in Paris, in the late fourteenth century. This must have been a common sight during the Hundred Years' War

Years' War, in particular, John Barnie writes: 'It [chivalry] is based almost entirely on caste solidarity and mutual self-interest.'[23] We cannot avoid the essential truth of this. No one now seriously believes that the chivalry of the fourteenth century was a corruption of a twelfth-century ideal. It is true that there were changes and developments; pre-eminently an increasingly elaborate sense of display. But the essence remained the same. Chivalry contained ideals and principles, but they operated largely in relations between knights and between knights and their superiors.

Although the sources concentrate upon the attitudes and behaviour of the most elevated soldiers, there is little reason to think that their knightly inferiors thought very differently. After all, chivalry was essentially a collective frame of reference, operating in a feudal world of personal superiority and personal dependence. Its values were reinforced at once from above and below. It follows that among the virtues that were most prized were the old ones of courage and loyal subordination. Although the chivalric ethos found a place for individual acts of bravery and flamboyance it was equally necessary for men to retain a sense of proportion in the interests of all. One of the great success stories of the Hundred Years' War, Sir John Chandos, for example, was believed to have possessed the four cardinal virtues of chivalry: prowess, loyalty, courtesy amd moderation (*mesure*). According to the chronicler Froissart, there was no knight living who was so *courtois* and *gentil*. Although he was perfectly capable of acts of knight-errantry, in general, '*mesure* and a strong sense of duty restrained him from romantic escapades'.[24] This is not to say that spectacular acts did not occur, nor that they were not applauded. Much of the same mentality as that of the Black Prince or Sir John Chandos is revealed in the *Scalacronica* of Sir Thomas Gray of Heaton in Northumberland. This is an extraordinary piece of work in that it was written by an actual fourteenth-century knight who, like his father before him, spent much of his active life defending the Scottish border. It is, in essence, a professional soldier's viewpoint. It does, however, contain one famous incident that seems to come straight out of the pages of romance. During the time of Edward II, when Gray's father was warden of Norham Castle, a Lincolnshire knight named William Marmion joined the garrison. He had been given a helmet of gold by his mistress and commanded to make it known wherever glory was most difficult to attain. When a small Scottish force appeared before the castle Marmion, attired for battle and wearing the helmet, approached Sir Thomas, who answered him thus:

> Sir knight, you have come here as a knight-errant to make that helm known and it is more fitting that chivalry be accomplished on horseback than on foot where that is practicable. Mount you horse; behold your enemies; spur on your horse and go and do battle in the midst of them. May I renounce God if I do not rescue your body alive or dead, or die in the attempt.

Marmion then charged into the Scottish host and fought until surrounded and on the point of death. Only then did Sir Thomas rescue and remount him with the aid of his own garrison forces.[25] Given that such acts were consistent with the code of honour to which the chivalric knight subscribed, they had to be

Norham Castle, Northumberland, the scene of a fourteenth-century act of gallantry by Sir William Marmion

accommodated. Occasionally, too, knights would actually die in acts of defiance. A case in point is the death of Sir William Felton in Castile in 1367, related by the Chandos herald. A small English detachment was surprised by a Spanish force and prepared to defend its position on a small hill. But Felton, 'a lion-hearted man', charged them on horseback with couched lance. He fought bravely but was surrounded and cut to pieces. It was an extravagant gesture, and militarily useless. But in chivalric, honorific terms, there could be no finer death.[26]

Although chivalry's essential social role was to validate an élite, the ultimate *raison d'être* of the chivalric knight was to fight. The consequences of the ideology that underpinned their privileged station in the world were inescapable. There were consequences of this that affected not only the knights but society as a whole. As has been convincingly argued 'one reason for the failure of this age to keep the social problem of war within bounds lay, ironically, in the idealism of its attitude to war and to the soldier, in what we may call the ethic of chivalry.'[27] There was a profound ambivalence in the attitude towards the mercenaries (the *routiers)* who ravaged France and elsewhere and towards the *condottieri*, those soldiers of fortune (many of them English) who operated in Italy. These men were able to draw upon the ideology of and around chivalry to validate their actions. Indeed, the most famous of them all, Sir John Hawkwood, was later, one of the models of chivalrous achievement for Caxton.

According to Maurice Keen 'Chivalry was an essentially upper-class mystique, and for just that reason its trappings and the chivalrous calling of arms had a particular significance and attraction for those at the fringes of nobility, heirs of insufficient estate, cadets, bastards.'[28] But the problem was wider even than that. 'We poor soldiers', wrote Jean de Bueil, 'are for the most part noble by birth, and those who are not are noble by the exercise of arms, for the *métier* of arms is noble in itself.'[29] This apparently prevalent idea was to cause consternation in England in the years after the great victory at Agincourt when ignobly born men-at-arms were claiming the right to coats of arms as a consequence of their participation in Henry V's war. Here the chivalric ideology of the nobility was being used against itself.

Chivalric knighthood had consequences, too, in the civilian sphere. As long as the *raison d'être* of the knight was primarily that he should live by the exercise of arms, then it was extremely difficult to deny his right to maintain his personal position by reaching for his sword. The aristocracy led the way. The chroniclers tell the story how, in response to Edward I's demands that those who exercise franchises (that is, rights of jurisdiction) should show by what warrant they held them, either the earl of Warenne or the earl of Gloucester (according to the chronicler one reads) presented the royal justices not with a charter but with a rusty sword, declaring: 'Look, my lords, here is my warrant. My ancestors came with William the Bastard, and conquered their lands with the sword, and I will defend them with the sword against anyone wishing to seize them.'[30] The story may well be apocryphal, but it is the thought process behind it that is significant. Where the aristocracy led, others followed. Much instability and tension surrounded the whole issue of inheritance, not least because of the increasing complexity of the land law. At times of political disturbance, in particular, these underlying tensions could spill over into actual disorder.[31] In extreme cases, members of the knightly class might take to banditry. Take, for example, the case of the mid-thirteenth-century Ralph Harengod, lord of Iklesham in Sussex. With insufficient income from his estates to satisfy his needs, Ralph became indebted to the Jews. In order to bolster his position he attempted to reduce his tenants to villeinage so that he could exploit them more. The royal courts, however, upheld their free status. When the prior of Hastings failed against the tenants of nearby Burwash in the same way, he employed Ralph and others to perpetrate acts of savage thuggery against them. Ralph later died fighting for Simon de Montfort against the king at the Battle of Lewes.[32] From time to time gentry gangs were in operation, such as the Folevilles and the Coterels who functioned during the 1320s and 1330s. Their most infamous escapade was the holding to ransom of Sir Richard de Willoughby, justice of the King's Bench, in 1332.[33] Their *modus operandi*, with its emphasis upon summary 'justice', came to be known as *Foleville's law*. Such men, however, were not the norm. Much of the potentiality for violence within landed society was actually contained, by arbitration for example and by other forms of self-regulation, and the seizures and attacks upon land that did occur were often controlled and tactical, an accompaniment to action at law.[34] Nevertheless, when all of these features have been allowed for, a predilection for violence was undeniably there, and it was reinforced by the chivalric mode of thought.

Having said all this, chivalric militarism heavily overlay but it could not entirely extinguish the service connotations of knighthood. One only needs to think of the aristocratic retinue that could not have functioned without it. Moreover, the •Crown continued to call upon the service of local knights. It may well be that it was their position as prominent landowners that the Crown was looking to, rather than their knighthood as such. They were no longer in such demand procedurally in the legal sphere. The grand assize, for example, had given way to newer and more adaptable judicial processes. Nevertheless, knights often took the lead in administration, sometimes perhaps with a sense of social obligation. Moreover, office itself reinforced local status. Sir John de Langley, for example, a knight with properties in both Gloucestershire and Warwickshire who was summoned to fight in the king's wars on five occasions between 1300 and 1322, performed a variety of functions on behalf of the Crown. He was twice sheriff of Gloucester. On five occasions he served on judicial commissions of oyer and terminer (to hear and determine) in cases of violence against persons and property. He was justice for gaol delivery at Warwick in at least five years of the reign of Edward II. In addition, he was appointed an assessor and collector of parliamentary subsidies; he was four times taxer in the county of Gloucester and at least twice in the county of Warwick. He was also a purveyancer (organizing supplies for the royal army) and a commissioner of array, selecting able-bodied men for military service. Not surprisingly, he was twice elected member of parliament for the county of Gloucester.[35]

As MPs for the counties, knights represented their communities in negotiations with the king in parliament. Increasingly during the late thirteenth and early fourteenth centuries they brought petitions from their constituents. The effect was not only to produce a wider public awareness of national politics but also to foster a deepening sense of community within the shires.[36] Leadership within local communities naturally fell principally to the knights.[37] This remains true despite the fact that not all county MPs, the knights of the shire, were in practice actual knights. However, the majority do seem to have been throughout the fourteenth century, and overwhelmingly so during the reigns of Edward I and Edward II.[38]

•Knighthood, however, had additional, latent functions in later medieval society. It acted at several levels as a cement, binding the social order. To understand how this could be it is necessary to examine the structure of society itself and the points or levels of potential fracture. To a considerable extent the landed society of the twelfth century had revolved around the honour, an amalgam of estates, rights and overlordships that gave the great lord much of his income, his power and his influence in the world. An honour had a head or *caput*, in practice a central estate or castle, and was regulated by the lord's private court. During the late twelfth and early thirteenth centuries the honour was in steady decline, its jurisdiction eroded by the new legal procedures introduced by the Angevin kings. These connected features were symptomatic of a growing emancipation of feudal tenants. Moreover, as the government's tentacles reached deeper and deeper into the localities, it drew local men, and pre-eminently local knights, into its orbit. Given this scenario, local knights could easily form themselves into social élites, along purely geographical lines. The county and its court provided one obvious basis for this.

The new knighthood that emerged during the course of the thirteenth century must have helped to prevent this working to the detriment of the great territorial lords. It provided, in fact, a bonding mechanism between them and those more solidly based local landowners who retained their knighthood and their social aspirations across the period of crisis and differentiation. Henceforth, the county knights faced two directions at once. On the one hand they were participants within chivalric society and were exponents of its values, while on the other hand they were the natural leaders within the localities. The result was a relatively stable polity, its major potential fracture effectively bridged.

Gentle society was further cemented, however, by the continuation of service as a social norm. Service was the institutionalized personal relationship between man and man which characterized feudal society. Such service was located primarily in the household, in the retinue and in administration. By the end of the thirteenth century these relationships were increasingly being expressed in written form, that is to say in an indenture: a formal document produced in duplicate with one copy being retained by each party under the other's seal. The development of the indenture was made possible by the level of legal and literate administrative activity in general and by the gradual spread of contractual agreements of various kinds in particular. Agreements to raise troops for specific periods or campaigns had existed since at least 1270, and no doubt long before. Moreover, even in the twelfth century, the fact that a man held an estate from a feudal superior was no guarantee of his service other than in the narrowly military sphere, that is when service was owed to the royal army as a condition of the tenure. Lords needed to operate a system of reward. As land became a scarce commodity they must increasingly have had recourse to paying fees. By the end of the thirteenth century the indenture had become a common way of expressing such an arrangement and an appropriate way of cementing the relationship. The magnate gained not only service but also a measure of security and control. The lesser lord gained access to a greater lord, to his influence and, of course, his income. It was, therefore, mutually advantageous.

Let us take just one of the earlier surviving indentures for close examination. The indenture in question is that drawn up (in French) between Robert de Montalt, hereditary steward of Chester, and Sir John de Bracebridge on 30 August 1310. It carries the Montalt seal, a lion rampant, indicating of course that it is the half of the indenture that remained in the hands of Sir John de Bracebridge. It exists today through the survival of his family's archive.[39] The Montalt arms are confirmed from the rolls of arms as *azure, a lion rampant argent.* Obviously, the half retained by Robert de Montalt would have carried Bracebridge's seal. His arms were *vairy argent and sable, a fess gules.*

The terms of the indenture were simple and straightforward. Bracebridge promised Montalt his loyal service as a knight (*son leal servise de chivalerie*) for life, in peace and in war, wherever he would have need of him, except in the Holy Land. He was to serve at Montalt's expense, and was to be fittingly horsed and attired by him. In time of war he and his valet (groom or esquire) were to be compensated for their lost horses, at a reasonable evaluation. Sir John was to receive an annual fee of £10 from the manor of Walton-on-Trent in Derbyshire. The tenants of the manor both free and unfree, from whom the money was to be taken (in

An indenture of retainer, between Lord Robert de Montalt and Sir John de Bracebridge, dated 30 August 1310

practice, of course, their rent) were named and the amounts specified. He was empowered to distrain them directly for the rent should there be a default. But, conversely, should Sir John himself fail to perform his service, without reasonable cause, then he would release all claim on the £10 fee or face a fine of £100, just as Robert de Montalt would if he defaulted. In either case the sum was to be levied by the king's stewards and marshals.

In reality, this indenture did not create a new relationship so much as cement an old one. Robert de Montalt (or Mohaut) took his name from the lordship and castle of Mold on the Welsh Marches. He had succeeded to his estates after the death of his brother in 1296. He fought for Edward I in Flanders and in Scotland, and was present at both the Battle of Falkirk in 1298 and the Siege of Carlaverock in 1300. His military activities continued through the troubled reign of Edward II when he largely avoided involvement in politics. He was regularly summoned to parliament as a lord by both kings. He died in 1329. His grandfather's marriage to Cecily, sister of Hugh d'Aubigny, earl of Arundel (d. 1243), had brought him the honour of Coventry. Among the knights' fees attached to this honour was that of Kingsbury, which was held by the Bracebridge family. Montalt and Bracebridge were thus tenurially linked.[40]

As has already been said, overlordship was no longer any guarantee of service; certainly not without further reward. But John de Bracebridge seems to have been linked with Robert de Montalt from about the time the latter succeeded his brother. He was in his company at the Battle of Falkirk, for example, where he was referred to as Robert's knight and where both men, incidentally, lost horses. In 1300 Robert acquired royal licence to make John de Bracebridge a life grant of £20 per annum from the rent he received from the prior of Coventry.[41] In 1310, as a result of his service in the Scottish wars, John was pardoned for his part in an attack upon the same prior's park at Coventry, an attack which was probably instigated by Montalt himself, since he and the prior were in contention over their respective rights in Coventry at this time. The pardon may well be referring back to an attack said to have been perpetrated by Montalt himself and a body of armed men in 1303 when they hunted in the prior's park and carried away his deer.[42]

Robert de Montalt's support was probably a vital matter for John de Bracebridge. His father had lost possession of the manor of Kingsbury as a result of his part in the civil wars of 1264–5 and his inability to make the necessary redemption payments. He was forced, in fact, to make a life-grant of his manor, to Robert and Eva de Tiptoft. He and his family were hardly destitute, however, for they had their less valuable manor of Bracebridge in Lincolnshire to fall back upon. Nonetheless, they must have been in relatively straitened circumstances. It seems most unlikely that the elder John de Bracebridge ever regained possession of Kingsbury; it was still in the hands of Eva de Tiptoft in 1298. In September 1301 John de Bracebridge II was in possession.[43] With such an inauspicious beginning, John must have found his relationship with his wealthier overlord of very considerable benefit.[44]

Knighthood, then, was part of the means by which the aristocracy bonded with the élite of the counties. Once knighthood had become a more exclusive commodity it gave the emerging territorial élites a clear-cut and collective expression of status that they had not enjoyed hitherto. Knighthood, therefore, bridged a potential chasm between the great feudal lord and the landowner of more local significance. This bonding was the more achievable, and dependable, because of shared lifestyle and outlook, however much their worlds differed in degree.

It is interesting in this context to note the appearance of service in the tournament in retaining contracts, especially during the early fourteenth century. In this respect it has been noticed that the surviving contracts of Humphrey de Bohun, earl of Hereford (d. 1322), tend to follow a pattern. In 1307 he retained Sir Bartholomew de Enfield for life in peace and war, at home and abroad and in the Holy Land. In peace he was to receive hay and oats for four horses and wages for three grooms, while his chamberlain had the right to dine in the lord's hall. During wars and tournaments this was increased to eight horses and seven grooms, with sufficient horses for himself being provided by the earl. For this he received land worth 40 marks per annum. Two years later, the same earl retained Sir Thomas de Maundeville on precisely the same terms, except that Thomas received only 20 marks per annum as his contract was not for life but for a fixed term.[45] Similarly Thomas de Beauchamp, earl of Warwick, contracted with Sir Robert Herle in 1339 whereby Herle would serve the earl as one of the knights bachelor of his household. He was to receive travelling costs, dining rights (*bouche de court*) for himself and his esquires, wages for his grooms, and fodder and supplies for his horses. The earl would provide a horse for Robert himself both in time of war and for attendance at tournaments. He was to have the wardenship of Barnard castle for life, including forests and lands, while his officers were to have their keep within the castle and hay for their horses.[46]

As for war so for the tournament, men could also serve under temporary contracts. Sir Robert fitz Payn was paid £100 to serve Aymer de Valence, earl of Pembroke, in tournaments for one year. The contract was concerned almost solely with tournaments, except that it also envisaged Robert supplying part of the entourage when the earl attended parliament.[47] Another contract emphasizing the tournament is that between Sir Stephen de Segrave and Sir Nicholas Cryel. Cryel was to serve as a knight bachelor with nine horses and nine grooms for tournaments, seven horses and seven grooms for war, and five horses and five grooms for peace including parliament. Tournaments involved Cryel in his highest level of service.[48]

Lords, then, regarded attendance at the tournament as an important part of the service they required.[49] Its direct connection with war is obvious enough, and the same men were often expected to appear with their lord at both. Indeed, it seems generally to be the case that those knights who are found to be most active in war are the same men who were most active in tournaments. These were the men who corresponded to the chivalric ideal, those who set the standard. It is not only a question of expected service, but also, no doubt, of shared interests.

The tournament had probably always been a rather exclusive affair,[50] and this becomes increasingly clear when the participants come more definitely into view with the two Dunstable tournament rolls of arms of 1309 and 1334. Until then what knowledge there is of tournament participation comes either from the

The tournament was an exclusive affair. The finely equipped Sir Geoffrey Luttrell sets out for a tournament, attended by his wife and daughter-in-law (from the Luttrell Psalter, fourteenth century)

haphazard mentions in the chronicles or from the evidence of the government's licences, fines and prohibitions. The roll of the Dunstable tournament, held most probably in June 1309, gives the names of 235 participants.[51] Six earls were present, those of Gloucester, Hereford, Lancaster, Warenne, Warwick and Arundel. The form of the roll, however, shows quite clearly that they were present with their retinues, and to a considerable degree these can be reconstructed. In many cases the individuals whose names follow those of the earls can be shown to have been in their retinues at other times or to have been otherwise connected with them. Thirteen names, for example, follow that of the earl of Hereford. This can be compared with the list of the retinue he proposed to take with him to Scotland a few months after the tournament, in October 1309. There were six knights among his nineteen men-at-arms, and four of them appear on the tournament roll. It is significant that none of those of lesser rank do, an indication of the exclusivity of the tournament. Only knights were supposed to take part; at least in a full capacity.[52] One of the four was none other than Bartholomew de Enfield who had been retained by the earl for life to serve in peace, war and tournaments two years before. The others were Walter de Beauchamp, Roger de Chandos and Thomas de Ferrers. In addition to the earls there were numerous others present of quite elevated status, either of baronial rank or bannerets. Present were John de Ferrers of Chartley, Robert de Clifford, William le Latimer, Hugh Despenser the younger, William the Marshal of Hengham, Bartholomew de Badlesmere, Nicholas de Segrave and Payn de Tibetot. They were also leading retinues, probably in many cases sub-retinues of the greater lords. The name of John de Ferrers, for example, follows those of the Bohun retainers. He seems to have brought his own retinue to Dunstable but he was himself closely associated with the earls of Hereford. Nicholas de Segrave and the nine men he brought with him very probably belonged to the earl of Lancaster's contingent, since it is known that he was himself among the earl's indentured retainers.

Not all of the knights present at Dunstable, however, were there as members of retinues. The latter part of the roll, entitled *De la Commune*, seems to consist of individuals who came to the tournament on their own.[53] In all probability the knights were divided in practice into two opposing camps so that the vigorous mock battle or *mêlée*, traditional in the tournament *à outrance*, could be properly conducted. It has been suggested that the mock battle was fought out by the earl of Lancaster and his contingents together with the greater part of the *Commune* against the knights of the remaining earls and barons and the rest of the *Commune*, but this is conjecture. When the social rank of the participants is examined it is found that there were very few knights who did not belong to either the county élites or the higher nobility. They included some young men of very high birth. Hugh Despenser the younger was there with a retinue which consisted of some of his father's men. Theobald de Verdon the younger, shortly to succeed to his father's lands, appeared as part of the earl of Hereford's retinue, while Thomas de Vere, son and heir of the earl of Oxford, was present with the earl of Lancaster. An interesting feature is the tendency for leaders of contingents to have close relatives in their retinues. The earl of Gloucester's retinue contained both Richard de Clare, his cousin, and Nicholas de Clare, while Nicholas de Segrave brought with him his brother, Henry, and his nephew, Stephen. It had been a matter of some prestige from at least the late twelfth century for the noblest families to boast more than one knight in any generation.

Another interesting feature of the Dunstable tournament is that knights of earls who were not themselves present had joined other retinues, just as they tended to do in actual military campaigns. For example, there were knights present who were normally associated with the earl of Lincoln. John de Bracebridge, who had joined Bartholomew de Badlesmere for the tournament, was among three knights of Robert de Montalt, who was on pilgrimage in Spain. Although the earl of Pembroke, too, was out of the country, no less than thirty-two of his retainers appear to have been present at Dunstable.[54] Other knights had associations with the king's favourite, Piers Gaveston, now earl of Cornwall. He was not himself present at Dunstable, being on his way back from exile; but he was a keen and skilful tourneyer, much to the consternation of many of the earls. In short, the tournament is shown to have been a highly exclusive activity, and it has been said with justice that the passionately exciting game of the tournament was much in the minds of the younger members of the governing class during this period.[55]

Of course, great lords did not merely participate in tournaments with their relatives and retinues, they also hosted them. Tournaments were spectacular events, and the element of lavish display was an important feature from the thirteenth century on, especially with the development of the tournament *à plaisance*, fought with blunted weapons as opposed to the more primitive and dangerous tournament *à outrance*, descendant of the twelfth and thirteenth century *mêlée*.[56] The programme was more varied, moreover, at the tournament *à plaisance*, and included jousts where knights in pairs would run a specific number of courses together. As these occasions became more spectacular, greater prestige must surely have attached to those who could afford to host and equip them. To arrange a tournament, then, was an expression of leadership in society. With fourteenth-century tournaments, in particular, there seems to have been much parading through the streets in livery, an expression at one and the same time of wealth, power and solidarity. It is a truism that this lavish display, its ceremonial character and its heavy symbolism, were drawn from romance. It has been argued that this factor combined with the increasing involvement of ladies, to produce an increase in the degree of pageantry. While this is probably true on one level, it is also the case that the increasing accent upon display stemmed from the tournament's social functions.

In the right hands the tournament could not only provide an opportunity for the exercise of royal leadership over the nobility, it could also lavishly display the wealth and power of the Crown. These features first become apparent during the reign of Edward I. Edward made his tournament debut at Blyth in 1256. In 1260 he followed convention by leading a company of newly dubbed knights on a two-year tourneying tour of Europe just as many princes before him had done. They included John of Brittany, Henry of Almain, two sons of Simon de Montfort, Roger Clifford, James Audley, Hamo Lestrange and Warin Bassingbourne.[57] A tournament in which he participated in 1270 was so indistinguishable from a full-scale battle that it became known as the 'Little War of Chalons'.[58] As king, his interest in the tournament by no means abated, but it took on other dimensions. He is known to have personally sponsored two round tables, one at Falkirk in 1302, the site of his victory over the Scots four years before, and the other at Nefyn in 1284 to celebrate his conquest of Wales.[59] Edward clearly shared the contemporary interest in King Arthur, although the extent to which he was an 'Arthurian enthusiast' has been questioned by the most recent authority.[60] Certainly he visited the supposed tomb of Arthur and Guinevere at Glastonbury and 'translated' the bodies to a position before the altar, almost as if they had been saints. After his defeat of the Welsh, what was known as Arthur's crown was presented to him. He used the Arthurian past as an argument for his domination of Scotland and he was himself compared to Arthur by the contemporary verse chronicler Pierre Langtoft. For Michael Prestwich the Arthurian parallel was 'no more than a conceit' which Edward 'toyed with occasionally.'[61] He did, however, understand the importance of symbolism and display. This is shown most clearly in his foundation of Caernarfon Castle in 1283. Among the Welsh legends of the

Mabinogion was the story of Maxen Wledig, supposed father of Constantine the Great. Maxen dreamt of a beautiful maiden who dwelt in a great castle, with multicoloured towers, at the mouth of a river. Having located the castle, he married the maiden. Edward's castle, with its coloured bands in the masonry, turned this legend into reality. Another striking, and specifically chivalric, spectacle was the famous Feast of the Swans in 1306, the occasion of the knighting of the king's eldest son, with approximately 300 companions. At the banquet that followed, a host of minstrels heralded the appearance of two gilded swans upon which the revellers, including the king himself swore extravagant oaths.[62]

The most extravagant patron of all was undoubtedly Edward III. It has been stressed recently that his accession to the throne coincided with 'an efflorescence of tournament activity', and that it was only natural that he should follow the role model of his martial grandfather rather than the repressive policy towards tournaments preferred by his own father.[63] Of Edward III's liking for tournaments there can be no doubt. They were held to mark royal occasions (births, betrothals and so on) and to mark the conclusion of chevauchées, sieges and campaigns. Moreover, the increasing pageantry of tournaments in his day mirrored his own inclinations. He greatly enjoyed dressing up and disguises, as the royal games that featured in celebrations at Christmas and Epiphany make abundantly clear. Indeed, the games seem to have exercised a strong influence upon the tournaments. The tournament processions, for example, involved the same fantastic dress.[64] His chamber knights, in particular, provided overlap of personnel. That Edward was an Arthurian enthusiast is also clear. The Second Dunstable Roll of Arms (of 1334) lists 135 participating knights including members of the royal household. It is headed by the king's brother, John of Eltham. The king himself is not recorded as present. The roll does, however, contain the arms of an otherwise unknown knight, 'Sir Lyonel'. The royal wardrobe accounts show that these arms were exactly the same as those supplied to the king for the occasion. The conclusion, therefore, is inescapable; Sir Lyonel was no less a person than the king himself appearing incognito, in the manner of the Arthurian knights.[65] In 1331 he had visited Glastonbury, the centre of the Arthurian cult, and in 1345 he ordered a search for the body of Joseph of Arimathea, Arthur's supposed ancestor.

Edward III was a remarkably image-conscious king. He was, in fact, 'a natural showman' who 'proved remarkably successful at manipulating public opinion through displays of majesty.'[66] He certainly utilized his shared interest in chivalric matters as an instrument of policy in dealing with the nobility. A great round table was held at Windsor Castle in 1344.[67] At the end of the festivities the knights who had taken part gathered in the royal chapel. There, in their presence, the king swore an oath that he would inaugurate a new round table in the manner of King Arthur to the number of 300 knights and that he would continue to maintain it at that level adding the most valiant knights to it as necessary. He then received the oaths of the 300 knights chosen to grace his order. It may well be the case that this oath mirrored that of the romance knights of the round table, that is to protect damsels, widows and orphans and all those seeking aid in just quarrels. But Edward went further, even, than this, for he promised to construct a noble building where the round table would permanently reside. In the end the idea

Fourteenth-century tournaments often involved fantastic dress. This rather extravagant miniature from the Luttrell Psalter of a knight defeating a Saracen seems to evoke this fashion

proved too extravagant and was abandoned. But his intention was clear enough. By such means he might marshal the interests and the loyalty of his higher born subjects.

More enduring was the Order of the Garter.[68] Although the order seems not to have come formally into being until 1349, it had its origins in Edward's great victory at Crécy in 1346 and his adoption of the garter device on that campaign. Almost all of the first knights of the Garter can be shown either to have taken part in the battle or in the campaign which followed in Guyenne. The twenty-six knights were divided into two groups each with a stall in St George's chapel, one headed by the king himself and the other by the Black Prince. It is probably the case that it was modelled upon tournament teams. As Juliet Vale writes:

Edward's achievement in the institution of the Order of the Garter was remarkable in its complexity. He drew up two finely-balanced tournament teams with a view to engaging in chivalric encounter of the very highest quality, yet at the same time exploited existing allegiances and groupings of the kind which . . . governed tournament structure. His simultaneous political achievement was two-fold: to provide a perpetual memorial to the justification of his own kingly claims; and also to create a prestigious chivalric élite comprising every section of society that could aspire to inclusion – established noble families and allies abroad, as well as members of his own household and family – who were characterised first and foremost by loyalty to the order's head.[69]

Edward III's Order of the Garter was the most striking manifestation of his *rapprochement* with the higher nobility that characterized the middle years of his reign. With it he created something enduring, which worked to the benefit of the monarch in helping to bind the nobility, and in particular its most martial elements to him. To some degree, however, it was a double-edged sword, for by tying the king so closely to chivalric valour it created a standard to which a monarch had himself to aspire. Nonetheless, the potentiality of knighthood as a binding mechanism between Crown and nobility had been strikingly proven.

It was not only at the most elevated levels, however, that knighthood could provide a powerful bonding mechanism. It is a well-known fact that there was considerable turnover in landed society. This is a phenomenon more closely studied for the aristocracy or higher nobility but it is also true within landed society in general. In addition to the loss of members through financial pressure, the instances of which were variable according to circumstance, there was the more constant feature of biological failure. Both the sale and purchase of land and marriage to heiresses brought new families from below and scions of older families to the fore. Where new families succeeded in rising from below one can sometimes chart their rise, often from the free tenantry and often involving the mechanism of service. Here knighthood performed an additional function, as a *rite de passage*. It marked the social acceptance of families into the higher reaches of local society, and since knighthood was now clearly predicated upon the attainment of a specific income level (generally £40 from land) it offered a safety valve in that it brought together social and economic criteria and thus helped to stabilize a somewhat shifting élite.

One example which has been closely researched recently is that of the Abberburys of North Oxfordshire and Berkshire.[70] This family is traceable back to 1208 as one of the leading peasant families of the north Oxfordshire village of Adderbury. They owed their rise from the ranks of the free peasantry to Master Thomas Abberbury, an Oxford graduate who had found his way into the service of the archbishop of York by 1280. After service to successive archbishops, he developed a connection with the treasurer of England, Walter Langton. This provided him with some profitable opportunities in the land market. From 1295 his investment began in earnest. By the time he died in 1307 he had consolidated a considerable estate in Oxfordshire and Berkshire.

The status of the family was uncertain, however, not least because of the means of acquiring the properties, which included for example buying out an indebted family and supporting a desperate litigant. Thomas was succeeded in turn by his brother, Walter, and then by his nephew, Richard. The former pursued a policy of active consolidation, concentrating upon Oxfordshire, and of making his titles more secure. Richard, following his uncle, embarked upon an administrative career but from a radically different base. He became prominent in Oxfordshire during the 1320s as a supporter of the government of Edward II and the Despensers. In 1325 he became a commissioner of array and one of the keepers of the peace for Oxfordshire. He was MP for the county in 1328. During the early 1330s he was again on the peace commission for Oxfordshire and then for Berkshire. He became sheriff for the two counties in 1333 and in the same year he was knighted. He was, of course, the first of his family to acquire the dignity and it marked their full arrival and acceptance upon the county scene. The Abberburys were now fully established among the leading figures in the two counties, and so they remained throughout the fourteenth century.

Many similar examples could be presented and there is little need to labour the point. One aspect does, however, require stressing. It was becoming an increasingly literate and professionalized society and, consequently, administration was becoming the chief means of upward mobility at all levels. It was necessary that those who rose sufficiently far to equal the county knights should be absorbed as much as possible within their culture. Many of the most spectacular of such rises were to be found within the legal profession. Here the Crown took a hand in ensuring that its servants were assimilated into the mainstream of society. There is evidence of Henry III knighting his judges: Walter Heliun and John de Lovetot were knighted by him in 1267 and 1269 respectively. The great majority of lay judges during the reign of Edward I were certainly knights.[71] Some judges were themselves from knightly stock; among them, the remarkable Scrope brothers, Henry and Geoffrey, founders of the illustrious dynasties of Scrope of Bolton and Scrope of Masham. They were the sons of William Scrope of Wensley in the North Riding of Yorkshire.[72] Henry became chief justice of the King's Bench (1309–17) and chief baron of the Exchequer (1330–6), while his younger brother, Geoffrey, was chief justice of the King's Bench from 1324–40.[73] It became established, however, that lawyers promoted to the bench, whatever their origins, should be knighted. Moreover, since it was generally assumed that maintaining themselves in their newly acquired social status would involve them in additional expenditure it also became customary for the king to make them an annual grant at the time of their creation. For example, on becoming a justice of the Common Bench Robert Parving was knighted by Edward III on 24 May 1340 and given 40 marks a year. William Thorp was made a justice of the King's Bench on 20 May 1345, was knighted and received an annual grant of £40 which seems to have become the normal allowance. Some were given the superior rank of banneret, for example John Fencotes at Christmas 1347, who was due to take up appointment as justice of the King's Bench on 14 January 1348, and John Mowbray and William Skipwith who were made justices of the Common Bench in 1359. Moreover, the king followed the practice of defraying the expenses of the ceremony for those he knighted. When Thomas Ingleby and John Knyvet were appointed to the King's Bench and Common Bench respectively in June 1361 they were each to receive for the ceremony of knighthood 'twenty ells of dyed cloth, twenty one ells of long-length coloured cloth, twelve ells of long-length russet cloth, four minever furs, four furs of popel, two capes and four hoods of tawed minever, twelve ells of tartaryn, four lengths of cloth with gold sequins, two pieces of silk of firm texture, forty eight ells of Paris linen, four pieces of card and four furs of doe-skin.'[74]

Another group for whom knighthood in the fourteenth century could be a mark of recognition was the London aldermen. According to Sylvia Thrupp there were three in the early years of the fourteenth century. One of them, John le Blound, Mayor of London, was among those knighted at the Feast of the Swans in 1306.[75] Similarly John Pulteney, then a London draper, was among the twenty-four knights created by Edward III in 1337. Having acquired extensive lands in the Home Counties and in the Midlands, Pulteney built a fine mansion at Penshurst in Kent.[76] Others seem to have included Richard de la Pole, the fish-mongers Robert Aleyn and John Wroth, and very probably John Gisors the pep-perer.[77] It may well be that Edward III wished to draw the London financiers, on whom in reality he was much dependent, into his chivalric world. The presence of a Genoese merchant, Antonio Pesagno, in a list of household knights at Woodstock in 1332 suggests this.[78] Tournaments were certainly much held in or near London in the early years of Edward III. The summer of 1331, for example, was dominated by a sequence of three tournaments held successively at Dartford, at Stepney and in Cheapside, the latter being the famous occasion when the queen's stand collapsed. The alliterative poem, *Wynnere and Wastoure*, belonging most probably to *c.* 1352, may also be indicative. The poem shows two hostile armies brought before the king to present their rival points of view. The army of Waster comprised the military classes, while that of Winner comprised merchants as well as friars and lawyers. The king's promise to knight Winner indicates that knighthood was not necessarily regarded as totally restricted.

A new dimension was added, however, in 1381 when the boy king, Richard II, knighted a number of London aldermen for their part in suppressing the lower-class rebellion. These were, according to both the Anonimalle Chronicle and a London Letter Book, William Walworth, the mayor, John Philipot, Nicholas Brembre and Robert Launde, to which list Henry Knighton added Ralph de Standish and Nicholas Twyford.[79] The Anonimalle also records that the king gave Walworth £100 in land and each of the others £40 in land, to themselves and their heirs. This was often done when men were raised in status by the king, to ensure that they had sufficient dignity to maintain it. In the case of the citizenry it probably also reflects the rule, generally present in the distraints of knighthood, that the income which qualified a man for knighthood should come from land (in the fourteenth century £40), a socially conservative position. In reality, though, some prominent Londoners certainly acquired considerable landed property.

It is perhaps surprising that more of London's most prominent citizens were not knighted. It is possible to argue, as Sylvia Thrupp did, that knighthood was, in fact, unpopular among the citizenry pointing to the paucity of knights among the higher reaches of London society and to those London merchants who were fined under the distraints. The recent researches of Caroline Barron have reaf-firmed that fourteenth-century Londoners had very little positive involvement in the tournaments, and indeed with chivalric culture more broadly, beyond their roles as spectators and suppliers.[80] As a consequence, for the most part they did not seek knighthood. They may well have been influenced in this, however, by the contemporary view that restricted the status of knighthood to the more elevated of the lesser nobility and above, as well as by the enduring conservatism that equated chivalry with landed estates. It is most certainly true that conservative aristocratic opinion was critical of giving knighthood to merchants. When this did happen the chroniclers sought to justify it in terms of men's military capacities. John Wroth, for example, was called '*miles strenuus et valens*', that is active and valiant knight.[81] John Philipot had equipped a fleet at his own expense in 1378 and had captured the notorious Scottish pirate, John Mercer. According to Walsingham his resultant popularity had made him enemies among the nobility to whom he replied:

> I would not have destined myself, nor my money, nor my men to the dangers of the sea on that account – in order to snatch the good name of knighthood from you or your colleagues and to acquire it for myself. But, pitying the afflictions of the common people and of our native land which now, through your indolence, has fallen from being the most noble kingdom and mistress of nations into such wretchedness that it lies open to plundering by whom it please of the most ruthless people; so long as none of you applies his hand to its defence, I have exposed me and mine for the salvation of my own countrymen and the liberation of my native land.[82]

Similarly, when the Anonimalle Chronicle depicts Walworth expressing reluctance to be knighted in 1381 he speaks of his unworthiness and the fact that he makes his living by trade. Whatever view the king might take, it is probable that conservative opinion did not in general favour the knighting of Londoners. If they in turn were reluctant, it is likely that they were feeling the force of this opposition. But all of this was transcended when knighthood was truly merited by extraordinary deeds.

What this begins to indicate is that the recognition implied in knighthood had a public dimension. It was beginning to be granted to those outside of traditional chivalric circles in cases where they had deserved the nation's respect. Needless to say, and notwithstanding the patriotic fervour indicated by Walsingham, the nation's generosity is not a socially neutral concept as the elevation of the aldermen who had assisted in putting down the 1381 revolt (in Walworth's case by murdering the peasants' leader, Wat Tyler) is eloquent witness. This public dimension, however, should not cause us to lose sight of the essential bonding function of knighthood. Like the higher reaches of the legal profession, the great London merchants were close in many ways to the Crown and the aristocracy. The inclusion of some of them within the circle of fourteenth-century knighthood reflects the increasing sophistication and complexity of contemporary society on the one hand and the realization, especially by the Crown, that their recognition was necessary for social stability.

Knighthood functioned as a social cement in another sense too. It has been argued above that knighthood provided a bridge between the aristocracy and local society where the knights themselves constituted an élite. One has only to reflect upon the English parliament where the knights of the shire sat with the burgesses from the towns as the Commons, whereas men with a personal summons sat separately as the Lords. Part of aristocratic society in some senses, and tied to the greater lords by service, local knights nevertheless spent much of their lives in the company of men of the same or lesser degree. This is true whether one is looking from a social perspective or in terms of service and administration. Moreover, they too had their estates and households to run, necessitating a further level of service association. And, finally, as has been seen, knighthood became confined to the aristocracy and the higher reaches of local society. There were many local landowners in the later thirteenth and fourteenth centuries who were not knights. It was from this basis that the graded English gentry took shape during the course of the fourteenth century. The values associated with knighthood played a major role in determining the outlook of the emergent gentry. It was impregnated with chivalric values. The key to understanding this lies with the rise of the esquires.

The starting point for observing this phenomenon is usually taken to be the sumptuary legislation passed by parliament in 1363. This attempted to regulate the apparel that the different groups in society should be allowed to wear. It was deemed to be necessary due to 'the outrageous and excessive apparel of divers people against their estate and degree to the great destruction and impoverishment of all the land'. With the aristocracy left out of account, at the top end were knights and ladies with land or rent to the value of 400 marks or more per annum. Second were to come knights, their wives and families, with £200 per annum from land and rent, with esquires of the same level of wealth to be treated in broadly the same way. Then came esquires and all manner of gentle men below the estate of knight (*esquiers & toutes maneres de gentils gentz desouth lestat de*

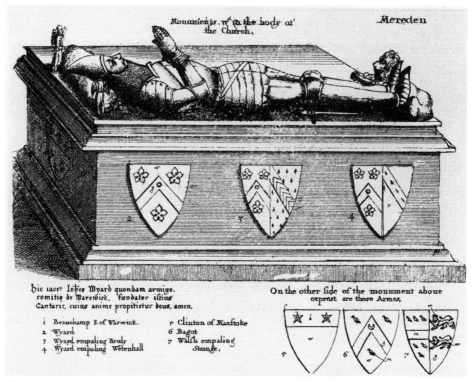

The effigy of John Wyard, esquire of the earl of Warwick (from Sir William Dugdale's Warwickshire). During the fourteenth century esquires inherited some of the chivalric aura that surrounded knighthood

chivaler) with less than £100 land per annum. Clerics, other than those high in Church and state who were not to be restricted, were to dress as knights and esquires of equal landed wealth, while merchants and other wealthy townsmen were divided into two groups, equivalent either to esquires and gentle men who had £200 or those who had £100 income from land or rents, but on the basis of the value of their moveable goods.[83]

It is often assumed that this legislation represents a widening of gentility to include groups in society that had not previously been acknowledged as such, and in particular that it recognized the arrival of the esquires into gentle ranks. This, however, is a misreading. Gentility certainly did not end at the level of the knight in the thirteenth century. The *Rules* of Bishop Robert Grosseteste of 1240–2, for instance, advised: 'Order your knights and your gentle men who wear your livery (*Comaundez a vos chivalers e a vos gentis hommes ki vos robes pernent*) that they ought to put on that same livery every day, and especially at your table & in your presence to uphold your honour, and not old surcoats, and soiled cloaks, and cut-off cloaks.'[84] The household account rolls confirm this. The Latin word *generosus*, meaning noble or gentle man, was commonly employed in them from around 1300. Earlier accounts had sometimes used *armiger*, a term normally translated as squire, in an equivalent sense.[85] Another word used for household service was valet (*valettus*), although it came to be used in preference to denote a rank below that of *generosus*. Early indentures of retainer equally indicate that gentility was employed quite widely. Knights and other men-at-arms had their own attendants – their *gentils gentz* – who shared the right to eat in the lord's hall.[86] Honourable service in the household or retinue of the gentle was held, therefore, to confer gentility.

However, this is not the whole of the story. Members of the social strata from which such followers were drawn were also held to be gentle. Those men the thirteenth-century government felt should be knights and were not, were commonly described in official and legal records as *valetti*. So, too, in the early fourteenth century, were those members of parliament for the counties who were not knights. When it came to paying their expenses, knights might be paid 4s. per day and *valetti* 2s.[87] Different government departments, and even different records from the same department, used alternative words to describe the same type of men. Edward I's paid household cavalry, for example, were variously described as *valetti, scutiferi, servientes* and *armigeri. Serviens* is usually translated as sergeant, *armiger* (originally armour-bearer) and *scutifer* (shield-bearer) as esquire, equivalent to the Old French *écuyer* or *escuier*.[88]

In origin, esquire denoted a knight's servant with particular responsibility for his horses and his arms. It was an ideal situation for a trainee or apprentice knight, as the romances show, but this was by no means invariably the case and less so, it seems, farther back in time.[89] No doubt, there was held to be prestige in having an esquire of high social rank and of obvious breeding, that is to say of gentle manners, although it cannot be concluded by any means that all esquires were from gentle stock even in the late thirteenth century.

The service role of the esquire is underlined by the *Statute of Arms* of 1292. This was concerned to regulate the conduct of armed servants at tournaments in

England, both esquires and others. Combatants were limited to a maximum of three armed esquires each and they had to be identifiable, that is to say they had to wear their lord's cap denoting his arms. They were to wear only specified pieces of defensive armour to protect them on the field, and they were to carry broadswords and no other weapons. They were to play only a limited role in the fighting. In certain circumstances they could drag a knight from his horse. But, clearly, they were not supposed to tourney as such. After the tournament only those esquires who were accustomed to carve their lord's meat were to attend the festivities.[90] The intention was probably to restrict admission to those who were regular and close attendants. Such a role would perhaps have appealed to an aspirant to knighthood.

There can be no doubt that gentility now, as in later centuries, was a condition dependent upon its recognition by others. In all probability not only those in honourable service but also many of those non-knightly cavalrymen who fought in Edwardian wars would have been acknowledged by contemporaries as gentle.

This, then, was the basis on which esquires came to be recognized as a social rung immediately below that of knight. The process by which this happened is as yet imperfectly understood. By the time of the sumptuary laws of 1363 it was more or less complete. By this time, too, they were being acknowledged as armigerous by the heralds in their rolls, that is to say as legitimate holders of coats of arms. The lists of men-at-arms as well as knights that the sheriffs drew up for their counties in 1324 show the process well underway. In some cases they are described as *armigeri*. In Warwickshire, for example, the names of nineteen *armigeri* were returned together with those of forty-two knights. Almost all of the nineteen can be readily identified. Three of them (John de Clinton of Coleshill, John Trussell and Richard de Whitacre) were young men who, although heads of major families, were as yet at the beginning of their careers; they would later be knights. A fourth, who originated from outside the county, was in the same position. Ralph de Arden of Curdsworth seem to have preferred to remain, for some time at least, as an esquire, although the head of his family was normally a knight. Five men held the same surnames as contemporary knights. Two of these were holding their own interests through marriage. Six of the others were lesser landowners whose ancestors had once been knights. In one case, that of Culy, the family was later to reacquire its lost knighthood.

During the early fourteenth century men of this bracket were already employing heraldic devices on their seals. One example is Robert de Langley, lord of Wolfhamcote in Warwickshire and younger brother of Sir John de Langley, who sealed with a heraldic device in 1317.[91] Some esquires and men-at-arms seem to have figured in tournaments at this time, judging by their inclusion in royal prohibitions. They were certainly doing so during the latter half of the fourteenth century.

Why esquire should have crystallized as a social rung seems clear enough. The surprise is that it should have taken so long to develop. It was a suitable title for those heads of families who had shed knighthood in the mid-thirteenth century while remaining landowners of some local consequence. It was useful, too, for cadet lines of more substantial families. And, finally, with its connotations of

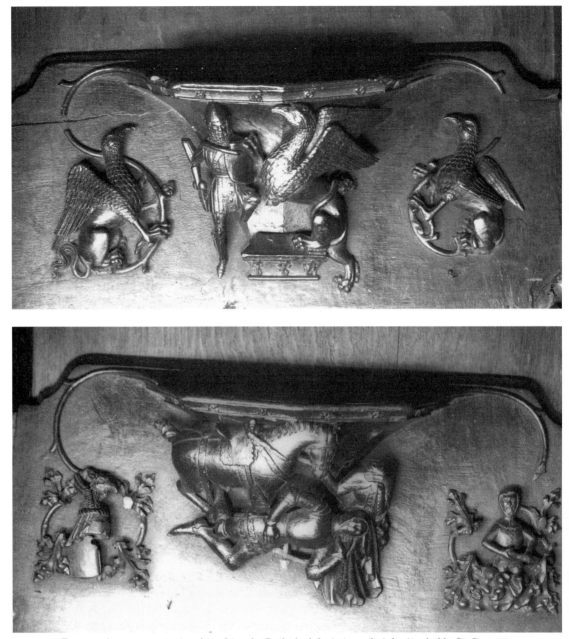

Fourteenth-century misericords in Lincoln Cathedral depicting a knight (probably St George) and a dragon (top), and a sleeping knight (above)

A fourteenth-century misericord in Lincoln Cathedral showing a wounded knight falling from his horse

noble service and traineeship, it was felt to be appropriate to the elder son of a knight before he came to be knighted himself. This, after all, is how Chaucer presents his 'yong Squier', the knight's son. About twenty years of age, he had already fought in Flanders, Picardy and Artois. The manner of his service is reminiscent of the esquires of the *Statute of Arms*:

> Curteis he was, lowely, and servysable,
> And carf biforn his fader at the table.
> *(Canterbury Tales, Prologue* ll. 99–100)

What is particularly significant is that the esquire was defined in essentially chivalric terms; without the title certainly but, nevertheless, with many of the attributes of knighthood. Very revealing is the famous grant of arms made by Richard II to John de Kingston in July 1389. Hearing that John had been challenged by a French knight the king received him into the estate of gentleman (*gentile homme*), made him an esquire and granted him the right to bear a specified coat of arms, viz. *argent a chapeau azure with an ostrich feather gules*. By this date the esquires had inherited some of the chivalric aura that had long surrounded knighthood.[92] In fact, the behaviour and thought patterns of chivalric knighthood permeated the English gentry from its very roots.

The influence of chivalric knighthood, however, went deeper still, for the esquires are not the whole of the story. The sumptuary legislation, it will be recalled, referred not only to esquires but to also to other gentle men. With the crystallization of the squires into a social rank, as it were, the question of who else was entitled to be considered gentle came to the fore. The situation was made more complex by the social dislocation which ensued following the arrival of the plague during the mid-fourteenth century and the profound changes which resulted within the rural economy. This led to an increasing reluctance to accept the social hierarchy from below and to a fear of upward mobility from above. The result was uncertainty and confusion. But this was not the only complicating factor. The increasing sophistication of society during the preceding two centuries meant that a host of literate administrators and professionals of various kinds needed to be accommodated within the social order. Some approximation to the social reality can be glimpsed in the preamble to the graded poll tax of 1379.[93] After the dukes, earls and countesses, come the barons, bannerets and more substantial knights. Then come the remainder of the knights (described here as bachelors, technically those knights who were not bannerets) and esquires who, in terms of income, ought to be knights. These are followed by esquires of lesser estate, and they in turn by esquires without land or rent but who were in service or had been armed. By beginning in this way the preamble implicitly asserts the primacy of the traditional landed sector. After the several ranks of the Order of the Hospital of St John, there follows a host of lawyers of various stations, urban office-holders, merchants, artificers and so on. Often they are required to pay tax at one of several levels, according to assessment, and on occasions the levels overlap with the payments made by the chivalric groups. Those described as sergeants and franklins of the countryside, for example, are to pay either 6s. 8d. or 3s. 4d., that is to say either at the level of the lesser esquire or at the level of the esquire in service, while those who had taken on manors at farm (in effect, on lease) were to pay at these levels or below.

Again, the ultimate outcome can be seen in a legislative act. The *Statute of Additions* of 1413 stipulated that in personal actions brought before the royal courts the plaintiffs should indicate in their writs the precise social position of the defendants, or in contemporary parlance their estate, degree or mystery.[94] In descending order these were knight, squire, gentleman, followed by yeoman, husbandman and so on. Some fluidity remained in the system, with individuals being variously described, and on occasions plaintiffs covered themselves by using aliases to ensure that they had accurately described their opponents. However, henceforth society would be perceived in terms of a clear divide. As Shakespeare has Somerset say to Richard Plantagenet (later, duke of York) in *Henry VI, Part One*:

> Was not thy father, Richard Earl of Cambridge,
> For treason executed in our late king's days?
> And by his treason stand'st thou not attainted,
> Corrupted, & exempt from ancient gentry?
> His trespass yet lives guilty in thy blood;
> And till thou be restor'd thou art a yeoman
>
> (Act II, Scene IV)

A statute of 1440 stipulated that no man should be elected as knight of the shire who 'standeth in the degree of Yoman and bynethe'.[95] This is not to say that the divide could not be bridged. As Thomas Fuller wrote in 1642: 'The good

Yeoman is a Gentleman in Ore, who the next age may see refined'.[96] Gentleman now had two senses. It was used both in the old sense of *gentil homme*, to describe anyone who was recognized as gentle, and in the new sense of the simple gentleman, the lowest rung of a graded gentry.

As with the esquires, so the gentlemen came to be regarded as armigerous. On 2 June 1417 Henry V instructed his sheriffs of southern England that:

> Whereas in recent expeditions abroad many persons have taken to themselves arms and tunics of arms called 'Cotearmures' when neither they nor their ancestors had used such in times past, proclamations should be made that no man, of whatever status, rank, or condition he might be, should take to himself arms or tunics of arms, unless he possess or ought to possess the same by ancestral right or by grant of some person having authority sufficient thereunto, [and] that all, except those who had borne arms with the king at Agincourt, should on a certain day declare their arms and by what grant they had them, on a fixed day to persons named or to be named for the purpose, under pain of exclusion from the expedition then about to start, loss of their wages and defacement of their said arms and tunics called 'Cotearmures'.[97]

The scene was now set for the heralds' visitations of the counties for precisely this purpose. How the gentlemen are to be related to Henry V's instruction is not at all clear. Were they the very people whose arms were seen as suspect? More probably, they were already coming to be accepted within armigerous ranks. Gentlemen were certainly accepted as bearing arms by the middle of the fifteenth century.[98] What is instructive, though, is that the context in which we first see chivalric lore residing in the lowest level of the gentry is once again a military one.

It was not only in the bearing of coats of arms, however, that the members of the lowest rung of the gentry aped the standards set by the knightly landowners of the past. Like the esquires they, too, wished to display their social prestige in public places. At the church of Much Marcle in Herefordshire there survives a remarkable fourteenth-century effigy. In oak polychrome, it is thought to depict the local franklin, Walter Helyon. With his beard, his *anlaas* and *gipser* (dagger and purse), he bears an extraordinary resemblance to Chaucer's Franklin; only the colour of his beard is wrong. In the same church there are the more conventional effigies of a military figure and his lady. They are of the late fourteenth to early fifteenth century, although their identity is uncertain.

The divide between gentleman and yeoman, however, should not lead us to believe that the former resulted simply from an unusual degree of upward mobility within the countryside. Many of those so designated in the early fifteenth century were civil servants and professional bureaucrats.[99] Others represented those local administrators and wealthy freeholders who had long lived on the margins of gentility.[100] It may be that as society emerged from the period of crisis that characterized the second half of the fourteenth century, the line between the gentle and non-gentle was drawn a little further down the scale. On the whole, though, it seems more likely that the grade of gentleman resulted from the need for sharper definition more than from a widening of gentility. With this sharper definition, older and vague social terms like sergeant and franklin gradually fell away. So, too, did banneret, which had threatened to become a social as well as a military rank during the fourteenth century. It became less necessary to differentiate within the ranks of knighthood when the number of knights declined further as the first, victorious, phase of the Hundred Years' War gave way to a period of desultory warfare and military failure and as the esquire became entrenched as an accepted chivalric status.

The decline in the number of knights after the reign of Edward III is imperfectly recorded. Sources from the 1430s suggest that, at most, there can hardly have been more than about two hundred in the country as a whole at that date.[101] Figures fluctuated somewhat during the course of the fifteenth and sixteenth centuries, but they were never again more than a few hundred.[102] Knights were by now a small élite, their position bolstered, as it were, by the more numerous esquires and gentlemen. The situation is once again best understood on a local basis. In Warwickshire in 1436 there were eighteen knights, fifty-nine esquires and something in the region of fifty-five gentlemen.[103]

One consequence of this decline was that fewer of the men who represented the counties in parliament as knights of the shire actually were knights. At the parliament of 1422, for instance, of seventy-four members representing the counties, only thirty-one were actual knights and twenty-six esquires, a great contrast with the situation a century earlier when the great majority of county MPs had indeed been knights.[104]

SIX

Knighthood, Literature and the Social Order

So far the discussion of chivalric knighthood has concentrated on its impact upon the gentle classes and its mode of dissemination within them. It is time now to look, more broadly, at the way in which chivalric knighthood permeated the thought-processes of society as a whole. It did so with considerable ideological consequences. This can be observed most confidently by means of vernacular literature.

It involves something of a change of direction. The book has been concerned less with the ideals of knighthood as drawn from chivalric manuals and romance literature and more with knighthood in practice within society. This approach has been chosen deliberately, and for good reason. It is all too easy to be drawn into the trap of seeing literature as simply reflecting reality, with unhappy consequences for our understanding of actual behaviour. As has been well said, if literature does reflect reality then it does so with distorted mirrors. Of course, ideas are embedded in social practice as well as in the text; they are thus social facts and themselves the objects of historical inquiry. Life, moreover, sometimes imitates art, as we have seen in the case of the tournament, and when it does so the ideological impact of the ideas embedded within the art is immeasurably strengthened. The nature of that impact, however, cannot be assumed, without further inquiry, from the text. Neither the ideas nor the texts in which they reside have a life of their own outside humanity. Nevertheless, used cautiously, literature is an invaluable source for the historian, not least in terms of understanding the dissemination of ideas.

This chapter will begin by examining romance in England and the means of its dissemination through society. It will then turn to the treatment of the knight in literature during the latter half of the fourteenth century, primarily in the works of Geoffrey Chaucer and William Langland and in the *Gest of Robin Hood*.

As is well known, the early French romances, pre-eminently the works of Chrétien de Troyes, were crucial in the formation of aristocratic manners. Courtly and élitist, as Duby has long emphasized, they were pivotal in the formation and dissemination of chivalric knighthood. It is clear enough that French romances circulated in twelfth-century England and that they were long to do so.

It is equally well known that romances were also composed in England, in a dialect known as Anglo-Norman and that the latter tended to display distinctive characteristics. Many of them were shortly to provide the basis and the inspiration for romances in Middle English. Native Anglo-Norman and Middle English romances share certain characteristics, despite the fact they tend to be stylistically divergent.[1]

The definition of romance is a difficult matter and one that need not be addressed in detail here.[2] For brevity's sake one can hardly do better than to follow Susan Crane in seeing romances essentially as 'secular fictions of nobility', or as Chaucer puts it in the prologue to the *Miller's Tale,* the 'storial thyng that toucheth gentillesse'.[3] What then were the particular characteristics of Anglo-Norman romance? For one thing, the love theme differs from the French romances in being more down to earth, less idealized, although there is much compliance with conventional motifs and with conventional standards of behaviour. The love motif often features, in fact, in terms of family stability and continuity. By contrast the often observed tendency to greater piety in romance in England may well have been exaggerated by literary scholars in the past. Certainly the piety is there, but it is clearly subordinate to other, more worldly concerns. As Crane puts it, 'The Christian faith remains a subsidiary aspect of knighthood whose goals are aggressively secular and political'.[4]

The most striking feature, however, is that the heroes of half the romances in Anglo-Norman dialect surviving today are in fact English. In this they have much in common with the twelfth-century chronicles. These lay stress upon continuity with pre-Conquest England, thereby reinforcing the Norman insistence on the legality of their rule. The English heroes were essentially Norman forebears. However, whereas the chronicles justify the power of rulers, the romances are concerned with their vassals. Their milieu is undoubtedly aristocratic, but essentially provincial and not inspired by the royal court. The central theme is the story of the loss and recovery of inherited lands and titles. They are infused with a firm belief in private right, in the justice of custom and in stability. These values tend to be presented as being beneficial to the nation, not just to the individual or family. This is clearly true in the cases of Horn and Havelock, who are in any case depicted as kings (though they control only part of England). But it is also the case with Boeve de Hamtoun, and with Gui de Warewic who defends all England against its enemies.[5]

In order to understand the dissemination of romance through society it is necessary first of all to grasp the circumstances of the production of Anglo-Norman literature.[6] To satisfy their appetite for works of vernacular literature members of the aristocracy commissioned authors, borrowed, purchased and kept books. The romances themselves were produced over a half-century or so, in late twelfth- to mid-thirteenth-century England. It is important to stress that the place where they were read was not the baronial hall but the private chamber where reading was a small group activity. This was made possible by the increasing emphasis upon privacy in domestic architecture with the elaboration of private apartments or solars.

It was natural enough that laymen of lesser standing, those whom we have become accustomed to calling the gentry, should have wished to emulate the higher nobility. After all, they enjoyed a broadly common culture, and there were many points of social contact between them. If few were able, or could afford, to commission works themselves they could at least use their aristocratic contacts to borrow manuscripts or have borrowed manuscripts copied. However, the country gentlemen of the thirteenth and fourteenth centuries, whatever their aristocratic connections, had their own households and estates to maintain. The design of their manor-houses indicates the same emphasis on comfort and privacy from servants as is found with their social superiors. Increasingly it was the chamber rather than the hall that provided the resident family with the available comforts of life. The hall by contrast is best conceived of in a more public sense. Grand enough to reflect the status of its owner, it was intended to function as a ceremonial and banqueting hall and to house courts and other assemblies. It was in the more luxurious *camera* or solar that the family and their guests would be most often entertained. Families would, of course, play host to others of the same or

Aydon Castle, Northumberland, built by Sir Robert de Reymes at the beginning of the fourteenth century. Looking across the inner courtyard, the hall is on the first floor facing and the commodious chamber block is on the left at right angles to it. It was the chamber which provided the landed family with the comforts of life

similar social standing. Such occasions provided opportunities for exchange of ideas, as did meetings in retinues, at courts and within administration. They also provided occasions for the reading of romances and other literature.

If the values and standards were primarily determined at the highest levels of society, however, they were nonetheless reinforced by social contacts further down the social scale. Emulation and the desire to share in cultural advantages did not end at the level of the upper gentry. Society was very localized and if social intercourse was lateral between families of equal or near equal degree it was also to an extent vertical. Even allowing for a fairly high incidence of temporary absence, many a knight and, later, esquire must have found himself the leader or among the leaders of a small local élite. England in the thirteenth and fourteenth centuries was an increasingly professionalized society, where service was all-pervasive. People rubbed shoulders with those above and below them on the social ladder in a host of administrative and professional capacities. Nor should too sharp a contrast be drawn between town and country in this respect. Urban administrators were often men of the same type, background and ambition as those who served lords in administrative and legal capacities. The élite of major towns tended to consist of an amalgam of administrators, *rentiers* and merchants, elements that were not necessarily separable. Some were drawn from established gentry families; others aspired to and achieved the life of the country gentleman. It was a mobile and aspirant society in town and country and, it should be stressed, an increasingly literate one. If professional scholars and men of letters remained comparatively few, literacy in a pragmatic sense and literacy for pleasure went increasingly deeply into society. From the thirteenth century, then, the gentry came to play a pivotal role in English society, and the gentry household arguably a pivotal role in the transmission of secular vernacular literature.

But if a true understanding of the diffusion of a literate culture is dependent upon an appreciation of the level of literacy, it turns equally on the relative status of the two vernacular languages. French was a widely used language of culture; it was the language of the common law, of management and lordship, of the king's court and of *gentils hommes*. Great prestige was attached to it. 'For unless a man knows French, he is thought of little account', wrote the chronicler Robert of Gloucester late in the thirteenth century. The language of instruction in formal schooling was French and remained so until the mid-fourteenth century.

Nonetheless, French as a spoken language was in decline throughout the thirteenth century. It is now clear that by the beginning of the thirteenth century, at the latest, French was already an acquired language. By mid-century treatises were being written for those who wished to improve their French. Most people's first tongue was English, and they thought in that language. The chronicler, Ralph of Coggeshall, tells the story of a spirit (*spiritus fantasticus*) that appeared in the house of a Suffolk knight during the reign of Richard I (1189–99). According to the knight's chaplain, from whom Ralph had heard the story, the spirit was accustomed to speak in the Suffolk dialect with the family of the knight but to argue on theological matters with the priest in Latin. If the members of the household of a country knight already spoke English as their first tongue, it is hardly surprising that a demand for entertainment in that language should have grown up in the course of time. Moreover, there was nothing disreputable about writing in English. Some quite sophisticated literary works were produced in that language during the late twelfth and early thirteenth centuries. The earliest Middle English romances, *King Horn* and *Floris and Blancheflur*, appear in manuscript around 1260, soon after the production of Anglo-Norman romances had largely ceased. By the time Middle English versions begin to proliferate, that is at the very end of the thirteenth century, there is likely to have been a demand for them for some time. Satisfaction of that demand was probably delayed by the greater prestige attached to Anglo-Norman as a literary language and by the real problems attendant upon the use of English, such as its dialectal nature. As soon as romances in English began to appear in any number, statements of self-justification issued from the writers just as they had done in the case of Anglo-Norman, a hundred years earlier. In both cases the choice of language was justified in terms of reaching a wider audience; in the case of Middle English because it was the language of the nation. Among the audience were families whose staple diet had once been exclusively French. The pattern was set by the gentle household and diffused by imitation and emulation.

It should not be imagined that an audience existed that was interested exclusively in Middle English romance. The greatest of all early miscellany manuscripts, Harley 2253, for example, contained works in all three languages, Latin, French and English. Comprising mostly lyrics, it also contained *King Horn*. Belonging to the 1330s, it was written by a scribe with strong contacts in and around Ludlow. It originated not in the household of the bishop of Hereford, as was once thought, but within local society. Digby 86, another trilingual manuscript, was compiled in or shortly before 1282 in the diocese of Worcester. Its marginal notation indicates that it was in the possession of a family of minor Worcestershire gentry early in the fourteenth century and suggests its probable earlier possession by a related family of similar station. The likelihood is that it was compiled for, if not indeed by, a layman and within a gentry milieu. It contains a wide variety of pieces, religious and secular, in prose and verse, about half of which are in French and a quarter each in Latin and English. Much of the material contained in these manuscripts is likely to have been actively circulating within society, and it is highly probable that families were already borrowing and copying such material, as is increasingly evidenced from the later fourteenth century on. Such manuscripts, however, were probably relatively scarce. Much material circulated rather in the form of booklets, some of which were probably being produced commercially, in Oxford for example. The romances were composed over a geographically wide area. While *Havelock the Dane*, for example, came from Lincolnshire, *King Horn* came from the south, possibly from Surrey. Moving forward to fourteenth-century romances, *Yvain and Gawain* came from the north or possibly north-east Midlands, while *William of Palerne* was composed in Gloucestershire. The four romances known collectively as the 'Kyng Alisaunder group' were composed in the London area, around if not before 1300, by well-educated men who were well versed in French literature. 'The London area', however, must be understood in its wider sense. The possible area of composition includes not only Essex but areas to the west and north-west of London. There is in fact no need to believe that they were composed in the capital itself and there is a strong probability that, like *King Horn* and *Floris and Blancheflur* before them, they were produced within and for local society.

There is, however, good reason why they should soon have been copied in and circulated from London. Buyers in a number of surrounding counties could be reached with some ease, quite apart from the possibility of an internal market. Moreover, Edwardian London was already a thriving capital. The central law courts and parliament brought many people into London for short periods. Men came, perhaps, with a certain amount of leisure time and with the opportunity to purchase. The opportunity was certainly there for commercial book or booklet production. The great Auchinleck Manuscript was certainly produced there during the 1330s. The first sizeable collection of Middle English romances to have survived, it may have been the product of a commercial undertaking which included the translating of French works as well as the collecting together of romances already in circulation. It includes, for example, in addition to the 'Kyng Alisaunder group', the Middle English versions of *Bevis of Hamton* and *Guy of Warwick*.

Commercial production in London was a response to a growing demand and represents a second stage in the dissemination of romance in the English language. It had important consequences. One was to draw texts in from outside. Among these was the *Tale of Gamelyn*, which was composed in the Midlands some time around 1350 and which has come down to us through its inclusion in Chaucer manuscripts, probably because he intended to rework it for *The Canterbury Tales*. Another consequence was the rapid production of Middle English translations, some of them of markedly inferior quality. The spectacular growth in the production of vernacular literature during the course of the fourteenth century helped London on its way to becoming the cultural capital of England. However, this should not be exaggerated. There were areas of the country where cultural interaction with the capital was not strong. *Sir Gawain and the Green Knight*, and the other works of its Cheshire poet, was almost certainly unknown there. Nevertheless, cultural traffic increased to and from London during the course of the fourteenth century, and there began to develop what has been called a literature of commonly shared concerns, within which romance was a major ingredient. The most important point of all is that the production of vernacular literature continued to expand throughout the fourteenth century both in London and in the provinces with an increasing tendency to downward dissemination as formal education and lay literacy continued to expand.

Too often despised in the past, the Middle English romances are enjoying something of a mini-renaissance at the moment. Their craftsmanship and their sheer vigour tend to be appreciated more than they were, although their inferiority to French and Anglo-Norman works in general remains undeniable, with their thematic simplification and their tendency to emotionalism. A few, it has always been recognized, are works of very high quality - the *Alliterative Morte Arthur*, for example, and the superlative *Sir Gawain and the Green Knight*, high in moral tone and as elegant and refined in its manners as almost any romance in any language. Many, however, are highly conventional in style and structure, in motifs and in depiction of behaviour.

A scene from English romance: Sir Gawain kneeling before Arthur and Guinevere (from the only surviving manuscript of Gawain and the Green Knight*)*

There is plenty of knight errantry, for example. As the opening of the Auchinleck's *Sir Degaré* puts it:

> Knightus that werey sometime in lande
> Ferli fele wolde fonde, [many wonders/find]
> And sechen aventures bi night and dai
> Hou they mighte here strengthe asai; [try]
> So dede a knyght, Sire Degaree.[7]

There are plenty of tournaments and knights fighting in disguise. There are those who would be lovers, setting out to prove they are the best knight in the world. There are black knights, red knights, white knights, anonymous knights, even humble knights; there are false knights, there are fairy or magical knights.

Jousters breaking lances, from a fourteenth-century manuscript of the Romance of Alexander

Knights jousting, in the Romance of Alexander, *fourteenth century*

The study of Anglo-Norman and Middle English romances side by side, however, not only allows for the examination of shared characteristics within romance
produced in England but also reveals ways in which ideas shifted or developed. In
particular, the heroes become more clearly national heroes. This is strikingly
revealed in cases where the Middle English romances are based on extant Anglo-
Norman antecedents. More than anything else this was accomplished by a shift in
emphasis. There is a much stronger sense of the hero's merit being a national one
in *Beves of Hamton*, for example, than in *Boeve de Hamtoun*; nevertheless the
hero's prime concern is still with his inheritance. In *Guy of Warwick* the baronial
perspective tends to fade in face of much stronger expressions of national feeling.
A crusading hero in *Gui de Warewic*, he now becomes more of a national crusading hero. This is the case, too, with *Richard Coer de Lion*, a Middle English
romance written around 1300 and perhaps based on a lost Anglo-Norman original. In this work there often seems little to choose between the vices of the French
and the Saracens or, to put it another way, between the prejudice offered towards
each of them:

> Frennssche men arn arwe and ffeynte, [cowardly/false]
> And Sarezynys be war, and queynte, [wary/artful]
> And off here dedes engynous; [skilful]
> The Frenssche men be covaytous.
>
> (ll. 3849–52[8])

Sir Tristrem, likewise, was 'a hero of English custom and history, as the originator
of hunting and gaming practices and the defender of England against Ireland'.[9]

It would be simplistic, however, to regard the stronger expression of national
feeling in the Middle English romances as resulting solely from the fact that the
audience for these was wider than for the romances in Anglo-Norman. This may
well have been a factor, of course, but it is also the case that the period of their full
flowering was the very time when the English were fighting their first truly
national wars: the war against the Scots which opened in the 1290s and the beginnings of the long struggle against the French. They were wars which impinged
upon the lives of civilians in ways that previous wars had not done and they were
wars which involved government-inspired propaganda as never before.[10]

There is no doubt of the popularity of the romances. Even without the manuscript evidence, the condemnation of ecclesiastical writers alone would be sufficient to confirm this. As a result knighthood, like kingship, became part of the
mind set, part of the common property of the nation. The knight was part of the
natural order of things. The identification of knighthood with national feeling and
with national concerns, moreover, further strengthened its ideological force.

It was not only knighthood itself which was validated. Among the by-products
was a reinforcing of the belief in the justice of inheritance, and in the role of law
and custom in upholding inheritance, a prominent feature of Middle English
romance that had been carried over from Anglo-Norman. The implication was
that the protection of property and inheritance was beneficial to all. Justice, moreover, was to be reinforced if necessary by recourse to the sword. Although the

potentiality for violence is often contained in practice by the operation of the law, the threat is always there in the background and at times it becomes actual. A striking instance of this is provided by the curious *Tale of Gamelyn*. In this sombre tale a third and youngest son, who is defrauded by the eldest of his rightful share of the inheritance and failed by the law and its agents, takes bloody and brutal revenge upon them all, bolstered by a belief in a natural justice.

Romances were not, of course, the only form of literature circulating within local society. Others included saints' lives and vernacular chronicles, genres which overlapped in many ways with romance. Another type of literature in circulation, from at least the beginning of the fourteenth century, was the poem of social protest.[11] Although the majority of these were most probably written by clerics, they were certainly in circulation within secular society; in terms of technique and of treatment of themes they owed a good deal to romance.[12] Among them is the *Simonie* or *Poem on the Evil Times of Edward II*. This is found in the great Auchinleck Manuscript itself as well as in two later ones. It belongs to the tradition of estates satire in its condemnation of the particular vices of specific social groups. Contemporary knights are satirized as 'lions in hall, hares in the field', an idea that is found again in the famous preachers' handbook compiled by John Bromyard around 1348. The sermon provided, of course, yet another and very important channel for the dissemination of stock ideas.[13] According to the *Simonie* knights tended to be proud and haughty, prone to extravagance in dress:

> Knihtes sholde weren weden in here manere, [garments]
> After that the ordre asketh also wel as a frere; [friar]
> Nu ben theih so degysed and diverseliche i-diht, [now/arrayed/clothed]
> Unnethe may men knowe a gleman from a kniht, wel neih; [scarcely/minstrel]
> So is meiknesse driven adoun, and pride is risen on heih. [meekness]
>
> Thus is the ordre of kniht turned up-so-doun,
> Also wel can a kniht chide as any skolde of a toun.
> Hii sholde ben also hende as any levedi in londe, [gracious/lady]
> And for to speke alle vilanie nel nu no kniht wonde for shame; [no knight will
>   forbear]
> And thus knihtshipe is acloied and waxen al fot lame. [debased/lame][14]
>
> (ll. 253–64)

The sense of the knight here is that of St Bernard, with its stress upon humility and membership of an order.[15] This is reaffirmed by the author's sense of the true role of the knight, which is a functional, and a Christian, one. He is to fight for the Church:

> And thilke that han al the wele in freth and in feld, [those/wealth/wood]
> Bothen eorl and baroun and kniht of o sheld,
> Alle theih beth i-sworne holi churche holde to rihte;
> Therfore was the ordre mad for holi churche to fihte, sanz faille;
> And nu ben theih the ferste that hit sholen assaille. [now]

Hii brewen strut and stuntise there as sholde be pes; [they/stir/strife]
Hii sholde gon to the Holi lond and maken ther her res, [their assault]
And fihte for the croiz, and shewe the ordre of knihte,
And awreke Jhesu Crist wid launce and speir to fihte and sheld.
And nu ben theih liouns in halle, and hares in the feld.

(ll. 241–52)

The higher nobility, the earls and barons, are bracketed with the knights, as, of course, they shared knighthood with them. However, this is essentially pre-chivalric knighthood, at least in the full, secular sense in which chivalric knighthood should be understood.

What was provided, then, was a paradigm against which contemporary knighthood might be judged to be falling short; a paradigm which stressed the social function of the knight. However, as with estates satire in general, it operated on the basis of a natural and pre-ordained order. Once again, it reinforced contemporary ideology in encouraging the belief that the way in which society was structured was incontrovertible and inescapable.[16]

Romance and allied genres, together with the literature of social protest, provided some stock images of the knight that were widely circulated and well understood in fourteenth-century England. A much deeper understanding of the ways in which knighthood was perceived in society can be gained, however, by interrogating some of the quite remarkable works of literature that were produced at the end of that century. Close attention needs to be paid to Geoffrey Chaucer's *Canterbury Tales*, to William Langland's *Piers Plowman* and to the anonymous *Gest of Robin Hood*. Before doing so, however, it is imperative to examine the specific context in which these works were produced.

By the second half of the fourteenth century England had a vibrant literary culture in the English language. To some extent it was a national culture, although this should not be exaggerated. It was certainly a literate culture of wide participation. The search for the consumers of the literature of this period over recent decades has suggested that audiences were rarely, if ever, discrete. True enough, writers must generally have had a primary audience, a point of attachment in society as the art historian, Arnold Hauser, once put it. One influence upon the composition of a work must always have been the author's sense of the understanding, appreciation and sensibilities of at least this primary audience. Nevertheless, audiences generally overlapped. The primary audience for one work of an author may well have differed in composition from another. Chaucer is a case in point where some works, such as the *Book of the Duchess*, were written for a narrowly courtly audience, while others were received in the first instance by what has been loosely called the 'Chaucer circle' of courtiers, diplomats, civil servants and other professionals, an audience of sophisticated *littérateurs* that was cosmopolitan and urbane.[17] The audience of William Langland's *Piers Plowman* encompassed literate laymen as well as secular clerics. His readers were often, no doubt, of a serious caste of mind, and with wide interests and sympathies.[18] The manuscript evidence, besides telling us that it was widely disseminated, shows that it was read in conjunction with a variety of other works, not only devotional ones but also histories and legends of various kinds and even romances. It was known to John Ball, the rebel preacher of 1381, and perhaps to some of his followers. *Piers Plowman* is hard to classify or to describe in a few sentences. Its subject was nothing less than an exploration of the contemporary state of humanity and the means of salvation. Its author's approach was eclectic and his sources, direct and indirect, were manifold. An acquaintance with a broad range of themes and motifs drawn from varieties of thirteenth- and fourteenth-century literature was clearly expected by him of his audience.

For the *Gest of Robin Hood* it is more difficult to speculate. By contrast with *The Canterbury Tales* and *Piers Plowman*, it was not written in London. However, the outlaw was certainly known there. William Langland refers to rhymes of Robin Hood in the B text of *Piers Plowman*, composed around 1377. The *Gest of Robin Hood* dates from around 1400, or perhaps just a little before, and is in a northern dialect. It is an amalgam of pre-existing tales, woven together with some skill by its fourteenth-century compiler. Its audience is likely to have been socially wide, but not aristocratic. The frequent reference to yeomen in the text, to describe the outlaws and others, probably holds the clue. In origin this meant young men and was used to describe men in service, especially in households, below the level of esquire. It still retained something of its service overtones in the later fourteenth century, but this sense was fast giving way to another, more general usage. It was employed increasingly to describe men drawn from the upper ranks of the peasantry, and this is the sense of the term that predominates in the *Gest*. It ought not to be supposed, however, that the audience of the *Gest* was exclusively rural; there is no reason why it should not have appealed equally to townsfolk.[19]

The content of these very different works indicates that their audiences were by no means hermetically sealed in terms of the cultural influences upon them. The *Gest of Robin Hood*, for instance, although it was not a romance, is predicated upon considerable knowledge of romance literature.[20] Furthermore, while the legend of Robin Hood undoubtedly did have an oral dimension, the *Gest* was very much a product of a literate culture; in broad terms, it was the same literate culture that gave rise to *The Canterbury Tales*. Within this literate culture, the image of the knight, and indeed many other images drawn from romance, continued to play a major part. It is the possibilities within and around this central image that are to be explored here.

There is, however, a further dimension to be considered. As is well known, the age of Chaucer and Langland was a time of profound social crisis, a crisis which had its roots within the rural economy and pre-eminently in the dislocation caused by the population collapse following the visitations of the Black Death from 1347–8 onwards. The most striking manifestation was the Peasants' Revolt of 1381. Among the long-term changes wrought by the crisis were the abandonment by landlords of their direct role in corn production and the withering away of serfdom in England. Reverberations of the crisis, however, were experienced throughout society and throughout the economy as a whole. It was a crisis from which the social order survived more or less intact but was never quite the same again. The most pervasive aspect of this crisis was the decline in acceptance of traditional authority and order that was experienced and perceived on several levels. The climate of tension was exacerbated, moreover, by problems in Church and state. There was factionalism in government, with kingship itself under considerable strain. An unusual level of disagreement over Christian practice and belief was experienced. Prompted by reactions to the unorthodox views of the Oxford scholar, John Wycliffe, the ecclesiastical authorities came to recognize heresy under the name of Lollardy and to seek its eradication.

In the literature of this age, then, one can expect to find not only inherited ideas open to view but also uncertainty in terms of social values, exploration of ideas and strident differences of opinion, features representing the tensions and ambitions that contemporaries were experiencing. Naturally enough, the central social concept of the knight figures prominently and affords an opportunity of examining closely the ways in which contemporaries perceived it.

What images of the knight do these works present? One of the best-known portraits from medieval literature is Chaucer's Knight; that 'verray parfit gentil knyght' who loved chivalry, truth and honour, freedom and courtesy. A few years ago a stimulating book from *Monty Python*'s Terry Jones attempted to overturn orthodox thinking and to argue that Chaucer's portrait was not to be taken at face value but ironically – the knight in his view was, in fact, a mercenary and the very antithesis of chivalry. Historians and literary critics, however, had no difficulty in showing that Jones was wrong.[21] He had misread not only Chaucer's tone in the *Prologue* to *The Canterbury Tales* but also contemporary knighthood. There could be no simple dividing line between mercenary and chivalric knight in an age when everyone, even the greatest aristocratic captains in the land, received pay. Without doubt Chaucer's portrait was intended to be read as a paradigm.

It is tempting to go on to elucidate the text, in the manner of traditional literary criticism, and to extol the virtues of the chivalric knight that Chaucer's paradigm exemplifies. He was loyal to his lord, in whose wars he had fought. Above all, he was a crusader, fighting for the faith. He had participated in a long list of campaigns, in the eastern Mediterranean, in Spain, in Prussia. In his manner he was as meek as a maiden:

> He nevere yet no vileyneye ne sayde [discourtesy]
> In al his lyf unto no maner wight [person]

(ll. 68–9)

He was a sober, purposeful man, whose horse was good, but who 'was not gay' (l. 74).

However, two major questions arise. One is the relationship between Chaucer's portrait and contemporary knighthood. Terry Jones has done a major service here, in focussing attention upon this particular issue. In response, Maurice Keen showed clearly that Chaucer's model was by no means redundant, but that on the contrary it had considerable contemporary resonance. One need think no further than Bolingbroke, the future Henry IV, and his northern crusading venture, in the footsteps as it were of Chaucer's Knight, or of the careers of various members of the Scrope family.[22] It is true enough that there are doubtful aspects of some of

The 'verray parfit gentil knyght':
Chaucer's Knight (from the Ellesmere
Manuscript)

the campaigns in which the Knight participated, but this had long been the case with most crusading. The second major question, however, is what was Chaucer attempting to do with this paradigm? And here, there is certainly more to be said.

The knight represents one of the three traditional orders of society, with the poor parson of the town and his brother, the ploughman, representing the other two. It may well be the case that these are intended to supply a standard against which the remaining pilgrims are to be judged and found wanting; they represent, that is, the traditional values against which the evils of the day are to be measured. There is, however, another dimension. Chaucer's *Prologue* draws heavily upon the genre of estates satire. Normally within this genre the model was not so much expressed as understood. As has been seen, each order of society was attacked in accordance with its tendency to particular vices. Those of the knight commonly included pride, haughtiness and love of finery and display. Chaucer's Knight, however, shows no concern for his attire:

> Of fustian he wered a gypon, [tunic]
> Al bismotered with his habergeon [hauberk, coat of mail]
> For he was late ycome from his viage, [journey]
> And went for to doon his pilgrymage

(ll. 75–8)

This lack of concern for display is reinforced by his very modest retinue. He travels with no more than a single squire (who is his son) and a single yeoman.

It is a striking fact about the portrayal of the Knight that there is not one specific allusion to the vices of contemporary knighthood. Why is this? It is very much in contrast with Chaucer's treatment of the parson, representative of the other 'responsible' order of society, where much is said of what he did not do, as well as what he did. Being a good shepherd, he did not, for example, leave his sheep, encumbered in the mire, while he went off to London in search of the easy life of a chantry priest.

The answer may be political. Chaucer was a royal servant, a friend of courtiers who had himself served in royal households. He was also, beyond doubt, a wise man and a political survivor.[23] It may well be that Chaucer was chary of any direct attack upon contemporary knighthood. While there is much heavy criticism of moral evil in the *Prologue* to *The Canterbury Tales* and a good deal of laughter at the expense of the corrupt, he avoids explicit comment upon the higher reaches of either Church or state. Strategy may well have marched hand in hand with his own inclinations. One of his earliest works, the *Book of the Duchess*, was written to commemorate Blanche, duchess of Lancaster and widow of John of Gaunt, and there can be little doubt that the disconsolate Black Knight of the poem[24] is intended to represent John of Gaunt himself, a reminder that knighthood was prized in the very highest social reaches.

On the other hand, this line of reasoning should not be taken too far. There is much criticism of aristocratic attitudes and behaviour in *The Canterbury Tales*, not least in the *Knight's Tale* itself where, for example, the aristocratic lady is treated merely as an object of knightly desire.[25] Nor is it to be imagined for one moment that late fourteenth-century knighthood was exempt from the traditional moral strictures; far from it! One has only to think of the contemporary poet John Gower or of the famous fourteenth-century preacher, Bishop Thomas Brinton. In his *Mirour de l'Omme*, written around 1376–8, Gower blames knighthood's failure for the present state of society. People are complaining, he says, that the world is getting worse by the day. 'But, to tell the truth, the knights with their misdeeds, along with the esquires of nowadays – some going off to make war, others staying at home – the proud and the covetous, are, in part, the evildoers through whom all the rest of the world is embroiled in madness.' Those who fight in foreign wars do so, most often, for the wrong reasons, while those who stay at home are valiant only in courts where they conquer not with their swords but with their tongues. When they do fight it is to support other people's quarrels or to oppress their poorer neighbours. Such a knight is called 'a hedgerow knight, for he will never besiege a castle. He unfurls his pennon only in a safe place, where no wound is to be feared nor peril that his body may be killed.' However, says Gower, his soul may be in great peril. Brinton recites the knights' usual misdemeanours, but lays particular stress on their lechery. Luxury, adultery and incest reign everywhere, he says, for the lords especially fail to content themselves with their wives.[26] The court of Richard II was well known for its courtiers' love of fashion and outlandish dress. The satirical work *Richard the Redeless*, for example, produced during the aftermath of that king's overthrow, makes a great deal of this particular feature. Much of the criticism from contemporaries, however, was stock criticism and as long as it was couched in traditional form it was probably not regarded as politically dangerous.

It can be argued, then, that Chaucer's portrait draws attention to the behaviour of contemporary knights, but does so indirectly, and that this may help to explain the paradigm. There is, however, another possibility. It may well be that at least part of Chaucer's intention was to promote a cause. Any interpretation of the

Temptation: the lady of the castle visiting Sir Gawain in his bedchamber (from Gawain and the Green Knight*)*

portrait must turn in the end on the role the Knight is performing. He has certainly participated in an enviable range of engagements, but what is strikingly lacking is any engagement whatsoever against England's, as opposed to Christendom's, enemies. Dating *The Canterbury Tales* is a difficult and hazardous matter, but it seems generally agreed that the *Prologue* was written some time around the late 1380s. By then a shift had occurred in attitudes towards the French war. For some time informed commentators had been concerned at the failure of the English to prosecute the war vigorously. From here opinion moved towards the view that the war itself was due to greed and vanity. In his later works, *Vox Clamantis* and *Confessio Amantis*, Gower held this view consistently, and similar anti-war sentiments have been detected (though less securely) in Chaucer. The *Tale of Melibee*, which Chaucer the pilgrim tells, warns against too swift a recourse to war and of the dangers of prolonged warfare.[27] The *Knight's Tale* itself can be read as an indictment of the worship of the god of war.[28] According to John Barnie; 'By 1380 there is not a single moralist or chronicler who wholeheartedly supports the war.'[29] A lobby for peace was gaining sway. From the royal government's point of view there were considerable advantages in this, not least in terms of a reduction in expenditure and an avoidance of the consequences of heavy taxation. In 1389 Richard II's government signed the first of a series of truces with the French, that of 1396 being intended to persist for a period of twenty-eight years. It would be surprising if Chaucer had not been inclined toward the royal policy. Among the spin-offs of a long-term peace policy might well have been a concerted effort against the infidel, a position that had been argued within the Church for some considerable time. Thus, it may well have been as a supporter of the peace policy with France that Chaucer chose to offer a paradigm that rested upon ancient teaching as to the proper function of the knight. In this light the Squire, described as the Knight's son, who had participated in recent chevauchées in Flanders, Artois and Picardy, might have been conceived as more characteristic of a contemporary, and historically younger, knighthood.

One is reminded also of the views of Sir John Clanvowe, friend of Chaucer and one of the so-called Lollard knights whose views some contemporary churchmen feared so much:

> . . . the world holt hem worsshipful that been greet werreyours and fighteres and that dstroyen and wynnen manye loondis, and waasten and geven muche good to hem that haan ynough, and that dispenden outrageously in mete, in drynke, in cloothing, in buyldyng, and in lyvyng in eese, slouthe, and manye oothere synnes. And also the world worssipeth hem muchel that woln bee venged proudly and dispitously of every wrong that is seid or doon of hem.[30]

He goes on to add that such men have books and songs made about their deeds so that they should be remembered long upon earth. Soldier, diplomat and courtier, Clanvowe seems to have written this towards the end of his life. In 1390 he participated in the Duke of Bourbon's crusade against Tunis and died in Constantinople the following year, probably on pilgrimage.[31]

However, there does seem to have been a view within contemporary radical opinion against the waging of crusades. The tenth of the *Twelve Conclusions* of the Lollards, which their opponents said were nailed to the doors of Westminster Hall and St Paul's while Parliament was in session in 1395, proclaims the New Testament's opposition to manslaughter – *Non occides* [Thou shalt not kill!]:

> The correlary is: it is an holy robbing of the pore puple qwanne lordis purchase indulgencis *a pena et a culpa* to hem that helpith to his oste [host, army] and gaderith to slen the cristene men in fer londis for god temperel [worldly gain], as we have seen. And knyythtis that rennen to hethnesse to geten hem a name in sleinge of men geten miche maugre [displeasure] of the King of Pes; for be [by] mekenesse and suffraunce our beleve was multiplied, and fythteres and mansleeris Jesu Cryst hatith and manasit [threatens]. *Qui gladio percutit, gladio peribit* [He who lives by the sword shall perish by it].[32]

There is a particular opposition here to crusades launched against fellow Christians, campaigns like John of Gaunt's in Castile and Bishop Despenser's in Flanders. But the crusade in general against heathens comes over as a very doubtful proposition indeed, for the Bible is quite explicit here. Charges of opposition to crusading and of pacifism featured, in fact, in Lollard trials, both in the 1380s and later in the 1430s.[33] These, no doubt, were very much minority opinions. Lollardy does not appear to have been opposed to knighthood as such; that is to say, it was not opposed to the secular social order. Indeed, Lollard plans for taking the temporal possessions of the Church often involved the funding of more knights with the proceeds. The *Lollard Disendowment Bill*, which most probably dates from the time of the Westminster Parliament of 1410, argued that this would allow for the creation of 15 more earls, 1,500 more knights and 6,200 more squires.[34]

At the other end of the spectrum, however, there remained a vocal pro-war party during the 1380s and 1390s, for whom the northern crusades were no doubt only second best. It was led by the king's uncle Thomas, duke of Gloucester. Gloucester's view of Richard II and his peace policy is reported by the chronicler Froissart: 'He is too heavy in the arse, he only asks for drinking and eating, sleeping, dancing and leaping about. That's no life for men-at-arms who ought to win honour through deeds of arms and put their bodies to work.'[35] His views were shared by some of the more warlike earls, such as Arundel and Warwick, and no doubt by many career soldiers and others who sought profit from the French wars. It is difficult to believe that men of this persuasion would have been particularly impressed by some aspects of Chaucer's portrait. The matter of the Knight's dress and demeanour, for example, makes one wonder. His lack of concern for his armour has caused one recent writer to argue that 'favourable "psychological" explanations (such as that the Knight was too concerned about his religious obligations to care about his appearance) seem to stretch credibility too far and to fly in the face of clearly stated medieval opinion.'[36] How, moreover, can the meekness of a maid have been expected to have maintained dignity and authority in an age when barriers were threatening to break down and the lower orders were notoriously truculent? Chaucer's Knight may conform to the traditional moralist's view of the world, but it certainly would not have conformed to the behaviour of, at least, the majority of contemporary knights, even of those who followed his crusade-orientated career pattern. Looked at from a patriotic point of view, it would have been possible to have argued, even in the 1380s, that Chaucer's Knight seemed to lack commitment to both the external and the internal defence of the realm. Perhaps, after all, Chaucer was neither criticizing knights indirectly nor purposefully championing a traditional exemplar, but asking even-handedly that his audience should reflect upon its adequacy for their own times? It is certainly possible. Nevertheless, the volatility of English politics during the late 1380s and the ascendancy of the opposition earls[37] gives some poignancy to the notion of an aligned but circumspect Chaucer!

Discussion of the Knight in *The Canterbury Tales* should not be limited, however, to an analysis of the portrait of the pilgrim knight. Chaucer himself shows that knighthood had become a common social property. This is illustrated in the content of the tales, many of which feature knights and knighthood. Furthermore, Chaucer's pilgrims, almost to a person, reveal themselves, in one way or another, as being heirs to the romance tradition, even if this is only through the telling of *fabliaux*, a genre that was dependent upon romance. We have to be careful, of course, not to treat Chaucer's pilgrims as though they are actual fourteenth-century people. They are representations, often quite complex representations; that is to say they are representations not merely of social functions and positions, and of social types, but of ideas and competing values. Nevertheless, the dramatic interaction between pilgrims can illustrate the downward dissemination of ideas and images which were discussed earlier in this work. Key figures, here, are the Squire and the Franklin.[38] The young squire is an aristocratic, courtly figure taken straight from romance. His early engagement in war was designed to impress his lady. He was fashionable in dress, he could dance, compose songs and write poetry. Everything about him was evocative of romance:

> Embrouded was he, as it were a meede [embroidered/meadow]
> Al ful of fresshe floures, whyte and reede. [red]
> Syngynge he was, or floytynge, al the day: [piping, playing the flute]
> He was as fressh as is the month of May.
>
> (ll. 89–92)

Not unexpectedly, the tale the Squire tells is a romance. It is a romance, moreover, of a rather fantastical kind, in which he reveals, quite self-consciously, his considerable knowledge of the art of rhetoric. In fact, he becomes so obsessed with his own powers of expression that it seriously impedes his narrative, so that it threatens to continue for an inordinate length of time. Worse than this, he uses his learning as a means of emphasizing the social distance between himself and his pilgrim audience. Unlike most of them, he is *gentil*. The irony is that he actually reveals himself as a rather inadequate storyteller. The tale has a superficiality, or at least an immaturity, which echoes that of the Squire himself. The net result is that he progressively alientates his audience, so much so that it is necessary to interrupt him. The pilgrim who does so is the Franklin.

The Franklin is one of the most fascinating of all Chaucer's pilgrims, and a

Chaucer's Squire, 'as fressh as is the month of May' (from the Ellesmere Manuscript)

figure much debated upon. He tells a story which he describes as a Breton lay, a variety, that is, of romance. It is the story of the doughty knight Arveragus who wins the hand of Dorigen, a lady of superior birth to his own and who, during the subseqent absence of her husband, is courted by a squire of her own social rank, Aurelius. Once the down-to-earth Arveragus has left the scene, an air of unreality pervades the land; it is the seductive landscape of romance, in which Dorigen is beguiled into making Aurelius a foolish promise. On his return, the noble Arveragus rescues Dorigen from the consequences of her own folly. In doing so, he reveals not only his sympathetic understanding, his moral superiority over the higher born Dorigen and Aurelius, but also the superficiality of the romance world, the dangers of too uncritical an adherence to it, and the inadequacy of some of its aristocratic values.

Throughout, the Franklin betrays an ambivalence towards the aristocracy. This ambivalence centres upon his attitude towards rhetoric and rhetorical devices. He is, he says, a *burel* man, who never learned rhetoric. He asks, therefore, to be excused for his rude speech. This is, in part, affectation, for he proceeds to reveal that he knows and understands rhetoric very well indeed, even though he may not have been formally schooled in the art. The central irony is that he shows himself to be a much more effective storyteller than the Squire, producing a better controlled narrative and a greater command of language.

It is often assumed that the Franklin is a product of upward social mobility in the changed economic circumstances of the post Black Death world. In fact, it may be more accurate to see Chaucer's pilgrim, or at least certain of his features, as a product of the contemporary fear of upward mobility, of declining respect for differences in rank on the one hand and the obsession with gentility on the other. The term franklin was one of wide social usage. Originally meaning no more than free tenant, it was used in Chaucer's time to cover a wide spectrum of people, as is shown for example by the evidence of the 1379 poll tax. Chaucer's Franklin by no means corresponds to the majority of franklins. He evinces, rather, a type of social figure that had long existed in rural society, though not necessarily under that name.[39] He is proud and confident in himself, but he is on the lower edges of gentility and hence liable to be the recipient of snobbery exercised against him by the higher born. Hence his ambivalence towards knightly culture. He is at times disdainful of its excesses and a plain thinking man, as the tale shows. At the same time he is steeped in that knightly culture to which he desires, and indeed enjoys, access. His portrait in the *Prologue* immediately reveals this, for it invokes the image of the vavasour of French romance, the well-provided hospitable host:

> An housholdere, and that a greet, was he;
> Seint Julian he was in his contree.
> His breed, his ale, was alweys after oon; [uniformly good]
> A bettre envyned man was nowher noon. [stocked with wine]
> Withoute bake mete was nevere his hous
> Of fissh and flessh, and that so plentevous,
> It snewed in his hous of mete and drynke,
> Of alle deyntees that men koude thynke.
> After the sondry sesons of the yeer,
> So chaunged he his mete and his soper.
> Ful many a fat partrich hadde he in muwe, [mew, coup]
> And many a breem and many a luce in stuwe. [pike/fishpond]
> Wo was his cook but if his sauce were
> Poynaunt and sharp, and redy al his geere.
> His table dormaunt in his halle alway
> Stood redy covered al the longe day.
>
> (ll. 339–54)

The world the Franklin inhabits is that of the country gentry. He was the lord of a manor who held his own court; he had been a sheriff, a tax assessor and a member of parliament (a knight of the shire). Nevertheless, he was not of the social rank of the Knight or the Squire. The latter is an esquire in the traditional sense of the term, that is to say a trainee knight and the son of a knight who will be dubbed himself in due course. The Franklin's position *vis-à-vis* the Squire would have been the same in essence had the latter been an esquire in the more recent sense of gentle landowner below the rank of knight, whose ancestors may well have been knights themselves. The tensions that are being played out revolve around the emergence of a stratified gentry.[40] In the *Franklin's Tale* itself the squire Aurelius,

'Whit was his berd as is the dayesye':
Chaucer's Franklin (from the Ellesmere
Manuscript)

who in response to the large-mindedness of the knight Arveragus, is shamed into releasing Dorigen from her promise to become his lover: 'Thus kan a squier doon a gentil dede,' he asserts, 'As well as kan a knyght.'

The complex emotions of the Franklin are manifested in the well-known passage where the Franklin interrupts the Squire to put an end to his long-winded tale. He conveys everything in just a few lines: condescension towards the young Squire, admiration for his rank, an obsessive concern that he and his family should be considered gentle, and an affected unconcern for wealth while revealing the opposite:

> 'In feith, Squier, thow hast thee wel yquit
> And gentilly. I preise wel thy wit,'
> Quod the Frankeleyn, 'considerynge thy yowthe,
> So feelyngly thou spekest, sire, I allow the!
> As to my doom, ther is noon that is heere
> Of eloquence that shal be thy peere,
> If that thou lyve; God yeve thee good chaunce.
> And in vertu sende thee continuance!
> For of thy speche I have greet deyntee.

Geoffrey Chaucer (from Harley MS 4866)

> I have a sone, and by the Trinitee,
> I hadde levere than twenty pound lond, [rather]
> Though it right now were fallen in myn hond,
> He were a man of swich discrecioun
> As ye been! Fy on possessioun,
> But if a man be vertuous withal!
> I have my sone snybbed, and yet shal, [rebuked]
> For he to vertu listeth nat entende; [give attention]
> But for to pleye at dees, and to despende [dice]
> And lese al that he hath, is his usage.
> And he hath levere talken with a page
> Than to comune with any gentil wight [person]
> Where he myghte lerne gentillesse aright.'
>
> *(Squire's Tale* ll. 673–94)

The intensity of the social tension expressed is, no doubt, specific to the latter half of the fourteenth century, but the contexts in which the downward dissemination of ideas and values takes place – social contact, shared lifestyle, and social aspiration – are common to a broader time-span, across the thirteenth to fifteenth centuries. This dissemination did not cease at the level of the mere gentleman, nor was it contained within rural society. It is Chaucer's Wife of Bath, for instance, who not only tells the romance-derived story of the knight and the loathly lady, but who also lectures her fellow pilgrims on the nature of gentility (*gentillesse*). Knighthood and romance images had become the common property of society, often in extended and mutated forms.

The pervasive influence of knighthood is given startling expression in Langland's *Piers Plowman*. In this work knighthood is shown to be ever present, running throughout history. Trajan, for example, the righteous heathen who was saved through the intervention of Pope Gregory the Great, is referred to as 'a trewe knyght'.[41] So, too, was Moses.[42] As an order, however, knighthood seems to have been founded by King David, who dubbed knights and made them swear to serve truth for ever. In this he mirrored heaven where ten knights had been created as archangels to rule over the retinue of the king of kings. One of these was the disobedient Lucifer who proved, in effect, to be a knight apostate to his order.[43]

The greatest of all knights, however, is Christ himself. In Passus XVI of the poem Will meets an *Old Testament* figure, Abraham, who foretells the coming of Christ, that is to say he announces the *New Testament*. Christ is pictured as the knight who is to joust with the Devil. This has already been intimated to Will in his inner dream:

> And thanne sholde Jesus juste therfore, bi juggement of armes,
> Wheither sholde fonge the fruyt – the fend or hymselve. [which should receive]
>
> (B XVI ll. 95–6)

Abraham is described as a herald and Christ is announced not just as a warrior but as a chivalric knight:

Christ himself could be portrayed as a knight. Here, in a fourteenth-century Apocalypse, he is shown as a warrior leading his crusading host

And thanne mette I with a man, a myd-Lenten Sonday,
As hoor as an hawethorn, and Abraham he highte. [hoary/was called]
I frayned hym fram whennes he come. [asked/from whence]
And of whennes he were, and whider that he thoughte. [meant to go]

'I am Feith,' quod that freke, 'it falleth noght me to lye, [man/befits]
And of Abrahames hous an heraud of armes. [herald]
I seke after a segge that I seigh ones, [man/saw once]
A ful bold bacheler – I knew hym by his blasen.' [blazon, arms]

(B XVI ll. 172–9)

He goes on to explain:

> 'Thus have I ben his heraud here and in helle,
> And conforted many a careful that after his comynge waiten;
> And thus I seke hym,' he seide.

(ll. 247–9)

and a little later,

> 'Crist is his name
> That shal delivere us som day out of the develes power'.

(ll. 265–6)

The chivalric imagery is extremely full, and is repeated when these events finally come to pass, in the account of the Harrowing of Hell that provides the substance of Passus XVIII. Christ is first portrayed as a young knight, or more correctly as a young man about to be knighted on the eve of his great trial:

> Barefoot on an asse bak bootles cam prikye, [riding]
> Withouten spores other spere; spakliche he loked, [spurs or spear/lively]
> As is the kynde of knyght that cometh to be dubbed,
> To geten hym gilte spores on galoches ycouped. [slashed shoes]
> Thanne was Feith in a fenestre, and cryde 'A! Fili David!' [window/son of
>   David]
> As dooth an heraud of armes when aventrous cometh to justes. [adventurous
>   knights]

(B VIII ll. 11–16)

Langland is here following a literary tradition, that of Christ the lover knight, where Jesus is portrayed as the knight who comes to rescue his lady, that is to say the human soul, even though she has been unfaithful to him. The central image was taken straight from romance, and is found in several thirteenth-century texts. It is to be seen, for example, in the English *Ancrene Riwle* and in an Anglo-Norman text of the poet Nicholas Bozon.[44] Langland, however, avoids the more profane overtones of romantic love, and the notion of the soul as captive lady is replaced by the image of Pier's gathering the fruit from the Tree of Charity. He does, however, retain the romance topos of the knight who tourneys in disguise. Christ comes as Piers the Plowman, that is to say in human form. As Faith explains:

> 'This Jesus of his gentries wol juste in Pieres armes, [nobility]
> In his helm and in his habergeon – humana natura. [coat of mail]
> In Piers paltok the Plowman this prikiere shall ryde.' [jacket/horseman]

(B VIII ll. 22–5)

Despite his obvious vulnerability, however, he will not be overcome in battle. This is because of the divine nature that he shares with the Father. Clearly, the image of the chivalric knight is evoked here because it is one that is universally understood and is of universal validity.

The imagery of knighthood is continued, moreover, with the legend of Longinus (or, as here, Longeus). The two thieves who were being crucified alongside Christ had their limbs broken to ascertain whether or not they were dead, but there was none who dared touch the body of Christ, 'knyght and kynges sone' (l. 76), until the blind knight Longinus was forced to 'justen with Jesus' (l. 82). There follows the most extraordinary scene in which Longinus pierces Christ's side with a spear at which he is immediately cured of his blindness by Christ's spurting blood. At this he yields to Christ as a recreant or faithless knight, by which act Christ is deemed to have won the joust. Death has been vanguished and Christ has freed all those who follow him.[45]

In all this, then, Christ's knighthood has a very specific purpose; it is nothing less than the salvation of mankind. There can be no greater expression of the pervasiveness of the image of the knight within later medieval culture.

Of course, Langland makes reference to knighthood in more worldly senses too. Knights, and indeed squires, figure as members of retinues. Knighthood also signifies the nobility, in the sense of rulers or ruling class. Of particular interest, however, is Langland's dramatic expression of the three estates theory, where the knight is portrayed as a landlord and the whole arrangement is seen as essentially consensual. Piers the Plowman says:

'I shal swynke and swete and sowe for us bothe,
And ek laboure for thi love al my lif tyme, [also/for love of you]
In covenaunt that thow kepe Holy Kirke amd myselve [agreement/protect]
Fro wastours and fro wikked men that this world destruyeth;
And go hunte hardliche to hares and foxes, [boldly after]
To bores and to bukkes that breken down myn hegges; [boars/deer/hedges]
And go affaite thi faucons wilde foweles to kille, [train/falcons]
For thei cometh to my croft and croppeth my whete'.

(B VI ll. 25–32)

The knight, of course, concurs with the arrangement:

Curteisly the knyght thanne conseyved thise wordes:
'Be my power, Piers, I plighte thee my trouthe
To fulfille this forward, though I fighte sholde; [agreement/have to]
Als longe as I lyve I shal thee maynteyne'. [support]

(ll. 33–6)

There is, however, some ideological strain here. It is first indicated in the idea that the nobility's love of hunting and falconry has a functional, indeed communal, purpose; in reality, of course, it was not only potentially destructive but actually denied others access to valuable assets. The sense of strain is reinforced when Piers goes on to advise the knight that he should avoid vexing his tenants unless he has just cause, and that when he does need to fine them he should do so with mercy, that is to say moderately. He should avoid taking gifts from poor men, lest they be not deserved, and he should not injure his serfs, 'And mysbede noght thi bondemen – the bettre may thow spede' (l. 45). Having received the knight's assent to abide by his words in these and other matters, Piers sets about the business of sowing. What has been shown, however, is that the actual relationship between knight and peasant, between lord and tenant, is regulated by the knight as landlord in his manor court, and backed by force. The only constraints upon the lord are his own sense of what is just and sensible, and the belief that he will be accountable, ultimately, at his life's end. In other words, the relationship is not in the last analysis consensual at all!

Langland was wedded to a conservative ideology. Yet, as has been pointed out,[46] his imaginative insights revealed both the true nature of that ideology and its inadequacy as a means of understanding the fourteenth-century social order. In his worries lest the landlords should push their rural dependants too far, Langland was undoubtedly attuned to the mood of the peasantry during the 1360s and 1370s. In the episode that follows the dramatic representation of the doctrine of the three orders, Langland pictures society threatened by those he calls wasters who refuse to work for their food. In fact, what is depicted is a rural economy dependent upon the wage labour of landless or near landless peasants whose increasing bargaining power in the circumstances of the population fall after the plague put upward pressure on wages. It is no longer just a question of individual lords and their tenants but of a mobile workforce prepared to move in search of higher wages. The government had responded with legislation, the *Statute of Labourers*, which both held down wages and restricted mobility. The reactions by landlords to the threat to their economy and the thwarted expectations of sections of the population provided the seedbed from which sprang the Peasants' Revolt of 1381. Langland provides a dramatic insight into the situation. Faced with a recalcitrant workforce who tell him to 'go pissen with his plowgh', Piers (who now appears as some form of overseer) appeals to the knight to fulfil his agreement. The knight's manifest failure to rectify the situation expresses the breakdown in respect for authority that so characterizes the period:

> Thanne Piers the Plowman pleyned hym to the knyghte,
> To kepen hym as covenaunt was fro cursede shrewes. . . .
> (B VI ll. 159–60)

> Curteisly the knyght thanne as his kynde wolde, [nature dictated]
> Warnede Wastour and wissed hym bettre: [counselled]
> 'Or thou shalt abigge by the lawe, by the ordre that I bere!' [be punished]
> 'I was noght wont to werche', quod Wastour, 'and now wol I noght bigynne!'–
> And leet light of the lawe, and lasse of the knyghte. . . . [set little store by/less]
> (B VI ll. 164–8)

The knight now withdraws from the scene, indicating perhaps an intuitive understanding on the poet's part of the extent to which local economies were already operating outside of the landlord's sphere of operations, and prefiguring the abandonment of direct arable farming by the lords and their agents that was well in train by the end of the century.

The knight is seen from a different perspective in the *Gest of Robin Hood*. Here one encounters the story of the sorry knight, who is later equated with the outlaws' friend Sir Richard at the Lee. He makes his debut as the victim of the famous charade in which the outlaws lie in wait for a 'guest' approaching from the Watling Street, some 'bolde baron', some knight or squire, or some rich ecclesiastic. The guest is stopped, invited to dine (sumptuously) with Robin in the greenwood and then robbed under the guise of paying for the repast. All of this is undertaken with an ironic courtesy in which the outlaws ape aristocratic manners. Robin himself is depicted as though he were a lord with a retinue who obey him at his will and who, to signify the relationship, wear his livery. More than this, Robin has obvious affinity with King Arthur of romance, for example in his refusal to dine before some strange happening, that is the appearance of some 'unketh gest', had occurred.

The guest on this occasion, however, was not quite what the outlaws might have expected:

> All dreri was his semblaunce, [appearance]
> And lytell was his pryde;
> His one fote in the styrop stode,
> That othere wavyd beside.
>
> His hode hanged in his iyn two; [hood/two eyes]
> He rode in symple aray; [simple dress]
> A soriar man than he was one
> Rode never in somer day.
>
> (Fytte 1, verses 22,23)

Despite his appearance and his state of mind, however, this 'gentyl knight' behaves impeccably. He is, indeed, as Little John has hailed him, 'hende' and 'fre'. Moreover, of the yeoman Robin he has heard good report, and he greets him graciously:

> 'God the save, goode Robyn
> And all thy fayre meyne' [retinue]
>
> (Fytte 1, verse 31)

The knight's behaviour in the greenwood might well cause the reader to reflect upon Robin's instruction to his outlaw band on the manner of their life at the beginning of the *Gest*:

'But loke ye do no husbonde harme
That tylleth with his ploughe.

No more ye shall no gode yeman
That walketh by grene wode shawe;
Ne no knyght ne no squyer
That wol be a gode felawe.

These bisshopes and these archebishoppes,
Ye shall them bete and bynde;
The hye sherif of Notingham,
Hym holde ye in your mynde.'

(Fytte 1, verses 13–15)

What is it that makes a particular knight or esquire a 'gode felawe'? Partly, it seems, his honesty. When Robin inevitably asks the knight to pay for his dinner, the latter replies that he has but 10s. in his coffers. Little John is immediately sent to assess the validity of this statement and finds it to be true enough. Robin then wishes to know why it is that the knight is in the state he is. Perhaps, he suggests, the knight has been profligate 'a sori husbande', or a userer or a lecher: 'Wyth wronge hast led thy lyfe?' The knight, of course, is none of these.

There seems to be more, however, to being a good fellow than honesty of life, important though this is. What the knight lacks is *hauteur*. He makes no attempt to lord it over the yeomen. On the contrary he accepts them as companions. Invited to dine:

'I graunte,' he sayde, 'with you to wende, [go]
My bretherne, all in fere;' [brethren/company]

(Fytte 1, verse 27)

This is despite the knight's social rank, a rank that is never, in fact, denied:

'But pay or ye wende,' sayde Robyn; [before you go]
'Me thynketh it is gode ryght;
It was never the maner, by dere worthi God,
A yoman to pay for a knyhht.'

(Fytte 1, verse 37)

The knight's status appears to be fully accepted as a legitimate one. Robin in his several attempts to understand the knight's present state wonders whether the knight has been forced to take on knighthood or whether he comes from yeoman stock and is pretending to something above his station, either of which would explain his state of penury. The reply is reassuring:

> 'I am none of those,' sayde the knyght,
> 'By God that made me;
> An hundred wynter here before
> Myn auncestres knyghtes have be.'
>
> (Fytte 1, verse 47)

He is of ancient stock, and his neighbours could vouch for the fact that he was worth no less than £400 per year. As he later insists to the abbot, he was also a proper strenuous knight who had seen plenty of action:

> 'In joustes and in tournement
> Full ferre then have I be, [far]
> And put my selfe as ferre in prees [as much in danger]
> As ony that ever I se'.
>
> (Fytte 2, verse 116)

The knight explains that his problem results from his own kindness. His twenty-year-old son, a lover of the joust, who was to have been his heir, had killed a knight of Lancaster (presumably, that is, of the earl of Lancaster). In order to save his son, he had secured a loan on the security of his land. Unless he pays the creditor, the abbot of St Mary's, York, the £400 he owes him on the appointed day, then he will forfeit his land. Clearly he cannot pay; hence his misery. The outlaws weep at his story, and inevitably Robin lends him the cash with which to pay. The outlaws, in short, appear to have no quarrel with the knight's status, nor do they seem to demand total equality with him. It is clear at several points in the *Gest* that inheritance is sacrosanct; men should be free from arbitrary disseisin (dispossession), even by the king, and disseisin should be physically resisted. The outlaws are shown, however, to be as capable as the knight is of courteous behaviour and of largesse (or generosity). As the knight departs they offer him presents that befit his dignity. He is given a livery, a fine suit of clothes in which he can cut the necessary figure, a grey courser with a new saddle, a palfrey, a pair of boots and gilt spurs. Furthermore, Little John is to go with him as his servant, for:

> 'It were great shame,' sayde Robyn,
> 'A knight alone to ryde,
> Without squyre, yoman, or page,
> To walke by his syde.'
>
> (Fytte 1, verse 80)

There is, of course, deliberate role reversal here, with the outlaws not only lending money but also kitting out their social superior. It is a role reversal patently enjoyed by the fictive outlaws, and also no doubt by the *Gest*'s audience. But there is also something more than this. An increasing affinity develops between knight and yeomen. The knight not only keeps faith with Robin and the outlaws in returning to pay his debt to them, but returns with fine presents too.

Furthermore, he intervenes to save a yeoman who is being maltreated in a wrestling match 'for love of Robin Hood'. The courtesy of the knight and the outlaws is subsequently contrasted with the discourtesy of the abbot of St Mary's and the high cellarer when the knight appears on the day appointed to pay them his debt, and again with the discourtesy displayed by the cellarer and his fellow monk when they are invited to dine by the outlaws in the manner the sorry knight had been twelve months before. The abbot, moreover, has been shown to be decidedly uncharitable in his treatment of the knight and in his attempt to deprive the knight of his lands, in alliance with the sheriff and with the chief justice of England. Their behaviour, in a word, is churlish.

Their religion differs too. Robin's devotion to the Virgin Mary is contrasted with the behaviour of the monks who claim to serve her. The knight, too, is a pious man. When Robin asks him (one should rather say tests him) as to what he will do should he lose his land, he replies that he will go on pilgrimage (or perhaps it is a crusade that is implied) to the Holy Land. Honesty and charity are displayed by knight and yeomen alike, in contradistinction to the behaviour shown by the high ecclesiastics and the corrupt officials.

The full implication of all this seems clear. Robin's men are outlaws, but they are also yeomen. What is envisaged is a world where there are gradations within secular society but no great gulf. There is no suggestion in the *Gest* of overturning the social order. But the events do have the decided effect of reducing social distance. When Robin Hood is subsequently pursued by the sheriff and in mortal danger, he calls upon Sir Richard at the Lee for aid. The gentle knight gives him refuge in his 'fair castle', which, we learn, is double ditched, moated and walled. Sir Richard himself was later captured, while hawking by the riverside, and it was now Robin's turn to affect a rescue from the sheriff and his men. Having loosed the knight's bonds, Robin gave him a bow, saying:

> 'Leve thy hors the behynde,
> And lerne for to renne, [run]
> Thou shalt with me to grene wode,
> Through myre, mosse, and fenne.'
>
> (Fytte 6, verse 352)

The knight held faith with Robin Hood, and both played their parts full courteously; but, it is Robin who held centre stage and determined events.

In many ways, Sir Richard at the Lee seems reminiscent of Chaucer's Knight. He is a pious, socially responsible man, not given to emphasizing his exalted rank. In reality, of course, an enormous social gulf remained between knight and yeoman. The *Gest*, however, does seem to prefigure the emergence of knighthood as a clear social rung above yeoman, gentleman and esquire, a social rung from whose members certain standards in terms of pedigree and demeanour were to be expected. The concept of knighthood as simply a synonym for nobility was finally giving way before this.

SEVEN

Conclusion

Knighthood had changed considerably during the course of these few centuries. Like all institutions, as it evolved, elements from its past were consistently to be found in its present. Even the fully-fledged chivalric knighthood of the fourteenth century overlay its many earlier connotations but without wholly absorbing them. Older ideas of service and of social obligation, for example, were embedded within it. After 1400 the role of the knight in society continued to evolve, but there were no new ingredients. Increasingly, it was the emphasis that was to change.

As a knight, Sir John Paston, with whom this book began, appeared at the end of a long process of evolution. The full history of knighthood could hardly have been comprehended in its entirety by him, or by any other contemporary for that matter. What he did understand, however, was that knighthood was linked strongly to the past as well as to contemporary social status and display. For him the emphasis was to be placed upon antiquity and heraldry, upon military valour and noble association. He was himself a full participant in all aspects of knightly culture. He saw active military service. He was a great collector of books, including romances and collections of arms, and he commissioned his own 'Grete Boke' of Knighthood which still survives.[1] A friend, Thomas Danvers, called him 'the best cheser of a gentell-woman that I know.'[2] Although his family clearly felt that he could have paid more attention to his estates, he did not neglect his status within the local community. He was a member of parliament and a justice of the peace. Not surprisingly, having been brought up in the royal household, Sir John Paston played his part in the chivalric revival associated with the court of Edward IV and much influenced by that of contemporary Burgundy. In 1467 he fought with Lord Scales on the king's side at a tourney at Eltham, where he hurt his hand. In the following year he and his brother, John Paston III, went to Bruges as part of the retinue of the king's sister, Margaret of York, for her marriage to Charles of Burgundy. John III wrote back to their mother of the celebrations, including jousts, that marked the event: 'And as for the Dwkys coort', he wrote, 'as of lordys, ladys, and gentylwomen, knytys, sqwyirs, and gentyllmen, I herd of non lyek to it save Kyng Artourys cort. By my trowthe, I have no wyt nor remembrans to wryte to yow halfe the worchep that is her [here]'.[3]

Jousts and tourneys, however, were not the most enduring aspects of knighthood. Whether or not the chivalric display of the fifteenth century was any more stagy than that of a century earlier is a matter of some debate. There is no doubt that it was taken seriously at the highest levels. The binding function of

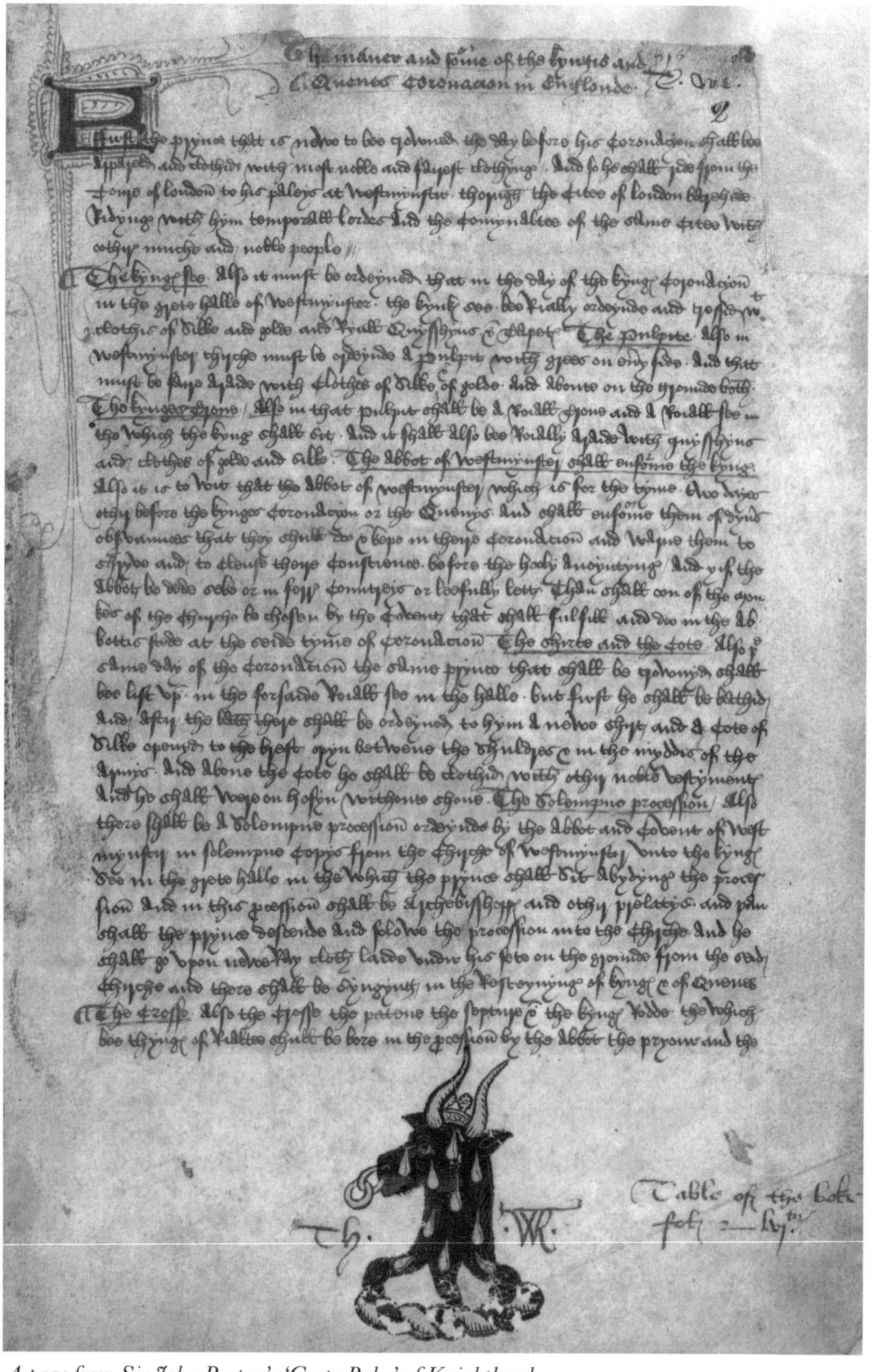

A page from Sir John Paston's 'Grete Boke' of Knighthood

A hermit instructing a would-be knight (from Ramon Lull's Order of Chivalry, *as published by William Caxton)*

knighthood was still well understood. From the time of Edward IV it became normal practice for the sovereign to knight the mayor of London either during or immediately after his term of office. On the other hand there was a lot of nostalgia in the air. William Caxton, England's first printer, who produced the first edition of Sir Thomas Malory's *Morte D'arthur* in 1485, was responsible for publishing numerous romances and chivalric works. His prefaces contain exhortations to contemporary knights that they should leave their current ways and return to the ancient customs of chivalry.[4] Of course, he had something of a professional interest in taking this line. The plain fact is, though, that military changes – the increasing use of infantry and artillery – were tending to make chivalric combat antiquated. The future of knighthood lay as a rank within the English gentry.

During the course of the fifteenth century the gentry hierarchy became more clearly defined. Although the *Statute of Additions* of 1413 had added the status of gentleman to that of knight and esquire, there remained a degree of confusion in the usage of these terms for some considerable time. Esquires came increasingly to proclaim their status in title deeds during the 1420s and 1430s, to be followed by the gentlemen before the middle of the century. By its close the several ranks had become more homogeneous so that it became clearer as to which layer a man did and should belong. It is significant, too, that the obligations to local office that each implied were also becoming clearer.[5] There can be no doubt that these gradations played a major part in the future stability of English society. And without knighthood, they would not have existed.

Social obligation to office is a strand that links back to the civilian duties of Angevin knighthood and, beyond that even, to the service connotations that were present from the very birth of knighthood. It was one of the ingredients that knighthood bequeathed to the gentry, and hence to the nation as a whole. Another was heraldry, which has had a further, and extremely long, life of its own. The visual legacy of the medieval past is, in fact, relatively easy to perceive within the modern world. The effects upon our thought-processes are not always so easy to discern, although some aspects can be grasped more readily than others. For example, the knight's code of honour became the code of honour of the officer class of less remote times.[6] What is certain is that knighthood and romance are deeply imbedded in our culture.

Finally, knighthood's most enduring role of all is as a reward for service to the nation. Among others, our most prominent historians can still aspire to being knighted.

Notes

1. Introduction

1. The Paston statement has been shortened and its language somewhat modernized here. The full statement is accessible in Norman Davis (ed.), *Paston Letters and Papers of the Fifteenth Century Part II* (Oxford, 1976), No. 897. The isolated quotation from Edward IV comes from the previous document, p. 896. For the status of the Paston statement, which purports to be in the king's name, and a discussion of its context see Colin Richmond, *The Paston Family in the Fifteenth Century: the first phase* (Cambridge, 1990), ch.I.
2. W. Caxton, *The Book of the Ordre of Chyvalry* (ed. A.T.P. Byles, Early English Text Society, 1926), pp. 18–20; it is quoted by M. Keen, 'Chivalry, Nobility and the Man-at-Arms', in C.T. Allmand (ed.), *War, Literature and Politics in the Late Middle Ages* (Liverpool, 1976), p. 38.
3. See Richmond, *op. cit.* p. 7.

2. The Origins of Knighthood in England

1. Sir Frank Stenton, *The First Century of English Feudalism* (Oxford, 1932), pp. 132–3.
2. For a different view see Janet L. Nelson, 'Ninth-Century Knighthood: the Evidence of Nithard', in C. Harper-Bill, C. Holdsworth and J.L. Nelson (eds.), *Studies in Medieval History presented to R. Allen Brown* (Woodbridge, 1989), pp. 255–66.
3. A great deal of the work on this subject has recently been reviewed by Jean Flori, in *L'Essor de la Chevalerie XIe – XIIe Siècles* (Geneva, 1986), ch.VI: *Milites*, where full references will be found.
4. P. van Luyn, 'Les *milites* de la France du XI siècle', *Le Moyen Age*, 1971, pp. 1–51 and 193–238.
5. G. Duby, *La société aux xi et xii siècles dans la*

region mâconnaise (Paris, 1953). See also his 'Lineage, Nobility and Knighthood: the Mâconnais in the Twelfth Century – a Revision', in *The Chivalrous Society*, trans. C. Postan (London, 1977), pp. 59–80.
6. Flori, *L'Essor de la Chevalerie*, p. 135.
7. *Ibid.* p. 123. For the work of Pierre Bonnassie, see Jean Birrell (trans.), *From Slavery to Feudalism in South-Western Europe* (Cambridge, 1991).
8. See below p. 9.
9. Flori, *Op. cit.* pp. 119–20.
10. For what follows see David Bates, *Normandy Before 1066* (London, 1982), pp. 109–11, and Lucien Musset 'L'Aristocratie Normande au XIe Siècle', in *La Noblesse au Moyen Age* (Paris, 1976), espec. pp. 89–96.
11. R. Allen Brown, 'The Status of the Anglo-Norman Knight', in J. Gillingham and J.C. Holt (eds.), *War and Government in the Middle Ages* (Bury St Edmunds, 1984), pp. 21–2. In this essay, however, the author is arguing for knighthood as an elevated status.
12. For Norman land tenures see Musset, *op. cit.* and Bates, *Normandy Before 1066*, pp. 122–8.
13. S. Harvey, 'The Knight and the Knight's Fee in England', *Past and Present*, No. 49 (1973), pp. 3–43; repr. in R.H. Hilton (ed.), *Peasants, Knights and Heretics* (Cambridge, 1976), pp. 133–73. A convenient précis of her views is to be found in H.E. Hallam (ed.), *The Agrarian History of England and Wales, vol.II 1042–1350* (Cambridge, 1988), pp. 81–2.
14. David Douglas (ed.), *English Historical Documents vol.II* (London, 1953), No. 219.
15. For criticism of the Harvey thesis see R. Allen Brown, 'The Status of the Anglo–Norman Knight', and most recently Donald F. Fleming, 'Landholding by *Milites* in Domesday Book: A Revision', in Marjorie Chibnall (ed.), *Anglo-Norman Studies XIII* (Woodbridge, 1990), pp. 84–98. The latter includes a reworking of the

statistics. However, his quarrel lies more with the interpretation which Harvey places upon them.

16. See below p. 24.

17. Harvey, 'The Knight and the Knight's Fee', p. 158.

18. See Fleming, 'Landholding by *Milites* in Domesday Book', pp. 94–5, Richard P. Abels, *Lordship and Military Obligation in Anglo-Saxon England* (London, 1988), p. 134 and references given there.

19. Stenton, *First Century of English Feudalism*, pp. 142–3.

20. For this and what follows see Stenton, *First Century of English Feudalism*, pp. 129–36.

21. *Ibid.*, p. 135.

22. Similarly, in northern England, the ministers whom documents call *drengs* had holdings very like those Domesday Book describes for the Norman *milites*. S. Harvey in Hallam (ed.), *Agrarian History*, p. 81.

23. Abels, *Lordship and Military Obligation*, p. 132. Similarly the *Life of Edward the Confessor* talks of Earl Tostig's military household as *milites*. Elsewhere they would be described as housecarls.

24. See, in particular, Georges Duby, *The Three Orders: Feudal Society Imagined* (Chicago, 1978).

25. N.P. Brooks, 'Arms, Status and Warfare in Late Saxon England', in David Hill (ed.), *Ethelred the Unready*, BAR British Series, 59 (1978), pp. 81–103.

26. Sir Frank Stenton, in particular, believed that *fyrd* duty belonged to the peasants and that they were recruited on a territorial basis. By contrast, the thegn's obligation to join the royal host was held to have been personal, stemming from his rank. Others, led by Eric John, have argued that the late Anglo-Saxon *fyrd* was essentially a feudal host of landed aristocrats and thegnly retainers, whose obligation to service derived from their possession of land. C. Warren Hollister maintains that there were in fact two types of *fyrd*, the 'select fyrd', a force of professional, noble warriors, each of whom answered for a five-hide holding, and the 'great fyrd' which was in effect the nation in arms. Michael Powicke argues something similar with the army divided into royal, provincial and county forces, the first two being closely related and comprising mounted, thegnly warriors whose obligation to service was assessed on the land they held according to a five-hide rule. County forces, on the other hand, were essentially peasant militias under the command of of the shire's thegns. For further details of the

debate, and for full references, see Abels, *Lordship and Military Obligation*, pp. 3–6, 97. In the argument that follows I have drawn particularly from this work.

27. Richard Abels argues further, and with vigour, that this obligation to provide military service to the king was derived from the possession of bookland, that is to say land held by royal charter.

28. For what follows see, in particular, Brooks, *op. cit.*

29. For the arms and armour depicted in the tapestry see David M. Wilson, *The Bayeux Tapestry* (London, 1985), pp. 219–25.

30. Abels, *Lordship and Military Obligation*, p. 147.

31. B. Griffiths, *The Battle of Maldon: Text and Translation* (Pinner, 1991), p. 59. For recent commentary see Donald Scragg, *The Battle of Maldon AD 991* (Oxford, 1991). See also Abels, *Lordship and Military Obligation*, pp. 146–8.

32. *Ibid.*, pp. 143–4.

33. See Brooks, 'Arms, Status and Warfare', p. 85.

34. R. Allen Brown, *The Normans and the Norman Conquest* (London, 1969), p. 230, and for a summary of knowledge on this point generally, pp. 230–2.

35. Frank Barlow, *William Rufus* (London, 1983), p. 174.

36. Abels, *Lordship and Military Obligation*, p. 135 and references given there.

37. *Ibid.*, pp. 155–6. For the social conditions that pertained in England during the eleventh century see, in particular, Robin Fleming, *Kings and Lords in Conquest England* (Cambridge, 1991).

38. C. Given-Wilson, *The Royal Household and the King's Affinity* (New Haven, 1986), pp. 7–8.

39. J.O. Prestwich, 'The Military Household of the Norman Kings', *English Historical Review*, vol. 96 (1981), p. 8.

40. For what follows see Marjorie Chibnall, 'Mercenaries and the *Familia Regis* under Henry I', *History*, vol. 62, no. 204 (1977), pp. 15–23.

41. *Ibid.*, p. 18.

42. Some of the chroniclers also indicate that these troops included mounted archers. In charters and Exchequer records the castle garrisons figure as *milites et servientes* (sergeants); therefore, they were not all fully armed knights. Some were clearly archers. There may also have been some lightly armed cavalry.

43. J.C. Holt, 'The Introduction of Knight-Service into England', in R. Allen-Brown (ed.), *Anglo-Norman Studies VI* (Woodbridge, 1984), pp. 89–106.

44. J.C. Prestwich, 'War and Finance in the Anglo-Norman State', *Transactions of the Royal Historical Society*, 5th ser., 4 (1954), pp. 19–43, and 'The Military Household of the Norman Kings', pp. 1–35.

45. Holt, 'Introduction of Knight-Service', p. 106.

46. *Ibid.*, pp. 104–6.

47. Harvey, 'The Knight and the Knight's Fee', p. 139.

48. See, for example, Edmund King, 'The Peterborough Descriptio Militum (Henry I)', *English Historical Review*, vol. 84 (1969), pp. 84–101.

49. Harvey, 'The Knight and the Knight's Fee', pp. 142–3.

50. *Ibid.*, pp. 135–44, and the examples given there. This is the heart of her thesis in which she argues, somewhat sweepingly, for two distinct levels of enfeoffment. Although overdrawn there is undoubtedly an element of truth here. Her characterization of this distinction as one between active or professional knights on the one hand and nominal or honorific knights on the other, however, seems to me to be unsound.

51. Quoted by Harvey, 'The Knight and the Knight's Fee', p. 144.

52. Richard Mortimer, 'Land and Service: The Tenants of the Honour of Clare', in R. Allen Brown (ed.), *Anglo-Norman Studies VIII* (Woodbridge, 1986), pp. 177–97.

53. See Thomas K. Keefe, *Feudal Assessments and the Political Community under Henry I and His Sons* (Berkeley, 1983), espec. pp. 42–3, 84–6. The figure of 7.5 per cent new fees is based upon those tenants-in-chief for whom sufficient information is available.

54. *Ibid.*, p. 229, n.177.

55. Quoted by Marjorie Chibnall, *The World of Orderic Vitalis* (Oxford, 1984), pp. 142–3.

56. Anne Williams, 'The Knights of Shaftesbury Abbey', in Allen Brown (ed.), *Anglo-Norman Studies VIII*, pp. 214–37.

57. Edmund King, *op. cit.* p. 97.

58. Keefe, *Feudal Assessments*, p. 21.

59. For castleguard the fundamental work is Sidney Painter, 'Castleguard', *American Historical Review*, 40 (1935), pp. 450–9, and references given there. For more recent discussions see C. Warren Hollister, *The Military Organization of Norman England* (Oxford, 1965), ch.5, John Beeler, *Warfare in England 1066–1189* (New York, 1966), ch.10 and D.J. Cathcart King, *The Castle in England and Wales* (London and New York, 1991), ch.2.

60. Beeler, *Warfare in England*, pp. 288–9.

61. See Stenton, *First Century of English Feudalism*, pp. 206–7.

62. Sidney Painter, *op. cit.* p. 451.

63. W.M. Delehanty (*Milites in the Narrative Sources of England, 1135–54*, University of Minnesota PhD, 1975) has studied the references to *milites*, *miles* or derivatives in 27 narrative works which contain them from the reign of Stephen. Of 769 occurrences, no less than 508 (66%) were in a context where nothing more than the generic meaning of soldier could be inferred. Of the others, 91 (12%) referred to cavalry or specialized arms, 52 to retainers. In 21 cases (largely those dealing with local affairs) the context was the fief, in 22 cases the context was religious, while in the remaining 75 cases the context was one defining a social group.

64. *Pace* Donald Fleming, *op. cit.*, pp. 93–8.

65. Michael Powicke, *Military Obligation in Medieval England* (Oxford, 1962), pp. 42–3.

66. Harvey, 'The Knight and the Knight's Fee', p. 159; Delehanty found 19 knights referred to by name in the narrative sources of Stephen's reign, excluding three who lived before the Conquest and the future Henry II who is referred to as *novus miles* towards the close of the *Gesta Stephani*. They differed widely in wealth and in the attributes which distinguished them. However, six were tenants-in-chief of the Crown and thirteen others were subtenants. The six include (in addition to Robert of Bampton) at the highest level Brian fitz Count (who is said to have received the belt of knighthood from Henry I) and Baldwin fitz Gilbert (de Clare) who is described as 'a men of great nobility and a very brave knight' (*Historia Anglorum*, p. 271). Among the other thirteen are an apparently landless knight 'using his skills as a fighter to make his fortune', an illegitimate member of the Percy family (Alan de Percy, who fought in the army of King David in 1138 and was described as *miles strenuissimus*) and Stephen's mercenary captain, Robert fitz Hubert, described by William of Malmesbury as the most savage of all men of his time. Another was the man who captured King Stephen at Lincoln in 1141, described by Henry of Huntingdon as *miles validissimus*.

67. Chibnall, 'Mercenaries and the *Familia Regis*', p. 19.

3. Angevin Knighthood and its Transformation c. 1150–c. 1250

1. K.R. Potter (trans.), *Historia Novella* (London, 1955), p. 6.

2. A point made by Delehanty, *op. cit.* Appendix B.

3. For vavasours see P.R. Coss, 'Literature and Social Terminology: the Vavasour in England', in *Social Relations and Ideas: Essays in Honour of R.H. Hilton* (Oxford, 1983), pp. 109–50, and references given there. For the honorial baronage see Stenton, *First Century of English Feudalism*, ch.III, and D. Crouch, *The Beaumont Twins: the Roots and Branches of Power in the Twelfth Century* (Cambridge, 1986), ch.IV.

4. Mortimer, 'Land and Service', pp. 180–1.

5. *Ibid.*, p. 180.

6. R.C. Van Caenegem (ed.), *English Lawsuits From William I to Richard* I, (I), Selden Society, vol. 106 (London, 1990), No. 346.

7. See, for example, Richard Mortimer, *op. cit.* pp. 194–7. However, it is also true that in many cases honour and locality must have reinforced one another. On this point see P.R. Coss, *Lordship, Knighthood and Locality: A study in English society c. 1180–c. 1280 (Cambridge, 1991)*, pp. 8–10.

8. Van Caenegem (ed.), *English Lawsuits*, (I), p. 283.

9. Only the barest outline is given here. For the full details see G.D.G. Hall (ed. and trans.), *Tractatus de Legibus et Consuetudinibus regni Anglie qui Glanvilla vocatur* (Oxford, 1965), pp. 26–37. A useful summary can be found in W.L. Warren, *Henry II* (London, 1973), pp. 352–4.

10. *Ibid.* pp. 99–102.

11. *Ibid.* pp. 11–12. See also p. 16.

12. *Curia Regis Rolls* vol. VI, p. 67.

13. For the foregoing see C.T. Flower (ed.), *Introduction to the Curia Regis Rolls, 1199–1230*, Selden Society, vol. 62 (1944), pp. 434–40, and A.L. Poole, *Obligations of Society in the Twelfth and Thirteenth Centuries* (Oxford, 1946), pp. 53–6. For a recent introduction to the operation of the English government at this period see W.L. Warren, *The Governance of Norman and Angevin England 1086–1272* (London, 1987).

14. For the text of this case see D.M. Stenton, *English Justice between the Norman Conquest and the Great Charter* (London, 1965), pp. 148–211, and for the section that is relevant here, R.C. Van Caenegem (ed.), *English Lawsuits from William I to Richard I*, (II), Selden Society, vol. 107 (1991), pp. 672–85.

15. See below p. 39.

16. For the case see D.M. Stenton (ed.), *Rolls of the Justices in Eyre for Lincolnshire 1218–19 and Worcestershire 1221*, Selden Society, vol. 53 (1934), No. 920. The details of the knights and their properties come from the *Victoria History of the County of Worcester*, vols. III and IV.

17. Always supposing that the name *Saudebroille* which figures on the roll stands for either him or a member of his family, as seems very likely.

18. See Coss, *Lordship, Knighthood and Locality*, p. 228.

19. He may be equatable with the Leonin son of Philip who held some property of the monks of Worcester at Debdale in Wolverley. Hugh de Belne held the manor of Belne in Belbroughton. Richard Pauncefoot held the manor of Bentley Pauncefoot in Tardebigge. Strictly speaking, the electors should also have been knights from the locality where the disputed property lay.

20. The Warwickshire material is taken from Coss, *Lordship, Knighthood and Locality*, ch.7, where full details may be found.

21. On this point see J. Quick, 'The Number and Distribution of Knights in Thirteenth-Century England: the Evidence of the Grand Assize Lists', in P.R. Coss and S.D. Lloyd (eds.), *Thirteenth Century England III* (Woodbridge, 1991) p. 116.

22. R.C. Palmer, *The County Courts of Medieval England, 1150–1350* (Princeton, 1982), p. 134.

23. An interesting case from Warwickshire in 1225 shows litigants ready to take advantage of procedural inaccuracies, including the election of non-knights. See P.R. Coss, 'Knighthood and the Early Thirteenth-Century County Court', in P.R. Coss and S.D. Lloyd (eds.), *Thirteenth-Century England II* (Woodbridge, 1988), pp. 47–8. See also Quick, 'The Number and Distribution of Knights in Thirteenth-Century England', pp. 114–18.

24. Coss, 'Knighthood and the early Thirteenth-Century County Court', pp. 47–8.

25. Sir William Dugdale, *The Antiquities of Warwickshire* (revised by William Thomas, London, 1730), vol. I, pp. 331–2.

26. Coss, 'Knighthood and the early Thirteenth-Century County Court', p. 53.

27. See Coss, 'Knighthood and the early Thirteenth-Century County Court', and references given there.

28. R.V. Turner, 'The Miles Literatus in the Twelfth and Thirteenth Centuries: How Rare a Phenomenon?', *American Historical Review*, vol. 83 (1978), p. 931. See also M. Clanchy, *From Memory to Written Record: England 1066–1307* (London, 1979), espec. pp. 175–6.

29. D.M. Stenton (ed.), *Rolls of the Justices in Eyre for Gloucestershire, Warwickshire and Shropshire, 1221–2*, Selden Society, vol. 59 (1940), No. 390.

30. However, they might be represented later on by the Nicholas son of Warin *alias* Nicholas

Warin who occurs in Coventry during the 1240s and 1250s.

31. Grant G. Simpson, 'The *Familia* of Roger de Quincy, Earl of Winchester and Constable of Scotland', in J.J. Stringer (ed.), *Essays on the Nobility of Medieval Scotland* (Glasgow, 1985).

32. A man of the same type, and with similar property interests to Warin de Coundon, was Hugh de Essebroc. From Kingsbury in North Warwickshire, he figured in grand assizes in 1221 and again in 1232. See Coss, *Lordship, Knighthood and Locality*, pp. 219–22.

33. Quick, 'The Number and Distribution of Knights in Thirteenth-Century England', p. 116.

34. See Coss, *Lordship, Knighthood and Locality*, p. 211.

35. Quick, 'The Number and Distribution of Knights in Thirteenth-Century England', p. 116.

36. See M. Powicke, *Military Obligation in Medieval England: A Study in Liberty and Duty* (Oxford, 1962), p. 49.

37. Charles Johnson (ed.), *Dialogus de Scaccario, The Course of the Exchequer* (Oxford, 1983), p. 111.

38. Eleanor Searle, *Lordship and Community: Battle Abbey and its Banlieu 1066–1538* (Toronto, 1974), p. 42.

39. See M.T. Clanchy, *From Memory to Written Record: England 1066–1307* (London, 1979), p. 177.

40. See, in particular, M. Prestwich, *English Politics in the Thirteenth Century* (London, 1990), ch.6, p. 101, which summarizes work done in this field.

41. What follows is based on Painter, 'Castleguard' and Beeler, *Warfare in England*, ch.10. See also N.J.G. Pounds, *The Medieval Castle in England and Wales: a Social and Political History* (Cambridge, 1990), pp. 44–50.

42. Beeler, *Warfare in England*, pp. 303–7.

43. S.D. Church, 'The Knights of the Household of King John: A Question of Numbers', in P.R. Coss and S.D. Lloyd (eds.), *Thirteenth-Century England IV* (Woodbridge, 1992), pp. 157–9. See also J.S. Critchley, 'Summonses to Military Service Early in the Reign of Henry III', *English Historical Review*, 85 (1971), pp. 79–95.

44. For the Lord Edward's crusade in 1270 indentures survive specifying the number of men some household knights were expected to bring with them. See below p. 104.

45. Church, 'The Knights of the Household of King John: A Question of Numbers', pp.

141–55, which also gives a summary of the material from the minority of Henry III.

46. In terms of the strength of armies, the one campaign waged by John for which there are reliable figures of knights is the Irish campaign of 1210, where the surviving praestita roll names nearly 800 knights. For the reign of Henry III, I.J. Sanders estimated the size of the armies mustered at Stamford in 1218 and at Portsmouth in 1229. On both occasions 500–600 knights could be put into the field (Sanders, *Feudal Military Service in England* (Oxford, 1956), pp. 108–29). Church argues that both kings could contribute between one-fifth and one-third of the knights mustered.

47. D. Crouch, *William Marshal* (London, 1990), pp. 137–8.

48. Simpson, 'The *Familia* of Roger de Quincy, Earl of Winchester and Constable of Scotland', p. 107.

49. K.J. Stringer, *Earl David of Huntingdon, 1152–1219* (Edinburgh, 1985), pp. 166–7.

50. Flori, *L'Essor de la Chevalerie*, p. 340.

51. See, in particular, Alan Forey, *The Military Orders: From the Twelfth to the Early Fourteenth Centuries* (London, 1992).

52. M. Keen, *Chivalry* (Yale, 1984), p. 76, and see below, ch.3 note 79.

53. Flori, *L'Essor de la Chevalerie*, pp. 119–20.

54. There is a good summary of the evidence on this issue in Keen, *Chivalry*, pp. 23–5.

55. Juliet R.V. Barker, *The Tournament in England, 1100–1400* (Woodbridge, 1986), pp. 4–6; Geoffrey of Monmouth refers to the mock battle (*simulachrum prelii*) in which knights competed on horseback at the coronation of King Arthur. I owe the later reference to Delehanty, *Milites in the Narrative Sources of England*, ch.V.

56. Flori, *L'Essor de la Chevalerie*, pp. 271–4.

57. Chibnall, *The World of Orderic Vitalis*, p. 137. Professor Chibnall has some very perceptive comments on the subject of early twelfth-century knighthood, *op. cit.* pp. 132–45.

58. J. Flori, 'La notion de chevalerie dans les Chansons de Geste du xiie siècle', *Le Moyen Age*, lxxxi (1975), pp. 436–8; quoted by Chibnall, p. 140.

59. C. Holdsworth, 'War and Peace in the Twelfth Century: the Reign of Stephen Reconsidered', in B.P. McGuire (ed.), *War and Peace in the Middle Ages* (Copenhagen, 1987), pp. 76–9; see also the same author's 'Ideas and Reality: some Attempts to Control and Defuse War in the Twelfth Century', in W.J. Sheils (ed.), *The Church and War*, Studies in Church History, vol. 20 (Oxford, 1983), pp. 59–78.

60. See, for example, L. Paterson, 'Knights and the Concept of Knighthood in the Twelfth-Century Occitan Epic', *Forum for Modern Language Studies*, 17 (1981); and Keen, *Chivalry*, pp. 42–3.

61. See Tony Hunt, 'The Emergence of the Knight in France and England 1000–1200', in W.H. Jackson (ed.), *Knighthood in Medieval Literature* (Woodbridge, 1981), pp. 1–22 and the works cited there.

62. Keen, *Chivalry*, p. 77.

63. *Ibid.*, pp. 70–1.

64. G. Duby, 'The Transformation of the Aristocracy: France at the beginning of the thirteenth century', in *The Chivalrous Society*, pp. 178–85.

65. G. Duby, 'Les transformations sociales dans le milieu aristocratique', in R.H. Bautier (ed.), *La France de Philippe Auguste: le temps des mutations* (Paris, 1982), pp. 711–16. See also G. Duby, *The Three Orders: Feudal Society Imagined* (English edn., Chicago, 1980), chs.22, 24.

66. David Crouch has recently attacked the Duby perspective from two angles. First, he doubts whether the attention paid to knighthood by the magnates really did produce a homogeneous ethos, arguing that this had been in process for centuries. More significantly, he suggests that the high nobility in England during this period was creating a superior knighthood for itself. See D. Crouch, *The Image of Aristocracy in Britain 1000–1300* (London and New York, 1992), p. 153.

67. Jean Flori has recently argued that it was the *milites* who copied the *nobiles* in the formulation of the chivalric code not, as has been generally thought, the other way round ('Chevalerie, noblesse et luttes des classes au Moyen Age: à propos d'un ouvrage récent', *Le Moyen Age*, No. 94 (1988), pp. 263–6).

68. *Historia Comitum Ghisnensium*. See Flori, *L'Essor de la Chevalerie*, pp. 294–7, and Keen, *Chivalry*, 19–20.

69. Flori, *L'Essor de la Chevalerie*, chs.XIII–IV. See also Duby, 'The structure of kinship and nobility: northern France in the eleventh and twelfth centuries', in *The Chivalrous Society*, which shows a relatively humble late twelfth-century knight, Lambert of Wattrelos, keen to enumerate the knights among his ancestry.

70. For what follows see J. Bradbury, 'Geoffrey V of Anjou, Count and Knight', in C. Harper-Bill and Ruth Harvey (eds.), *The Ideals and Practice of Medieval Knighthood III* (Woodbridge, 1990), pp. 21–38. See also Keen, *Chivalry*, pp. 64–5.

71. I have used Bradbury's translation, p. 32.

72. Keen, *Chivalry*, p. 24.

73. Barker, *The Tournament in England*, p. 114.

74. For what follows I have relied, in particular, upon Jean Flori, *L'Essor de la Chevalerie*, ch.III. See also his earlier essays, 'Sémantique et société médiévale: le verbe adouber et son évolution au XII siècle', *Annales*, 31 (1976), and 'Les origines de l'adoubement chevaleresque: étude des remises d'armes et du vocabulaire qui les exprime', *Traditio*, 35 (1979), and Keen, *Chivalry*, ch.IV.

75. Keen, *Chivalry*, ch.IV. Likewise, the delivery of arms to the prince seems to have its ultimate origins in the ceremony attendant upon the young man's coming of age.

76. The significance of Henry's knighting is discussed by Flori, *L'Essor de la Chevalerie*, pp. 58–61. See also Chibnall, *The World of Orderic Vitalis*, p. 144.

77. See also Barlow, *William Rufus*, pp. 24–5. It may well be of significance that although the Anglo-Saxon chronicler uses the word *ridere* he nonetheless avoids the term *cniht* since this was undoubtedly of too lowly a connotation to describe a king at this juncture.

78. Marjorie Chibnall (ed.), *The Ecclesiastical History of Orderic Vital*, 6 vols. (Oxford, 1969–80), e.g. III, pp. 112, 114, 242; IV, pp. 121, 136, 138, 264, 274; VI, pp. 132–4, 190, 328.

79. Knighting at the altar and the liturgy of dubbing appear, on the whole, to have been secondary developments, despite some antecedents. On this complex subject, see Flori, *L'Essor de la Chevalerie*, chs.IV–V and pp. 319–29, and Keen, *Chivalry*, ch.IV.

80. Barker, *The Tournament in England*, p. 7; Coss, *Lordship, Knighthood and Locality*, p. 281n.

81. Potter, *Historia Novella*, p. 49; quoted by Chibnall, *The World of Orderic Vitalis*, p. 138.

82. Barker, *The Tournament in England*, p. 7.

83. *Ibid.*, pp. 117–20.

84. See J.M.W. Bean, *From Lord to Patron: Lordship in Late Medieval England* (Manchester, 1989), p. 133, and references given there. See also Crouch, *William Marshal*.

85. C. Tyerman, *England and the Crusades 1095–1588* (Chicago, 1988), p. 85.

86. *Ibid.*, p. 70.

87. For, what follows see Simon Lloyd, *English Society and the Crusade 1216–1307* (Oxford, 1988), espec. ch.3.

88. *Ibid.*, pp. 98–9.

89. For analysis of this see Simon Lloyd's case study in *English Society and the Crusade*, ch.4. The Lord Edward's crusade strongly reinforces

the impression given from the evidence of the earlier crusades; 225 knights were contracted to serve with him.

90. For what follows I have drawn heavily on Coss, *Lordship, Knighthood and Locality*, ch.7.

91. For details of the distraints see M.R. Powicke, 'Distraint of Knighthood and Military Obligation under Henry III', *Speculum*, 25 (1950), pp. 457–70, Powicke, *Military Obligation*, ch.4, and Scott L. Waugh, 'Reluctant Knights and Jurors: Respites, Exemptions, and Public Obligations in the Reign of Henry III', *Speculum*, 58 (1983), pp. 937–86.

92. For the armour of this period see Claude Blair, *European Armour* (London, 1958), espec. ch.I, and the same author's contribution to J. Alexander and P. Binski (eds.), *Age of Chivalry: Art in Plantagenet England 1200–1400* (London, 1987), pp. 169–70. On armour shown on seals see C.H. Hunter-Blair, 'Armorials upon English Seals from the Twelfth to the Sixteenth Centuries', *Archaeologia*, 89 (1943) and, looking beyond England, B.B. Rezak, 'Medieval Seals and the Structure of Chvialric Society', in H. Chickering and T.H. Seiler (eds.), *The Study of Chivalry: Resources and Approaches* (Kalamazoo, 1988), pp. 313–72.

93. On this subject see R.H.C. Davis, *The Medieval Warhorse*, (London, 1989).

94. On this point see Crouch, *The Image of Aristocracy*, p. 137.

95. Hall (ed.), *Glanvill*, p. 122; J. C. Holt, *Magna Carta* (Cambridge, 1965), pp. 218–19, 321–3.

96. Powicke, *Military Obligation*, p. 70.

97. *Pipe Roll 4 Henry II*, p. 113.

98. See below pp. 73–8.

99. See Coss, *Lordship, Knighthood and Locality*, pp. 249–50.

100. A.C. Chibnall, *Sherington: Fiefs and Fields of a Buckinghamshire Village* (Cambridge, 1965), pp. 50–1.

101. The extent of economic difficulty among members of the knightly classes during the first half of the thirteenth century is a matter of some debate. In addition to the acute problems faced by many lesser knights, it seems that there was an usually high incidence of difficulty experienced by better endowed knightly families. Clearly, problems by no means extended to all; there were some who were doing very well. It is, however, a period of some stress in local society. See, in particular, P.R. Coss, 'Sir Geoffrey de Langley and the Crisis of the Knightly Class in Thirteenth-Century England', *Past and Present*,

No. 68 (1975), repr. in T.H. Aston (ed.), *Landlords, Peasants and Politics in Medieval England* (Cambridge, 1987), pp. 166–202 with appendix; D.A. Carpenter, 'Was there a Crisis of the Knightly Class in the Thirteenth Century? The Oxfordshire Evidence', *English Historical Review*, 95 (1980), pp. 721–52; Coss, *Lordship, Knighthood and Locality*, ch.8.

102. Quick, 'The Number and Distribution of Knights in Thirteenth-Century England', pp. 114–23.

103. For Oxfordshire see Carpenter, 'Was there a Crisis of the Knightly Class in the Thirteenth Century?', pp. 726–7. I owe the Buckinghamshire figure to Dr Anne Polden.

104. W.H. Blauuw, *The Barons' War*, 2nd ed. (London, 1871), p. 373; N. Denholm-Young, 'Feudal Society in the Thirteenth Century: the Knights' in *Collected Papers of N. Denholm-Young* (Cardiff, 1969), p. 84.

105. The Shropshire figures are derived from Stenton (ed.), *Rolls of the Justices in Eyre for Gloucestershire, Warwickshire and Shropshire* and Alan Harding (ed.), *The Roll of the Shropshire Eyre of 1256*, Selden Society, vol. 96 (1981). The Warwickshire figures are from Coss, *Lordship, Knighthood and Locality*, ch.7 and P.R.O. Just 1/954. The Bedfordshire figures are from G.H. Fowler (ed.), *Calendar of the Roll of the Justices in Eyre*, Bedfordshire Record Society, vol. 21 (1939), and K.S. Naughton, *The Gentry of Bedfordshire in the Thirteenth and Fourteenth Centuries* (Leicester, 1976), pp. 79–80.

106. See Waugh, 'Reluctant Knights and Jurors', pp. 955–6.

107. P.A. Brand, 'Oldcotes versus d'Arcy', in R.F. Hunnisett and J.B. Post (eds.), *Medieval Legal Records in Memory of C.A.F. Meekings* (London, 1978). Additionally, Roger was to provide him with his maintenance and find him a squire, two grooms and three horses for the term of his life.

4. The Triumph of Chivalry in England

1. Thirteenth-century effigies have been magnificently surveyed recently in H.A. Tummers, *Early Secular Effigies in England in the Thirteenth Century* (Leiden, 1980).

2. For what follows see A.R. Wagner *et al.* (eds.), *Aspilogia II: Rolls of Arms Henry III*, Society of Antiquaries (London, 1967). This contains editions of the Matthew Paris Shields

by T.D. Tremlett and of Glover's and Walford's Rolls by H.S. London.

3. *Ibid.*, p. 91.

4. Wagner (ed.), *Aspilogia II*, p. ix. For a detailed discussion of the heraldry contained in Glover's and Walford's Rolls see *ibid.*, pp. 103–13.

5. A.R. Wagner, *Heralds and Heraldry*, 2nd edn. (Oxford, 1956), p. 12.

6. For the early history of heraldry see Wagner, *Heralds and Heraldry*, ch.iii, and Keen, *Chivalry*, ch.vii.

7. An enamel plaque in the church of St Julien, Le Mans, which has been dated to 1151–8, is indeed blue with gold lions. See A. Ailes, 'Heraldry in Twelfth-Century England: the Evidence', in D. Williams (ed.), *England in the Twelfth Century* (Woodbridge, 1990), pp. 1–16.

8. Keen, *Chivalry*, p. 127. Family symbols, however, appear to have pre-dated heraldry, and the earliest medium for their expression was often the banner rather than the shield. On this point see Crouch, *The Image of Aristocracy*, pp. 220–6.

9. J.H. Round, *Geoffrey de Mandeville* (London, 1892), pp. 388–96.

10. For other arms which are or may be connected with this group see A.R. Wagner, *Aspilogia I: A Catalogue of English Medieval Rolls of Arms* (London, 1950), p. 17.

11. *Ibid.*, p. 120.

12. *Ibid.*, pp. 395–6.

13. For what follows see, in particular, M. Maclagan, 'The Heraldry of the House of Clare', *Papers of the XIII International Congress of Genealogical and Heraldic Sciences* (1982), pp. 2–12.

14. It appears that originally the chevrons numbered six, but that the number became fixed at three during the second half of the twelfth century. A shield which has an equal number of chevrons is described as chevronny.

15. *Ibid.*, p. 4.

16. William Camden Esq., *Remaines Concerning Britaine* (London, 1636), pp. 205–29; see also F.P. Barnard, 'Heraldry', in H.W.C. Davis (ed.), *Medieval England: A new edition of Barnard's Companion to English History* (Oxford, 1924).

17. Wagner (ed.), *Aspilogia II*, pp. 52, 143, 197.

18. See Maclagan, 'Heraldry of the House of Clare', pp. 5–6. In the Pecche and d'Aubigny cases there had been marriage with the Fitz Walter family so that the line of transmission might perhaps have been kinship rather than tenancy.

19. Fawley was part of the escheated honour of Giffard which was divided between the earl of Hertford and William Marshal (as heir by marriage of the Clare earl of Pembroke). The honour came to these, however, because the daughter of Walter Giffard I had married Richard fitz Gilbert, the founder of the Clare family in England.

20. Camden, *Remaines*, pp. 210–14.

21. A good start has been made by Dr David Crouch. See *The Image of Aristocracy*, pp. 228–33, where some further early examples may be found.

22. Wagner (ed.), *Aspilogia II*, pp. 22, 60–1.

23. On different occasions Matthew Paris gives him these arms and the alternative *sable, three garbs or, bands and ears gules* (Wagner (ed.), *Aspilogia II*, pp. 27, 67).

24. See above p. 79.

25. See Wagner (ed.), *Aspilogia II*, pp. 26, 61, 66, 116.

26. See the revised list by Wagner in *Aspilogia II*, pp. 260–2.

27. For what follows see Wagner, *Aspilogia I*, *passim*.

28. Denholm-Young believed that the Dering Roll was based on a castleguard roll for Dover. See N. Denholm-Young, *History and Heraldry* (Oxford, 1965), ch.IV.

29. Wagner continues to assign a date of *c.* 1312, but Denholm-Young argued persuasively that the roll belonged to the time when Robert Clifford was acting marshal (3 September 1307 – 10 March 1308), most probably to 1308. See 'The Song of Carlaverock, the Parliamentary Roll of Arms and the Galloway Roll', in *Collected Papers of N. Denholm-Young*, pp. 121–32.

30. For heralds see in particular, Wagner, *Heralds and Heraldry*, Denholm-Young, *History and Heraldry*, ch.III and Keen, *Chivalry*, pp. 134–42.

31. Denholm-Young, 'Feudal Society in the Thirteenth Century: the Knights', p. 86.

32. Revd C. Moor (ed.), *Knights of Edward I*, 5 vols., Harleian Society (1929–35).

33. M. Prestwich, *The Three Edwards: War and State in England 1272–1377* (London, 1980), p. 139.

34. See below p. 106.

35. For a discussion of these and other returns for Gloucestershire see Nigel Saul, *Knights and Esquires: The Gloucestershire Gentry in the Fourteenth Century* (Oxford, 1981), pp. 30–5.

36. For a recent discussion of the Feast of the Swans see Constance Bullock-Davis,

Menestrellorum Multitudo: minstrels at a royal feast (Cardiff, 1978), pp. ix–xli. The list of Swan knights is given in an appendix to this work, pp. 185–7.

37. *Ibid.*, p. xvi.

38. Keen, *Chivalry*, p. 134.

39. See J. Vale, *Edward III and Chivalry: Chivalric Society and its Context 1270–1350* (Woodbridge, 1982), pp. 22–3 and references given there. The same author notes a sharp contrast between late thirteenth/early fourteenth-century rolls and those from the second half of the fourteenth-century which show a far higher proportion of native arms.

40. For a discussion of the content of these see Vale, *Edward III and Chivalry*, ch.I.

41. For the chivalric activities of Edward I see also below pp. 122–3.

42. Vale, *ibid.* pp. 66–7.

43. See J. Cherry, 'Heraldry as Decoration in the Thirteenth Century', in W.M. Ormrod (ed.), *England in the Thirteenth Century* (Stamford, 1991), pp. 123–34.

44. On these points see also Anne Payne, 'Medieval Heraldry', in Alexander and Binski (eds.), *Age of Chivalry*, pp. 55–9. A psalter recently dated to 1230 contains no less than 21 shields painted in the margins. If the date is correct then it becomes the earliest known collection of arms, predating Matthew Paris.

45. Cherry, *op. cit.* pp. 129–31 and references given there. The list has many names in common with those depicted by Matthew Paris. See also Nigel Saul, *Scenes from Provincial Life: Knightly Families in Sussex 1280–1400* (Oxford, 1986), pp. 26–7, where it is doubted that all of the baronial families who figure there can have been benefactors to the abbey.

46. See Y.E. Weir, *A Guide to the Heraldry in York Minster* (York, 1986).

47. See Peter Gibson, *The Stained and Painted Glass of York Minster* (Norwich, 1979), pp. 19–21, 40–1.

48. For an introduction to the history of medieval stained glass see Richard Marks, 'Stained Glass *c.* 1200–1400', in Alexander and Binski (eds.), *Age of Chivalry*, pp. 137–47. In general, of course, religious motifs dominated, but heraldic glass became increasingly significant.

49. Jonathan Hughes, *Pastors and Visionaries: Religion and Secular Life in Late Medieval Yorkshire* (Woodbridge, 1988), pp. 13–22.

50. See H.C. Colvin, *The White Canons in England* (Oxford, 1977), p. 108, and Hughes, *op. cit.*

51. M. Keen, 'Chaucer's Knight, The English Aristocracy and the Crusade', in V.J. Scattergood and J.W. Sherborne (eds.), *English Court Culture in the Later Middle Ages* (London, 1983), pp. 53 and 59; see also the same author's remarks in Keen, *Chivalry*, pp. 131–2.

52. The extent of the loss is shown in particular by P.A. Newton, *Schools of Glass Painting in the Midlands 1275–1430*, 3 vols. (University of London PhD thesis, 1961).

53. See Alexander and Binski (eds.), *Age of Chivalry*, No. 744.

54. See Marks, 'Stained Glass *c.* 1200–1400', p. 146, and G.McN. Rushforth, 'The Baptism of St Christopher', *The Antiquaries Journal*, vol. VI (1926), pp. 152–8.

55. See Sarah Crewe, *Stained Glass in England 1180–1540* (London, 1987), p. 73.

56. The glass is in two series; the second, of the fifteenth century, is more stylized. For an account of the glass see *Transactions of the Bristol and Gloucestershire Archaeological Society*, vol. 39, pp. 217–31. Sadly, there is now neither glass nor effigies *in situ*. Some pieces of the glass were incorporated in the east window of St Peter's, Cirencester.

57. John de Newmarch died in 1310. See Alexander and Binski (eds.), *Age of Chivalry*, No. 227.

58. For the Mancetters see *Victoria County History of Warwickshire*, vol. IV, pp. 119–20. I owe the date and the Crophull details to Newton, *Schools of Glass Painting in the Midlands*, vol. I, ch.2.

59. P.W. Fleming, 'Charity, Faith and the Gentry of Kent', in A.J. Pollard (ed.), *Property, and Politics: Essays in Late Medieval English History* (Gloucester, 1981), p. 51.

60. Saul, *Scenes from Provincial Life*, pp. 148–52. Note also references given there.

61. *Ibid.*, p. 151.

62. The indispensable works here are the essay by Paul Binski in John Coales (ed.), *The Earliest English Brasses: Patronage, Style and Workshops 1270–1350* (London, 1987), pp. 69–131, and the books by Malcolm Norris, namely *Monumental Brasses: The Memorials*, 2 vols., (1977) and *Monumental Brasses: The Craft* (1978). See also Binski's contribution to the *Age of Chivalry*, pp. 171–3.

63. It is thought to belong to *c.* 1323.

64. F.J. Furnivall and W.G. Stone (eds.), *The Tale of Beryn*, Early English Text Society, Extra Series vol. 105 (1909), ll. 147–56.

65. W.W. Skeat (ed.), *Pierce the Ploughman's Crede*, Early English Text Society, Original Series vol. 30 (1867).

5. The Role of Chivalric Knighthood in English Society

1. For what follows see the following works by M. Prestwich: *War, Politics and Finance under Edward I* (London, 1972), espec. chs.II–III; 'Cavalry Service in early Fourteenth Century England', in Gillingham and Holt (eds.), *War and Government in the Middle Ages*, pp. 147–58; *The Three Edwards: War and State in England 1272–1377*; *English Politics in the Thirteenth Century*, ch.6.

2. Prestwich, *War, Politics and Finance*, p. 42.

3. The earliest survivals in this respect date from the end of Henry III's reign and are contracts to serve the Lord Edward on crusade. See S.D. Lloyd, 'The Lord Edward's Crusade, 1270–2: its setting and significance', in Gillingham and Holt (eds.) *War and Government in the Middle Ages*, pp. 120–33.

4. Prestwich, 'Cavalry Service', p. 157.

5. In fact of the 713 names in the lists that have survived only 76 seem to have set sail for Flanders.

6. A good précis of work in this area is to be found in W.M. Ormrod, *The Reign of Edward III* (London, 1990), pp. 149–51. Detailed studies include: A.E. Prince, 'The Strength of English Armies in the Reign of Edward III', *English Historical Review*, 46 (1931); J.W. Sherborne, 'Indentured Retinues and English Expeditions to France, 1369–1380', *English Historical Review*, 79 (1964), pp. 718–46; see also M.C. Prestwich, 'English Armies in the Early Stages of the Hundred Years War: A Scheme in 1341', *Bulletin of the Institute of Historical Research*, 56 (1983), pp. 102–13.

7. These details are derived from G. Wrottesley (ed.), *Crécy and Calais from the Public Records*, William Salt Archaeological Society, 18 (2), (1897), pp. 193–203.

8. See Powicke, *Military Obligation*, ch.10. The number of knights was also swollen by dubbings on the field of battle.

9. For Calveley and Knollys see J.C. Bridge, 'Two Cheshire Soldiers of Fortune of the Fourteenth Century: Sir Hugh Calveley and Sir Robert Knollys', *Journal of the Chester Archaeological Society*, XIV (1908), pp. 112–231. Sais is dealt with by A.D. Carr, 'A Welsh Knight in the Hundred Years' War: Sir Gregory Sais', *Transactions of the Honourable Society of Cymmrodorion* (1977), pp. 40–53. For Norbury see M. Barber, 'John Norbury: An Esquire of Henry IV', *English Historical Review*,

68 (1953), pp. 66–76. And for all of them see Philip Morgan, *War and Society in Medieval Cheshire, 1277–1403*, Chetham Society, 3rd ser., 34 (1987), a splendid example of what the author, following Philippe Contamine, calls the sociology of war.

10. Ormrod, *The Reign of Edward III*, p. 149.

11. For what follows see A. Goodman, 'The Military Subcontracts of Sir Hugh Hastings, 1380', *English Historical Review*, 95 (1980), pp. 114–20.

12. Goodman, *ibid.*, p. 118.

13. Morgan, *War and Society*, pp. 107, 150–4. The delegation of recruitment to the Black Prince's indentured retainers began in 1347. Such retinues, however, were by no means permanent affairs. A number of those who served with Sir Ralph Mobberley in 1355 can be shown to have served abroad later in different retinues. For the Mobberleys and their estates see *ibid.*, pp. 115–20. Sir Ralph died of sickness during the siege of Rheims in 1360.

14. Morgan, *War and Society*, pp. 164–5.

15. Simon Walker, 'Profit and Loss in the Hundred Years' War: the subcontracts of Sir John Strother, 1374', *Bulletin of the Institute of Historical Research*, 58 (1985), pp. 100–6.

16. Morgan, *War and Society*, p. 169.

17. *Ibid.*, pp. 16–17. For the institution of brotherhood-in-arms, more generally, see M. Keen, 'Brotherhood in Arms', *History*, No. 47 (1962), pp. 1–17 and K.B. McFarlane, 'An Indenture of Agreement between Two English Knights for Mutual Aid and Counsel in Peace and War, 5 December, 1298' and 'A Business-Partnership in War and Administration 1421–1445', in *England in the Fifteenth Century: Collected Essays of K.B. McFarlane* (London, 1981). Soon after acquiring lands in Herefordshire Sir David Hulgreve married Helen Bertram, heir to the castle and lordship of Bothal in Northumberland. As a result the arms of a Cheshire knight featured in the glass of a Northumberland parish church. See Roland Bibby, *Bothal Observed: A Survey of a Northumbrian Castle, Village and Church* (1973). He was now the neighbour of his erstwhile companion, perhaps brother-in-arms, John Cresswell.

18. Ormrod, *The Reign of Edward III*, p. 151; M. Jones, 'Edward III's Captains in Brittany', in W.M. Ormrod (ed.), *England in the Fourteenth Century* (Woodbridge, 1986), pp. 109–15.

19. Morgan, *War and Society*, pp. 128–31.

20. *Ibid.*, p. 129.

21. Saul, *Knights and Esquires*, ch.II; G.G. Astill, *The Medieval Gentry: A Study in Leicestershire Society, 1350–1399* (University of Birmingham PhD Thesis, 1977), ch. 6.

22. Julian Pitt-Rivers, quoted by John Barnie in *War in Medieval Society: Social Values and the Hundred Years' War 1337–99* (London, 1974), p. 75. For what follows see, especially, Dr Barnie's third chapter, 'Aristocracy, Knighthood and Chivalry', a particularly perceptive discussion of the subject.

23. *Ibid.*, p. 82.

24. *Ibid.*, p. 89.

25. *Ibid.*, pp. 93–4.

26. *Ibid.*, pp. 90–1.

27. Keen, 'Chivalry, Nobility and the Man-at-Arms', p. 34.

28. *Ibid.*, p. 43.

29. *Ibid.*, p. 39.

30. M. Prestwich, *Edward I* (London, 1988), p. 259.

31. See, for example, S.L. Waugh, 'The Profits of Violence: the Minor Gentry in the Rebellion of 1321–22 in Gloucestershire and Herefordshire', *Speculum*, vol. 52 (1977), pp. 843–69.

32. Searle, *Lordship and Community*, pp. 163–5.

33. Much of the evidence on the subject of gentry gangs was drawn together by John Bellamy, *Crime and Public Order in England in the Later Middle Ages* (London, 1973), ch.III.

34. For a recent review of the situation, see Nigel Saul, 'Conflict and Consensus in English Local Society', in J. Taylor and W. Childs (eds.), *Politics and Crisis in Fourteenth-Century England* (Gloucester, 1990), pp. 38–58.

35. P.R. Coss, 'The Langley Family and its Cartulary: a study in late medieval "Gentry"', *Dugdale Society Occasional Papers*, No. 22 (Oxford, 1974), pp. 6–7.

36. On these matters see, in particular, the several works by J.R. Maddicott, viz. 'The County Community and the Making of Public Opinion in Fourteenth-Century England', *Transactions of the Royal Historical Society*, 5th ser., 28 (1978); 'Parliament and the Constituencies, 1272–1377', in R.G. Davies and J.H. Denton (eds.), *The English Parliament in the Middle Ages* (Manchester, 1981), pp. 61–87; 'Edward I and the Baronial Lessons of Reform', in P.R. Coss and S.D. Lloyd (eds.), *Thirteenth-Century England I*, (Woodbridge, 1986), pp. 1–30; and 'The Crusader Taxation of 1268–70 and the Development of Parliament', in Coss and Lloyd (eds.), *Thirteenth-Century England II*, pp. 93–117.

37. The county community is a much debated issue. For a warning against envisaging too strong a sense of community before the mid-thirteenth century see Coss, 'Knighthood and the Early Thirteenth-Century County Court' and Prestwich, *English Politics in the Thirteenth Century*, ch.3. For a critique of the concept of county community as applied to the fourteenth century see Astill, *The Medieval Gentry*, ch.3. Nevertheless some degree of community at county, or sub-county, local level is undeniable, even if it was often overlain by magnate power.

38. See, for example, Margery Bassett, *Knights of the Shire for Bedfordshire during the Middle Ages*, Bedfordshire Record Society, vol. 29 (1949); Astill, *The Medieval Gentry*, ch.4; and Saul, *Knights and Esquires*, p. 119–28. See also, K.L. Wood-Leigh, 'Sheriffs, Lawyers and Belted Knights in the Parliaments of Edward III', *English Historical Review*, 46 (1931), pp. 372–88.

39. See M. Jones, 'An Indenture between Robert, lord Mohaut, and Sir John de Bracebridge for life service in peace and war, 1310', *Journal of the Society of Archivists*, 4 (1972), pp. 384–94, which includes both text and commentary. For a discusion of the early indentures in general, including this one, see also Bean, *From Lord to Patron*, ch.II.

40. Coss, *Lordship, Knighthood and Locality*, p. 44.

41. The licence was necessary because Montalt held directly from the Crown, so that royal rights were affected.

42. *Calendar of Patent Rolls 1301–7*, p. 188 and *1307–13*, p. 293.

43. For the history of the Bracebridge family and their circumstances during the thirteenth century see Coss, *Lordship, Knighthood and Locality*, pp. 280–8.

44. There is some suggestion, moreover, of a previous association with Robert de Montalt's late brother (Jones, 'An Indenture between lord Mohaut and Sir John de Bracebridge', p. 387), in which case the Bracebridge/Montalt relationship had indeed begun before the Bracebridge family reacquired its Kingsbury estate.

45. Barker, *The Tournament in England*, pp. 27–8. A third Bohun contract, similar but not identical, survives only in transcript. See also Bean, *From Lord to Patron*, pp. 43–7.

46. *Ibid.*, pp. 63–4.

47. Barker, *The Tournament in England*, pp. 28,122.

48. *Ibid.*, p. 122–3. Barker points to some curious features of this indenture and argues,

interestingly, that Cryel may have been repaying a debt to Segrave.

49. Barker suggests (pp. 27–8) that the comparative rarity of tourneying clauses in indentures may be because few lords felt the need to make the commitment explicit. She also suggests that the tourneying clauses of the time of Edward II may have much to do with the fact that this was the point at which tournaments were at their highest point of significance in terms of political discontent. She is wrong to say that they were completely absent after 1332 (see Bean, *From Lord to Patron*, pp. 64, 89) but is nonetheless probably right to connect the decline in the tournament's relative prominence in the indenture with the decline of the great *mêlée* tournament.

50. See above p. 56.

51. The text was printed by C.E. Long in *Collectanea Topographica et Genealogica*, IV (1837), pp. 63–72. There are numerous manuscripts of this roll; one of them gives fourteen additional names and shields. Long also edited the roll of the 1334 Dunstable tournament (*ibid.*, pp. 389–95.) For what follows see, in particular, A. Tomkinson, 'Retinues at the Tournament of Dunstable, 1309', *English Historical Review*, 84 (1959), pp. 70–89. For the political context of the tournament, see J.R. Maddicott, *Thomas of Lancaster* (Oxford, 1970), pp. 90–106.

52. Esquires, grooms and others also participated but in limited roles. Edward I's *Statuta Armorum* of 1292 was designed primarily to regulate the conduct of these. See Barker, *The Tournament in England*, pp. 57–60, 191–2, here correcting the pioneering study by N. Denholm-Young, 'The Tournament in the Thirteenth Century' repr. in his *Collected Essays*.

53. Several manuscripts show a division after No. 186, and it seems likely that those outside the retinues begin here rather than with No. 165 where the title *De la Commune* begins; the presence of figures like Robert de Tony and Roger Mortimer le Filz suggest that we have further retinues here, although it is not so clear cut.

54. Barker, *The Tournament in England*, p. 123 and pp. 193–4.

55. Tomkinson, 'Retinues at the Tournament of Dunstable', p. 80.

56. It is the practice these days to use the generic, though rather ugly, term hastilude, *hastiludum*, a contemporary term that subsumes all of these sub-categories.

57. Barker, *The Tournament in England*, pp. 114–15.

58. Prestwich, *Edward I*, p. 85.

59. Barker, *The Tournament in England*, pp. 66–7, 91.

60. For what follows see Prestwich, *Edward I*, pp. 120–2.

61. *Ibid.*, p. 122.

62. See, in particular, Bullock-Davies, *Menestrellorum Multitudo*, pp. ix–xli.

63. Vale, *Edward III and Chivalry*, p. 60. For what follows see, especially, chapter 4 of this work.

64. *Ibid.*, p. 71.

65. *Ibid.*, p. 68.

66. See Ormrod, *The Reign of Edward III*, pp. 44–5.

67. For what follows see Barker, *The Tournament in England*, pp. 92–4 and Vale, *Edward III and Chivalry*, pp. 67–8.

68. The most recent discussion of the foundation of the order and the difficulties of interpreting its documentation is that by Vale, *Edward III and Chivalry*, ch.5.

69. *Ibid.*, p. 91.

70. Simon Walker, 'Sir Richard Abberbury (*c.* 1330–1399) and His Kinsmen: The Rise and Fall of a Gentry Family', *Nottingham Medieval Studies*, 34 (1990), pp. 113–40.

71. I owe this information to the kindness of Dr Paul Brand.

72. See Bridget Vale, 'The Profits of Law and the "Rise" of the Scropes: Henry Scrope (d.1336) and Geoffrey Scrope (d.1340), Chief Justices to Edward II and Edward III', in Michael A. Hicks (ed.), *Profit, Piety and the Professions in Later Medieval England* (Gloucester, 1990), pp. 91–102; E.L.G. Stones, 'Sir Geoffrey le Scrope, *c.* 1280–1340, Chief Justice of the King's Bench', *English Historical Review*, 69 (1945), pp. 1–18.

73. Barker, *The Tournament in England*, p. 129.

74. G.O. Sayles, *Select Cases in the Court of King's Bench under Edward III*, (VI), Selden Society, vol. 82 (1965), pp. xxiv–xxv.

75. Bullock-Davis, *Menestrellorum Multitudo*, p. xix.

76. See *Dictionary of National Biography*, vol. 47, pp. 25–6, and Ormrod, *The Reign of Edward III*, p. 172.

77. Sylvia Thrupp, *The Merchant Class of Medieval London* (Michigan, 1962 edn.), pp. 277, 345.

78. Juliet Vale believes it probable that 'something of the social integration between patriciate and knightly classes' which has been observed in Northern France and the Low Countries 'may also have existed in the England of Edward III', *Edward III and Chivalry*, pp. 62–3.

79. R.B. Dobson, *The Peasants' Revolt of 1381* (London, 1970), pp. 168, 186, 211.

80. I am extremely grateful to Dr Barron for allowing me to use her, as yet unpublished, paper 'How chivalrous was medieval London?'

81. Thrupp, *Merchant Class*, pp. 277–8.

82. Barnie, *War in Medieval Society*, p. 108.

83. The text is printed in J. Strachey (ed.), *Rotuli Parliamentorum* (London, 1783), vol. 2, p. 278, and *Statutes of the Realm*, I (Record Commission, London, 1810), p. 381. See also W.H. Dunham and S. Pargellis, *Complaint and Reform in England 1363–1533* (Oxford, 1938) and Frances E. Baldwin, *Sumptuary Legislation and Personal Regulation in England* (Baltimore, 1926).

84. Dorothea Oschinsky (ed.) *Walter of Henley and other Treatises on Estate Managing and Accounting* (Oxford, 1971), p. 403.

85. Kate Mertes, *The English Noble Household 1250–1600* (Oxford, 1988), pp. 26–9.

86. Bean, *From Lord to Patron*, pp. 56–7.

87. See Helen Cam, *Liberties and Communities in Medieval England* (Cambridge, 1944), p. 239.

88. Matthew Bennett, in C. Harper-Bill and R. Harvey (eds.), *The Ideals and Practice of Medieval Knighthood I* (Woodbridge, 1986), pp. 2, 8–9.

89. The subject has been explored by Matthew Bennett, *op. cit.*, by Linda M. Paterson, 'The Occitan Squire in the Twelfth and Thirteenth Centuries', in Harper-Bill and Harvey (eds.), *The Ideals and Practice of Medieval Knighthood I*, and by Crouch, *The Image of Aristocracy*, pp. 164–73.

90. Barker, *The Tournament in England*, pp. 56–9.

91. For this and some other examples see Saul, *Knights and Esquires*, pp. 20–2.

92. Saul, *op. cit.* p. 23.

93. Strachey (ed.), *Rotuli Parliamentorum*, vol.3, pp. 57–8.

94. *Statutes of the Realm*, II, p. 171.

95. *Ibid.*, p. 340.

96. T. Fuller, *The Holy State* (1642). Quoted by R.H. Tawney, *The Agrarian Problem in the Sixteenth Century* (London, 1912, repr. New York, 1967), p. 35.

97. *Calendar of Close Rolls 1413–19*, p. 433. See Wagner, *Heralds and Heraldry*, pp. 63–4.

98. See, for example, Saul, *Knights and Esquires*, p. 28.

99. See R.L. Storey, 'Gentlemen-Bureaucrats', in Cecil Clough (ed.), *Profession, Vocation and Culture in Later Medieval England* (Liverpool, 1982), pp. 90–129. See also Rosemary Horrox, 'The Urban Gentry in the Fifteenth Century', in J.A.F. Thomson (ed.), *Towns and Townspeople in the Fifteenth Century* (Gloucester, 1988), pp. 22–44.

100. See Christine Carpenter, *Locality and Polity: A Study of Warwickshire Landed Society* (Cambridge, 1992), pp. 73–4; see also Coss, *Lordship, Knighthood and Locality*, pp. 310–19.

101. H.L. Gray, 'Incomes From Land in 1436', *English Historical Review*, 49 (1934), pp. 607–39; Thrupp, *Merchant Class of Medieval London*, p. 276.

102. J.P. Cooper, 'The Social Distribution of Land and Men in England 1436–1700', in R. Floud (ed.), *Essays in Quantitative Economic History* (Oxford, 1974), pp. 107–32.

103. Carpenter, *Locality and Polity*, p. 55.

104. J.S. Roskell, *The Commons in the Parliament of 1422* (Manchester, 1954), ch.V, and see above, note 38.

6. Knighthood, Literature and the Social Order

1. The subject has recently been re-examined, in masterly fashion, by Susan Crane, *Insular Romance: Politics, Faith and Culture in Anglo-Norman and Middle English Literature* (Berkeley, 1986). In what follows I am much indebted to this work.

2. See, for example, John Stevens, *Medieval Romance: Themes and Approaches* (London, 1973); W.R.J. Barron, *English Medieval Romance* (London, 1987).

3. G. Chaucer, *Miller's Prologue*, l. 3179; Crane, *Insular Romance*, pp. 10–11.

4. Crane, *Insular Romance*, p. 105.

5. The idea that these romances indicate general baronial preoccupations and concerns seems to me to be much more tenable than the view of Mary Dominica Legge who saw some of them at least (*Boeve, Gui, Waldef,* and *Fouke le Fitz Waryn*) as 'ancestral romances' commissioned by families at points of crisis in the rights of those families to their titles and lands. See Crane, *Insular Romance*, pp. 16–18, and references given there.

6. What follows is a précis of my arguments in 'Aspects of Cultural Diffusion in Medieval England: The Early Romances, Local Society and Robin Hood', *Past and Present*, No. 108 (1985), pp. 35–79, where further details and full references may be found.

7. W.H. French and C.B. Hale (eds.) *Middle English Metrical Romances* (U.S.A., 1930).

Quoted by John Stevens, *Medieval Romance: themes and approaches* (London, 1973), p. 213.

8. Quoted by Crane, *Insular Romance*, p. 106.

9. *Ibid.*, p. 195.

10. For an intriguing discussion of how Anglo-French rivalry in the crusades and the xenophobic response of chroniclers could help to make a 'national' crusading hero, see S.D. Lloyd, 'William Longespée II: the Making of an English Crusading Hero, Part I', *Nottingham Medieval Studies*, 35 (1991), p. 41–67. William Longespée, who was killed at Mansurah in the Nile Delta in 1250, became the subject of a short Anglo-Norman poem which seems to belong to the early fourteenth century. For the text (edited by Tony Hunt) see the appendix to Lloyd, 'William Longespée II: the Making of an English Crusading Hero, Part II', *Nottingham Medieval Studies*, 36 (1992), pp. 79–125.

11. For what follows see J.R. Maddicott, 'Poems of Social Protest in early Fourteenth-Century England', in W.M. Ormrod (ed.), *England in the Fourteenth Century: Proceedings of the 1985 Harlaxton Symposium* (Woodbridge, 1986), pp. 130–44.

12. On this point see Janet Coleman, *English Literature in History 1350–1400: Medieval Readers and Writers* (London, 1981), pp. 92–5.

13. Maddicott, 'Poems of Social Protest', pp. 136–70.

14. For the text see T. Wright (ed.), *The Political Songs of England*, Camden Society (London, 1839); the knight figures on pp. 334–5.

15. See, for example, Jill Mann, *Chaucer and Medieval Estates Satire* (Cambridge, 1973), pp. 106–15.

16. Ruth Mohl, *The Three Estates in Medieval and Renaissance Literature* (New York, 1933), pp. 6–7; Mann, *Chaucer and Medieval Estates Satire*, p. 3.

17. For discussion of the composition, and the implications, of Chaucer's audience, see Paul Strohm, *Social Chaucer* (Harvard, 1989), ch.3, and the full references given there.

18. See Anne Middleton, 'The Audience and Public of Piers Plowman', in D. Lawton (ed), *Middle English Alliterative Literature and its Literary Background* (Cambridge, 1982).

19. There has been considerable discussion and scholarly debate around the issue of Robin Hood in recent years. Both the text and the debate are best encountered in R.B. Dobson and J. Taylor (eds.), *Rymes of Robyn Hood* (London, 1976). The preface to the second edition published in 1989 brings the discussion up to date.

20. The *Gest*'s debt to romance can be seen in its metrical form, in its language and its content. The repetition of incident that we find here is a well-known characteristic of romance. The portrayal of Robin Hood himself is reminiscent of Arthur and Gawain. Moreover, many of the incidents themselves (for example, the king's visit to the outlaws in disguise) can be found within thirteenth-century romance.

21. Terry Jones, *Chaucer's Knight: The Portrait of a Medieval Mercenary* (London, 1980). For criticism see, for example, J. Burrow, *Times Literary Supplement*, 15 February 1980, p. 168; M. Keen, *History*, vol. 66, no. 218 (1981), pp. 501–2.

22. See above pp. 88–9.

23. For Chaucer the political survivor, see Paul Strohm, *op. cit.* ch.2.

24. *A wonder, wel-farynge knyght*, as Chaucer, the narrator, describes him.

25. For the most recent analysis of the *Knight's Tale* see P. Brown and A. Butcher, *The Age of Saturn: Literature and History in the Canterbury Tales* (Oxford, 1991), ch.5, where previous major studies are referenced. See also David Aers, *Chaucer, Longland and the Creative Imagination* (London, 1980).

26. For Gower's views see John Gower, *Mirour de l'Omme*, trans. W.B. Wilson (East Lansing, 1992), pp. 310, 316. For Brinton see Barnie, *War in Medieval Society*, p. 117. Chapter five of this latter work contains a particularly fine discussion of contemporary views on war.

27. See V.J. Scattergood, 'Chaucer and the French War: Sir Thopas and Melibee', in Glyn S. Burgess (ed.) *Court and Poet* (Liverpool, 1981), pp. 287–96.

28. See, for example, Aers, *Chaucer, Langland and the Creative Imagination*, ch.7 'Imagination, Order and Ideology: The Knight's Tale'. See also Terry Jones, *op. cit.* ch.4 'The Knight's Tale'.

29. Barnie, *War in Medieval Society, op. cit.* p. 129.

30. J. Clauvowe, *The Two Ways*, ll. 485–93.

31. See V.J. Scattergood (ed.), *The Works of Sir John Clanvowe* (Cambridge, 1975), pp. 25–7, 69.

32. For the *Twelve Conclusions* see Anne Hudson (ed.), *Selections from English Wycliffite Writings* (Cambridge, 1978), pp. 24–9, with commentary on pp. 150–5. The *Conclusions* survive only in the works of enemies of Lollardy, but they seem to have preserved a reasonably accurate version of Lollard views.

33. See R.N. Swanson, *Church and Society in Late Medieval England* (Oxford, 1989), p. 331 and references given there.

34. See Hudson, *op. cit.* pp. 135, 203–5, and M. Aston, 'Caim's Castles: Poverty, Politics and Disendowment', in R.B. Dobson (ed.), *The Church, Politics and Patronage in the Fifteenth Century* (Gloucester, 1984), pp. 45–57.

35. Barnie, *op. cit.* p. 127.

36. G.A. Lester, 'Chaucer's Unkempt Knight', *English Language Notes*, 27 (1989), pp. 25–9.

37. Particularly during and after the Merciless Parliament of 1388, when some members of the government and its supporters paid the ultimate price.

38. For what follows on the Squire and Franklin I am much indebted to P. Brown and A. Butcher, *The Age of Saturn; Literature and History in the Canterbury Tales* (London, 1991), ch.2 and the references given there.

39. For the various interpretations of the Franklin's social position see, to quote only the most recent works, M. Carruthers, 'The Gentilesse of Chaucer's Franklin', *Criticism*, 23, pp. 283–300; Susan Crane, 'The Franklin as Dorigen', *Chaucer Review*, vol. 24, no. 3 (1990), pp. 236–52; N. Saul, 'The Social Status of Chaucer's Franklin: A Reconsideration', *Medium Aevum*, 52, pp. 10–26; H. Specht, *Chaucer's Franklin in the Canterbury Tales* (Copenhagen, 1981).

40. See above pp. 133–6.

41. B XI l. 141, and again l. 281. Quotations are taken from A.V.C. Schmidt (ed.) *The Vision of Piers Plowman: A Complete Edition of the B Text* (London, 1978).

42. *Ibid.*, B XVII ll. 1–2.

43. *Ibid.*, B I ll. 102–14.

44. See Malcom Godden, *The Making of Piers Plowman* (London, 1990), p. 143.

45. I am concerned here with the startling use of the imagery of chivalric knighthood. Langland's work is rich in doctrinal implications. For recent discussions of Langland's interpretation of the Redemption see Godden, *The Making of Piers Plowman*, ch.8, and references given there. See also James Simpson, *Piers Plowman: An Introduction to the B-Text* (London, 1990), pp. 194–5, 209–12.

46. By David Aers, who provides the best introduction to these issues. See his *Chaucer, Langland and the Creative Imagination*, ch.I 'Imagination and Traditional Ideologies in Piers Plowman'.

7. Conclusion

1. For a discussion of the Paston books see my 'Aspects of Cultural Diffusion', pp. 54–6. For the book of knighthood, which includes ordinances governing war, judicial combat and tournaments, details of specific feats of arms, and a translation of the treatise on military matters by the classical writer Vegetius, see G.A. Lester, *Sir John Paston's 'Grete Boke'* (Woodbridge, 1984).

2. N. Davis, *Paston Letters and Papers*, No. 745.

3. *Ibid.*, Nos. 236, 330. For the court of Burgundy see, in particular, Malcolm Vale, *War and Chivalry* (London, 1981).

4. See, for example, J.R. Goodman, 'Caxton's Publications of 1480–85', in H. Chickering and T. Seiler (eds.), *The Study of Chivalry: Resources and Approaches* (Kalamazoo, 1988), and references given there.

5. On these points see Carpenter, *Locality and Polity*, pp. 82–92. See also D.A.L. Morgan, 'The Individual Style of the English Gentleman', in Michael Jones (ed.), *Gentry and Lesser Nobility in Later Medieval Europe* (Gloucester, 1986), pp. 15–35.

6. Keen, *Chivalry*, p. 240.

Further Reading

The foregoing notes contain full citations to the scholarly work consulted in the writing of this book. Readers wishing to explore aspects of the subject further might wish to begin with the following recent books:

Abels, Richard P., *Lordship and Military Obligation in Anglo-Saxon England* (London, 1988)

Alexander, J. and Binski, P. (eds.), *Age of Chivalry: Art in Plantagenet England 1200–1400* (London, 1987)

Barber, Richard and Vale, Juliet, *Tournaments: Jousts, Chivalry and Pageants in the Middle Ages* (Woodbridge, 1989)

Barker, Juliet R.V., *The Tournament in England, 1100–1400* (Woodbridge, 1986)

Brown, P. and Butcher, A., *The Age of Saturn: Literature and History in the Canterbury Tales* (Oxford, 1991)

Carpenter, Christine, *Locality and Polity: A Study of Warwickshire Landed Society* (Cambridge, 1992)

Coales, John (ed.), *The Earliest English Brasses: Patronage, Style and Workshops 1270–1350* (London, 1987)

Coss, P.R., *Lordship, Knighthood and Locality: A Study in English Society c. 1180–c. 1280* (Cambridge, 1991)

Crane, Susan, *Insular Romance: Politics, Faith and Culture in Anglo-Norman and Middle English Literature* (Berkeley, 1986)

Crouch, David, *The Image of Aristocracy in Britain 1000–1300* (London and New York, 1992)

Flori, Jean, *L'Essor de la Chevalerie XIe–XIIe Siècles* (Geneva, 1986)

Godden, Malcolm, *The Making of Piers Plowman* (London, 1990)

Hopkins, Andrea, *Knights* (London, 1990)

Keen, Maurice, *Chivalry* (Yale, 1984)

Lloyd, Simon, *English Society and the Crusade 1216–1307* (Oxford, 1988)

Morgan, Philip, *War and Society in Medieval Cheshire, 1277–1403*, Chetham Society, 3rd ser., xxxiv (1987)

Saul, N., *Scenes from Provincial Life: Knightly Families in Sussex 1280–1400* (Oxford, 1986)

Simpson, James, *Piers Plowman: An Introduction to the B-Text* (London, 1990)

Strickland, M. (ed.), *Anglo-Norman Warfare* (Woodbridge, 1990)

Strohm, Paul, *Social Chaucer* (Harvard, 1989)

Tummers, H.A., *Early Secular Effigies in England in the Thirteenth Century* (Leiden, 1980)

Tyerman, C., *England and the Crusades 1095–1588* (Chicago, 1988)

Vale, Juliet, *Edward III and Chivalry: Chivalric Society and its Context 1270–1350* (Woodbridge, 1982)

Index